Go in Peace

Reflections on the use of confession yesterday, today and tomorrow

by Michael Hollings

McCrimmons
Great Wakering Essex England

Go in Peace first published in Great Britain in 1984, and *A Penitent's Prayerbook* first published in Great Britain in 1976 by Mayhew McCrimmon Ltd.

ISBN 0 85597 445 1

Cover Design: Paul Shuttleworth
Typesetting: Fleetlines, Southend-on-Sea
Lithographic artwork: Graphitti, Southend-on-Sea and McCrimmon Publishing Co Ltd.
Printed by Black Bear Press Limited, Cambridge

Contents

Foreword

I AM faced with an embarrassment of acknowledgments! From the time of beginning this book, every page has turned into a co-operative effort. The theme of the book was given to me. I then required a longish time to sort ideas and material and collect information. This tested the patience of those who live and work with me in the parish house of St. Mary of the Angels. So also, the long suffering parishioners and others who wanted time with me for confession, counselling, prayer, home and hospital visits and so on, found less time available, myself less approachable. They showed me lessons in understanding, tolerance and selflessness. I hope I learned something from them which will be more valuable for pastoral work in the future. I received great support from their prayers.

In a way, I am ashamed to admit that one essential requirement was the means to escape from the tight, busy, inner-city London where I live and work. Yet how stupid to be ashamed. The Lord made the sabbath. A great need today is space for rest, silence and reflection. All these I had at intervals through the generous kindness of Mrs Etta Gullick who opened to me the peace and beauty of her Isle of Man home. At the same time, she helped to research the history of confession and gave me leads towards discovering the practice of churches other than Roman Catholic.

Nor was hers the only help. I have been advised, guided and corrected by priests, ministers and lay people from various denominations. I cannot name them all, but I must mention Dr Richard Price who kindly read the historical chapter and made suggestions. If I have in any way misinterpreted what he or others offered I am sorry. Sister Joseph Camac has patiently and reliably managed to decode a series of my practically illegible manuscripts, typed them up and prodded me to give her the next section to get on with. Latterly, Miss Joan Cooley checked the final draft, laid out and re-typed the copy for the publishers.

Dr Anthony Baxter has given me incalculable assistance. He has gone to great pains to read all I have asked him, to make positive recommendations on the theological content I have submitted to him, and to suggest ways to make it more easily comprehensible. I know on many occasions he has steered me away from possible pitfalls through his theological knowledge and insight. If there are errors and inaccuracies, they are mine and not his.

As you will realise, I am very blessed in my friends and companions.

Week of Prayer for
Christian Unity, 1984

MICHAEL HOLLINGS
St Mary of the Angels,
Bayswater

All scripture quotations are taken from the *Revised Standard Version.*

Come now, let us reason together,
says the Lord;
though your sins are like scarlet,
they shall be as white as snow;
though they are red like crimson,
they shall become like wool.

Is. 1.18

PART ONE

Genesis

WHEN I said 'yes' to the request that I should write a book about confession, I did not fully realise what a formidable task I was undertaking. All too readily I agreed. I was influenced in this decision by paradoxically contrary personal experiences. The first experience was my own difficulty with confession, beginning in my childhood. This was backed up by hearing and reading of the problems others have had, and indeed are still having, to the extent of driving individuals from the practice of their faith and even from belief itself.

In apparent contradiction, I have personally gained a great deal from confession later in my life, as I hope will become clear as this book proceeds. This side of the paradox is also weighted by the widespread benefit which I know flows from the proper use of confession; this knowledge has come over the years from my work as pastor and confessor, as well as from discussing with fellow pastors and many members of religious orders and lay people their appreciation and gratitude for the sacrament of penance in various Churches.

Another factor was that confession today is at a low ebb generally speaking among Roman Catholics, is only used in parts of the Church of England, and does not feature as such in a number of other Churches. Because I believe in confession, I would like to make as sure as I can that it may be better understood. This for me is particularly important as regards the development of those in priesthood, ministry, pastoral care and counselling roles. I hope this will also benefit the growth of the ordinary person in the town or the country.

During my thirty or so years since ordination, one of the great aids I have had is that I have almost all the time been working in close contact with psychiatrists, psychotherapists and counsellors. This has been an invaluable source of learning and understanding. Although I have never done a specialised course in psychology, psychiatry or counselling, I can say without a blush that that continual contact and more or less continual field work has taught me a great deal. The book is essentially about confession, but in my exposition of this you will find that a significant amount of space is devoted to counselling.

I am a Roman Catholic and a priest. What I write stems from this background. However, I should broaden from simply giving the Roman Catholic viewpoint, and try to cover something of the ideas and practices of other Churches. Moreover, I have looked into the earlier history of confession. Certainly it has been true in the past among Roman Catholics that there has been very little familiarity with the history of confession before the provisions of the Council of Trent in the post-Reformation period. My questioning among members of other denominations led me to conclude that many of them also knew little of the growth of penitential practice in the early Church and into medieval times. It seemed useful, therefore, to include a chapter specifically on history in order to get some background and perspective that can assist discussion of the present and future position of confession.

Confession, in the sense broadly accepted by those

Churches which regard it as having a sacramental character, includes a priestly role, which will be discussed. It seemed to me that this led naturally to my sharing with the reader certain ideas and insights which I have accumulated, sifted and modified in the course of my own experience of working with people who do make use of confession, seek spiritual guidance or ask for counsel. Equally importantly, I have also drawn on personal knowledge of confessors, pastors and spiritual directors to outline some of the qualities necessary in my opinion for a priest or minister to fulfil such a role.

Before I go any further I want to give an outline of my own personal pilgrimage through the practice of confession. I believe this will be helpful as a picture of one man's way, with its various low and high points. With variations, each person who has encountered confession over a period could tell a similar story. Some would be more straightforward than mine, some much the same, and some ending abruptly.

A personal encounter with confession

I was instructed and coached towards my first confession about the age of seven. I was not going to a Roman Catholic school at the time, so I had to go every Saturday morning to a kind of Sunday School. This was held in a tin hall which had been the old church before a new stone church was built in front of it. Here, with about a dozen others, I was put through what I believe was the fairly normal pattern of instruction in those days. This mainly consisted after the first class of being sent home each week to learn by heart some questions and answers out of the current *Catechism of Christian Doctrine*. The following week, each of us in turn was asked to repeat one of these word-perfectly in front of the rest of the class. Great emphasis was put upon the absolute correctness of our repetition of what we had been set to memorise. I will say for the system that even today I can quote many of the catechism answers. It is true that the teacher, having gone round the circle and coaxed or scolded us into answering correctly, spent the last part of the class in explanation. But the lasting impression in my mind from then until now is that the word-perfect answer was given higher priority.

When we had completed the required sections of the catechism, the next and seemingly even more important lessons were on the detail of the form which confession would take when the day arrived. This, too, needed to be absolutely correct, because, we were told, the priest would expect us to use this form and this form only. I was very shy and timid as a boy and I dreaded Saturday mornings and the classes; but the thought of my first confession was worse. What I had to confess seemed relatively unimportant compared with the fear that I would forget the correct words in the form, or dry up altogether.

In the event, the first confession was just as terrifying as I had feared! Subsequent confessions did not get better, especially after the occasion when I went into the dark confessional, having arrived first in church at the time advertised for confessions, and went through all I had to say – only to realise after a long pause that there was no priest the other side of the grill! I came out red-faced to the grins of the queue which had now formed and the alarming figure of the priest arriving, which meant my return to the box and a repeat of everything.

From this young viewpoint, my going to confession and going to the dentist were about equally unpleasant. The teenage period was especially difficult. I was at boarding school, Mass and Holy Communion were every day, confession was expected to be every week or so, and a sharp eye was kept to make sure we came to Mass and Holy Communion each day unless we were sick. I got through these years painfully and under tension, though this was not simply centred on confession. Later, I fell away from both belief and practice. My subsequent return when it came about was not easy. After God had resurrected my belief, I had to face confession after a long and by no means sinless period of army life.

Once back to faith, prayer and practice, I went on very quickly to train for the priesthood. It was at this period that I really came to discover more about what I might call the dual possibility in confession of receiving absolution and gaining the benefit of counselling from an older, wiser and holier person. In the college in Rome there was a system by which a priest came in each week to hear confessions and to give a spiritual talk to the students. Most students seemed to go to confession to him. He was very gentle and kind but dry as dust in his spiritual talk to the college. In the confessional he did no more than give a penance and pronounce the words of absolution. However, at the same time, I was given an introduction to an elderly priest whom I took to visiting regularly each week. I always went to his room; he was a mine of interest and information, expecially on prayer and parish life. Gradually I took to making a periodic confession to him, asking him at the same time for counsel and guidance. I still continued, in between these occasions, to go to the college spiritual director for absolution.

The openness of my visits to the elderly priest and the way in which, over two or three years before he died, he allowed me to get to know him was a new experience. I was able in turn to be open with him, so that he also got to know me. I am sure in retrospect that this was one seed which among others widened my mind to different approaches to confession. It was new to find a priest willing to give me time, to understand my hang-ups and depressions and visions of priesthood while he expounded his ideas on the priestly life. His interest encouraged me in black times, when to me there was a question mark over God's call to serve him through ordination. All this set me to wondering about the availability of such help to the man and woman in the street, in the life I had lived before coming to the college.

Another small but enlightening discovery in Rome was that men and boys were allowed confession openly in the church sacristy or the priests' house, while women were only received for absolution in the confessional box. But even this had exceptions in Rome. On the occasions of big feasts and pilgrimages it was common before an open air Mass to find priests dotted anywhere, while men, women and children alike came to kneel or stand near them to tell them their sins.

After ordination, I came back to the normal situation of hearing confessions each week at set hours, and usually in church and in the confessional. However, it very soon became apparent that there were all kinds of exceptional situations, from visiting the sick and housebound at home to striking up an acquaintance on a train journey and being asked for confession before the end of the journey. A period at Westminster Cathedral during the middle nineteen-fifties raised another problem. Many people perhaps came to the anonymity of the Cathedral, where there were duty priests each day. Now and then it was clear that a particular person really needed much more than a quick in-and-out. I would tell them my feeling and give them the option of coming to see me some time in clergy house for a longer discussion of their particular difficulty. That worked well for most of the year, but special feasts and seasons produced impossible numbers. At seasons like Christmas and Easter almost unbelievably in the English setting I have been ten and more hours in the confessional box without a break.

The newer and more open ideas of Vatican II were much welcomed by me, not least when the practice grew of making provision for face-to-face confession. Later the introduction in the nineteen-seventies of the new rite of penance emphasised the community aspect and made it more possible to cope with large numbers.

From the development in my own life and experience which has coincided with the remarkable changes suggested in, and following from, Vatican II, these pages have been written. At the same time, as part of the movement of history, many steps have been taken towards re-establishing unity among the churches.

It is my hope that this book will have some practical value, not only for Roman Catholics, but also for those who serve Jesus Christ in other Christian churches.

Sin and Guilt, Love and Forgiveness

CONFESSION is about sin and guilt. It is also about love and forgiveness. In the professional sense of the term, 'counselling' does not necessarily recognise the existence of sin, though confession does recognise counselling. The confessor is not always, nor perhaps even often, a trained counsellor, but he will normally have studied morality, the distinctions in religious terms between good and evil, and so the nature of sin.

The Oxford English Dictionary defines sin as: 'a transgression of divine law and an offence against God; a violation (especially wilful or deliberate) of some religious or moral principle'.

The Roman Catholic Catechism, which was much used since the counter-reformation Council of Trent, defined sin as: 'an offence against God'. It went on further to specify sin in terms of the Ten Commandments, and laws of the Church and other ways in which the law of God might be broken. Sin from this teaching emerged as related to rules and laws which were to be kept 'under pain of sin'. Often it seemed as though the emphasis was on the rule rather than upon the violation of God's love. It is true that the summary of the law was expressed in the two so-called Great Commandments: 'You shall love the Lord your God with all your heart, and with all your soul, and with all your might'[1]; and 'You shall love your neighbour as yourself'.[2] However, the rules and provisions and elucidations which came in such profusion in Leviticus and Deuteronomy and elsewhere through the Old Testament tended to the impression which was later voiced by Jesus Christ[3] when he says to the Pharisees:

> But woe to you Pharisees! for you tithe mint and rue every herb, and neglect justice and the love of God; these you ought to have done, without neglecting the others . . . Woe to you lawyers also! for you load men with burdens hard to bear, and you yourselves do not touch the burdens with one of your fingers.[4]

Not so long ago, a woman came to me in distress and anger about the education of her child. 'This school', she said, 'is not a good Catholic school.' 'Why?' I asked. 'Because it doesn't teach the Catholic Faith.' 'What doesn't it teach?' I asked. 'It doesn't teach the Ten Commandments.' 'What does it teach?' 'Oh, something very strange,' she said, 'about loving God and your neighbour.'

Her reply underlines the continued impression that the faith we are to live by, the measuring rod of practical Christianity, is in keeping the rule of law. How often the Ten Commandments were painted on the wall behind the altar in English churches and formed an integral part of the Prayer Book services. But her reply also brings the newer emphasis which more positively looks to the love of God, and can cause concern because of seeming vagueness or lack of definite, detailed rules.

This very emphasis upon the law rather than the love of God, though the two are in a sense indivisible, has been a cause of tension leading to some of the problems arising in and around the practice of confession: inevitably, guilt had a way of getting greater prominence than the healing nature of forgiveness.

Guilt seemed to regain the upper hand all too quickly after the experience of forgiveness in confession. Sadly, not only the general line of teaching but also the attitude of the confessor could contribute to a dread of going to confession. This dread could then war with the duty-call to repent and the built-in desire for forgiveness.

In recent years and modern teaching, the effort has been made to re-direct the teaching and therefore understanding of the individual to the creative love of God, putting failure, sin and guilt into a newer perspective which is closer to the mind of Christ.

The place of the law

It would be foolish to dismiss the central importance of the law in God's plan for the human race. Some have tried to do so. Yet Christ, as he is recorded in the sermon on the mount, is forthright:

> Think not that I have come to abolish the law and the prophets; I have come not to abolish them but to fulfil them. For truly, I say to you, till heaven and earth pass away, not an iota, not a dot, will pass from the law until all is accomplished. Whoever then relaxes one of the least of these commandments, and teaches men so, shall be called least in the kingdom of heaven; but he who does them and teaches them shall be called great in the kingdom of heaven.[5]

The law is established for mankind, to fulfil the loving purpose of God in his creation. It is for growth, not for an excuse to punish. Therefore, without going into arguments on the whole subject of original sin, suffice it to say at this point that the law presupposes the imperfection of man. It also presupposes God's will for the completion of man to a state of perfection in the world to come, so that the union with God may be as complete as possible between creator and creature. But, in Christian teaching, another aspect of God's love for mankind is that he gives a freedom to each individual to choose self or God. This freedom is essential if man is to grow to full stature, because he is not created a slave by God and to God, but is created with an intelligence and will. He has this freedom, even if sometimes in a very limited way. We believe that ordinarily there is always sufficient freedom in man to say 'yes' to good and 'no' to evil. But there may not be explicit knowledge of God, and so the question of 'sin' for a particular individual may not in a strict sense arise. One definition of sin reads: 'The purposeful disobedience of a creature to the known will of God; unlike moral evil, it is fundamentally a theological concept.'[6]

This combination of knowledge and freedom is fundamental to the Christian teaching on confession and counselling. Any discussion on these two topics must make clear that confession and counselling within the Christian Church are meaningless without God. However, ordinary counselling in relation to psychology and psychiatry does not necessarily need this God-dimension, though it may well have it – and at that point draws much closer to the theological attitude. For instance, murder is very generally seen as morally evil but, for the Christian, murder is theologically evil, since it is accepted that God is the author of life and only he has the right to bring living innocent life in this world to an end. In revelation, among the Ten Commandments is the clear command: 'You shall not kill'.[7] The will of God will normally be to some extent known by one who believes in God. The degree of knowledge may vary, as may the degree of 'purposeful disobedience'. Confession and counselling in a theistic context are there to take into account the fact that we are all at different stages of development and to help and guide the individual penitent to discover the will of God, and to relate his or her own will to God.

Of course, the law was originally given for the good of the society – the right order and running of a people who live and work better together in community when there is some background of law – as well as being for the fulfilling of God's will.

Being imperfect, we each have to be instructed in the law, not coming automatically to knowledge of it. For this instruction, some elucidation is constantly needed, and from this elucidation there has grown up an absolute labyrinth of laws and bye-laws. The sheer strength and detail of the exposition of the law in the earlier books of the Bible is staggering. It seems to cover every possible evil conduct or misdemeanor by any possible person.

Towards the end of the Old Testament and the beginning of the New, exposition and dispensing of the law came into the hands of the scribes and Pharisees and doctors of the law. Here twin dangers soon arose – growing complication of the law and growth of an authoritarian attitude to the law-dispensers over the law-abiders. It was a pattern which was to be repeated down the ages, and still today is current in the more authoritarian churches. In confession, for instance, there are those who are strict interpreters of the law, very directive and dominating over the penitent. However, the law is made for the ordinary person. Christ summed up the situation when he said:

> The sabbath was made for man, not man for the sabbath.[8]

When this is forgotten, the law-dispenser may do his best to pre-empt any freedom of thought and decision from the penitent. Such an attitude inhibits the true growth of the individual, as well as inducing fear and sometimes a scrupulous conscience.

The law, however, still should remain central, and it can have a very positive effect upon individuals and communities when it is properly understood and administered as a support for growth. But it is interesting to look at one result of the exposition of the law as seen from outside.

Years ago I spent many months listening once a week to a sad and rich widow who came from the south coast to talk with me in London. She had much to pour out in bitterness, which was not aided by having nothing to live for, loneliness and no belief in God. The hours spent with her were as much a therapeutic session for desolation as an input of doctrine, though that was the object of her visit. However, she suddenly asked me one day to send her a catechism of Christian doctrine so that she could go over the basic doctrines at home. I sent her one. It is usually covered in red. A few days later, I received a short note from her. In capital letters she wrote: RED SPELLS DANGER! And went on to say she had found inside the cover some three hundred rules and regulations. That was too much to take . . . Goodbye!

Whether looking at the Old Testament, the New, or down the centuries to the present time, it seems that the effect of the law in its various interpretations and rigidity of enforcement has also had a variety of outcomes in the lives of individuals and communities. By no means can it be said that the application of the law has been overwhelmingly successful. Some of the repercussions from confession for instance can be traced into many a psychiatrist's waiting room. On the other hand, there have been million upon million who have gone happily and holily through life, not a few reaching the heights of sanctity. Though there have been brilliant developments in psychiatry and the social sciences, in human growth programmes and so on, a very considerable part of what is now taught in the name of science was and is already contained in the law and living theology of the Christian Church. It has not always been effective. It has had bad results as well as good. It has time and again been wrongly handled and the wrong emphasis given. Yet . . . yet, it would be a sad mistake to be totally disenchanted. Let us then look at a more positive approach which has always been there and been preached before and after Christ, but has often been obscured by the strong emphasis on conformity to rules.

The law of love

From the earliest stories in the Bible, with their many interpretations, there is a strong theme running through the revelation. This theme is that God's creation was and is good in essence. It has flaws indeed and for this reason it cannot be said that the world or human beings are perfect. Nevertheless, the theme brings with it a continuing hope, which is sometimes lost in particularly difficult periods, but re-emerges with even greater strength as time goes on.

God has created from his very being. That being, writes St. John, is very simple: 'Let us love one another; for love is of God, and he who loves is born of God and knows God. He who does not love does not know God; for God is love'.[9]

The work of God's love is seen especially in Jesus Christ, and God's purpose works out through him: 'We are all to come to unity in our faith and in our knowledge of the Son of God, until we become the perfect man, fully mature in the fullness of Christ himself . . .

'If we live by the truth and in love, we shall grow in

all ways into Christ, who is the head by whom the whole body is fitted and joined together, every joint adding its own strength, for each separate part to work according to its function. So the body grows until it has built itself up, in love'.[10]

Now, though we see God's love especially in Jesus Christ the love is very clearly there from the beginning. It continues through all the vicissitudes of the individual and community lives which are chronicled in the Old Testament. It is of extreme importance to be categorically certain in our minds that God wills to build up all human beings into unity and love together in this world, and even more fully in the world to come. For our purpose in the discussion of confession and pastoral care, anyone who is priest, penitent or critic must come to accept that in the eyes of faith the law is the law of love, created by God who is love, for the loving purpose of bringing all into the fulness of his love.

This is fundamental, because it should set the tone of law dispensing. It should set the tone for counselling and the basis for the conducting of confession. God is the God of love, not of fear. He is ultimately responsible for us because he has created us. But his plan for the growth of his people into love, though simple in its purpose, is complex in its unfolding. This is because we are not perfect, but have the built-in possibility of growth; and within this possibility there is also a built-in freedom.

The early expression of this imperfection and freedom is illustrated through the books of the Old Testament, beginning with Genesis. Here the story is of the battle for growth, the conflict of good and evil in human nature, as human nature wrestles to choose one or other with its God-given freedom. The history is one of ups and downs, triumphs and calamities as the intricate and sensitive nature, generation after generation, continues the evolution towards God's ultimate plan. Each generation begins from its mother's womb, but begins not altogether from the beginning, because of all that is inherited from the parents. In the history of the people, the immediate environment of family and other physical, mental, psychological, or spiritual factors may play a part in what God wills to be a development into full maturity.

It is in the story of Noah[11] that we find a very beautiful picture of the symbol of God's continuing love for his creation: 'I set my bow in the cloud, and it shall be a sign of the covenant between me and the earth'. The rainbow depicts the lasting light and warmth and power of God's love. However, it is only possible to see the full beauty of the rainbow when rainfall and sunshine combine together. So it is in the existence of human beings that the clouds and rain of our sorrows, failures and tears bring into relief in all its multi-coloured splendour the glory of God's everlasting love. Far from being the disaster some would emphasise, the imperfection of our nature is the seedbed for the flowering and fulfilment desired by God. In our present existence, to be without clouds and rain is for the earth to become a desert. In our present existence, not even the holiest most saintly man, woman or child fully responds to the command attributed to Jesus: 'You must therefore be perfect just as your heavenly Father is perfect'.[12] Our perfection is limited this side of death. Much of the misunderstanding and excessive imputation of guilt can grow from the error of viewing ourselves in some other-worldly perfection, which has in fact never existed in us, yet from which we picture ourselves falling.

It is very natural for us as individuals and whole communities to get into depression and even despair, because we feel that God has withdrawn or even ceased to exist. This is well illustrated again and again in the psalms and the writings of the prophets, so that the theme brought out by the iniquities and failures of Israel, her leaders or individuals, continually reveals once more the covenant rainbow:

> Behold, the Lord's hand is not shortened, that it cannot save,
> or his ear dull, that it cannot hear;
> but your iniquities have made a separation
> between you and your God,
> and your sins have hid his face from you
> so that he does not hear.
> For your hands are defiled with blood
> and your fingers with iniquity;
> your lips have spoken lies,
> your tongue mutters wickedness.[13]

Jeremiah gives this reassurance from God:

> I have loved you with an everlasting love;
> therefore I have continued my faithfulness to you.[14]

And the psalmist pursues the same line:

> It is he who remembered us in our low estate,
> for his steadfast love endures forever;
> and rescued us from our foes,
> for his steadfast love endures forever;
> he who gives food to all flesh,
> for his steadfast love endures forever.
> O give thanks to the God of heaven,
> for his steadfast love endures forever.[15]

These illustrations are given to show the continuity of the law of love through all the time of the law and the prophets which Jesus said he had come to fulfil.

> At various times in the past and in various different ways, God spoke to our ancestors through the prophets; but in our time, the last

days, he has spoken to us through his Son.[16]

God's love for us was revealed when God sent into the world his only Son so that we could have life through him; this is the love I mean: not our love for God, but God's love for us when he sent his Son to be the sacrifice that takes our sins away.[17]

Jesus, forgiveness, reconciliation and love

Scripture tells us the purpose of Jesus Christ:

> Sacrifice and offering thou dost not desire;
> but thou hast given me an open ear.
> Burnt offering and sin offering
> thou hast not required.
> Then I said: 'Lo I come;
> in the scroll of the book it is written of me;
> I delight to do thy will, O my God;
> thy law is within my heart.[18]

When Jesus talks of this himself, he says according to the evangelist:

> My food is to do the will of the one who sent me, and to complete his work.[19]

When we see the purpose of Jesus as simply to do the will of his Father, and when we know that God's will is the maturing into his love and kingdom of the whole of the human race, we can take Jesus's words to his disciples at the last supper as an explicit command for the growth and maturing of our own individual and community lives:

> As the Father has loved me, so I have loved you. Remain in my love. If you keep my commandments you will remain in my love, I have told you

> this so that my own joy may be in you and your joy be complete ... This is my commandment: love one another, as I have loved you.[20]

However, in order to strengthen our own understanding of what is demanded of us, and what therefore will be the guidelines for our development, for our need for counselling and for our use of confession, we must look briefly at Jesus. He was sinless, but this does not mean to say that humanly he did not grow and mature in this world. He was subject to all human frailty, he had to go through the natural growth from the womb to full manhood. He may have been a quick developer, but there is no reason to suppose that he did not go through the trauma of leaving the womb, the beginning of perception through the senses, and the gradual evolution of his relationship with Joseph and Mary and his own peer group. It is wrong and unhelpful to place Jesus so far removed from us and our situation that he really is no guide or example to us. He was not immune from temptation, from growing pains and from the need to be obedient:

> Since then we have a high priest who has passed through the heavens, Jesus, the Son of God, let us hold fast our confession. For we have not a high priest who is unable to sympathise with our weaknesses, but one who in every respect has been tempted as we are, yet without sin.[21]

Our 'vision' of sin can prove to be too closely aligned to our wrong concept of the perfect me, and not sufficiently closely taking into account the built-in imperfection which gives rise to the proverb: 'For though the virtuous man falls seven times, he stands up again'.[22] It is not in our present nature to be without sin: but with the grace of God and our own efforts to be at one with his will, we can live lives free of sin in the sense specified earlier: namely, 'The purposeful disobedience of a creature to the known will of God'.[23] In other words, starting from and living with the imperfect, we should be better able to realize who we are, the enormous potential which is ours because of God's love, and the limitations which are to be overcome by our growth and maturing through the combination of our own personal effort and the enabling love of God.

From the very little we know about the early life of Jesus we are entitled to surmise that nothing very extraordinary was evident about him or his behaviour. He did not stick out like a sore thumb. He did not apparently gain a reputation in Nazareth, other than being the son of the carpenter (cf. Mt. 13.55) – either for wisdom or miraculous powers (however, note Lk 2.41–51). This should be very helpful to us, if we are to believe that he continued to live in Nazareth for about thirty years. It is surely enlightening and of great importance that Jesus was living an ordinary life, just as any one of us may be doing.

After his silent and hidden years at the start of his so-called public life, Jesus is given a public token of God's love and the assurance that he is indeed doing the will of his Father: 'This is my beloved son, in whom I am well pleased'.[24]

Having come to that point of fulfilment of his purpose, Jesus continues his reconciliation with all mankind. He goes into the waters of the Jordan, not symbolically to have his sins washed away, because we understand he was sinless. He goes into the waters to take on in symbol all the sin of mankind from the dirtied waters of Jordan. When he comes out of the water again he has taken on the mantle of all human sin and suffering . . . imperfection, guilt, failure, bitterness, loss, old age, death itself. As if to confirm this, the Spirit of God's love leads him to be tempted in the desert. He becomes like the scapegoat, driven into the desert carrying the sins of the people:

> The spirit immediately drove him out into the wilderness. And he was in the wilderness forty days, tempted by Satan; and he was with the wild beasts.[25]

Here we have the element of the scapegoat, earlier prophesied of him by Isaiah:

> By his sufferings shall my servant justify many, taking their faults on himself.[26]

He is also tempted, so that he can really be one of us, but so close is the union of his human will to that of his Father, his reaction is to make the choice which will fulfil God's purpose – summing up the whole of his mission thus:

> You shall worship the Lord your God and him only shall you serve.[27]

But this does not mean that he does not have to go on, humanly making choices: as a human being, his nature demands to be allowed to be angry, to be sorrowful to feel rebellion against his Father's will, to be tired and despondent. All this is on the way, which is the way of the cross. We are to follow him, at his command, so we should clearly understand what it took to make even Jesus Christ's humanity ready for resurrection:

> During his life on earth, he offered up prayer and entreaty, aloud and in silent tears, to the one who had the power to save him out of death, and he submitted so humbly that his prayer was heard. Although he was Son, he learnt to obey through suffering; but having been made perfect, he became for all who obey him the source of eternal salvation.[28]

For Jesus, as for each of us, the resolution of the conflict of good and evil, the daily battle through imperfection towards perfection, is ended in this life by the final imperfection of death:

> It is accomplished[29]
>
> Father, into your hands I commit my spirit.[29]

One last word at this stage about Jesus and the law of love. Because of his Father's will for the human race, Jesus was all the time intimately connected with the reconciliation of individuals and the community to the love of his Father. Jesus gave the new covenant of faithfulness and love established by God as the rainbow had been given to Noah, and the promise to Abraham. Only this covenant was so much more. It was different in kind, because now Jesus was not only the sign or the promise, he *was* the covenant itself, the uniting principle of love. As he moved through the towns and the countryside he was being the sacrament of reconciliation, the effective means of bringing individuals to the loving forgiveness of his Father. His very first call in Galilee announced:

> The time is fulfilled, and the kingdom of God is at hand; repent, and believe in the Gospel.[30]

Jesus was not only saying words of reconciliation and exhorting to repentance. His own presence was sacramental in the wide sense, because the effect of his presence was to reveal secret things in the hearts of men, women and children – touching, healing, bringing new life and reconciling. This dimension is of the essence of who Jesus was and is. It is also essential for any Christian, and especially those who are by their calling involved in the ministry of growth and maturing which reconciles man to God. Such a person can assist in the often delicate, often lengthy, always demanding opening to self-awareness and God-awareness, which also needs to be followed by neighbour-awareness for full reconciliation.

Jesus's power is in and through himself. The power of the confessor and of the penitent is that power of which the Lord spoke to St. Paul:

> My grace is enough for you: my power is at its best in weakness.[31]

The basis, then, for both priest and penitent is the willingness to try to do the will of God – following in Christ's steps. In the Gospel there is no promise of success by human standards in this world. But each of us as part of our willingness has to try to understand that God is love. In addition each of us must try through study, through prayer, through humility, in living and self-denial, through openness to the Spirit to be available both for God and for our fellow human beings, so that we may be channels of his peace.

NOTES

1 Deut. 6. 5.
2 Lev. 19.18.
3 Lk. 11. 37–52.
4 Lk. 11. 42, 46.
5 Mt. 5. 17–19.
6 *The Dictionary of the Christian Church.* Ed. F. L. Cross. p. 1259. Reprinted 1971. Oxford University Press.
7 Deut. 5. 17.
8 Mk. 2. 27–28.
9 I Jn. 4. 7–8.
10 Eph. 4. 13, 15–16.
11 Gen. 9. 13.
12 Mt. 5. 48.
13 Is. 59. 1–3.
14 Jer. 31. 3.
15 Ps. 136. 23–26.

16 Heb. 1. 1–2.
17 I Jn. 4. 9–10.
18 Ps. 40. 6–8.
19 Jn. 4. 34.
20 Jn. 15. 9–12.
21 Heb. 4. 14–15.
22 Prov. 24. 16.
23 *The Dictionary of the Christian Church*. Ed. F. L. Cross. p. 1259. Reprinted 1971. Oxford University Press.
24 Mt. 3. 17.
25 Mk. 1. 12–13.
26 Is. 53. 11.
27 Mt. 4. 10.
28 Heb. 5. 7–9.
29 Jn. 19. 30; Lk. 23. 46.
30 Mk. 1. 15.
31 2 Cor. 12. 9.

What is the Priest or Minister called to be?

WHEN a person is called to love and serve God, the wide sense of the call should be that it is universal for all and each of the human race, because each individual is the much loved creation of the God of love. In this sense the call is there in our very nature, though it may take a long time, even a lifetime for anyone to realise the call and answer it. Moreover, it may seem never to be realised at all in an overt way. There are those who may never have known God in a specific, revealed sense such as is claimed by the followers of Mohammed or Jesus Christ; those who have had some smattering of knowledge almost in family folklore, and those who have been deliberately brought up without a mention of God.

This book cannot go into the complexity of God's loving purpose for the growth to maturity and to ultimate union with himself of all mankind. All true religion must contain mystery, because God himself cannot be fully comprehended; he is beyond or excels the human potential. He can and does assist the human potential through revelation, but mystery remains:

> Just as you were once disobedient to God but now have received mercy because of their disobedience, so they have now been disobedient in order that by

> the mercy shown to you they also may receive mercy. For God has consigned all men to disobedience, that he may have mercy on them all.
>
> O the depth of the riches and wisdom and knowledge of God! How unsearchable are his judgements and how inscrutable his ways!
>
> For who has known the mind of the Lord, or who has been his counsellor?[1]

To quote that may well be infuriating to someone who has no belief, but it is the simple statement of truth as understood by believers. This leaves endless room for further exploration through the intellect, through science and through prayer. Nevertheless, 'the upright man finds life through faith',[2] so that when we come to believe in Jesus Christ, the call to love and serve is universal through baptism and is seen in this sense as a universal priesthood:

> You are a chosen race, a royal priesthood, a consecrated nation, a people set apart to sing the praises of God who called you out of darkness into his wonderful light.[3]

As far as confession is concerned, in some churches it is part of what a priest is ordained to and for. Counselling with reference to general behaviour in relation to what a person is can be done in varying degrees by anyone simply by being willing to sit and listen. Greater depth of counselling needs greater training and know-how. But when it comes to relationship to God and Christian behaviour, it is not easy for anyone who is not 'into' Christianity to be a truly Christian counsellor. That said, it is possible for those other than priests to counsel. In earlier days even confession could be made for lesser sins to anyone, ordained or non-ordained. These confessions were accepted as valid. However, in more recent times, the hearing of confessions in the church sense became restricted to the priest.

For this reason, what follows in this section is specifically considering the ordained priest or minister. The text employs the pronoun 'he', because this has been the traditional priestly sex. However, writing for a wide public, I acknowledge that there are women ordained as priests and ministers. It is not for me to attempt to argue here where the future lies in regard to ordination. But I think it is important that those who are ordained or may be in the future should take a look at what I am saying, whether it is immediately applicable or not. There are fairly hard lines drawn in the Roman Catholic Church and the Orthodox Churches about the ordination of women. Other Churches have already accepted women for ordination, or are hoping to do so soon. It may be good to state here that anything I write for the 'traditional' priest is intended to be useful for the ordained woman priest or minister.

I am also not trying to analyse the 'whole' of a priest, because that would take a different book. What I do want to do is to make clear something about the priest and the confessional, and the outreach from his priesthood into the local community. For instance, in the confessional the priest brings himself alongside whoever the penitent or penitents may be. He is not just a robot churning out words of absolution, which have no significance because God has already forgiven the penitent. God has a way of involving us in his purposes. The person and spiritual dimension of the priest have a real significance. This is more evident in the modern developments in the West, but has always been clear in the Orthodox approach. The actual meeting of confessor and penitent with its successful outcome of pardon and peace depend essentially upon the merciful love of God reaching out to enfold the penitent in forgiveness. However, Roman Catholic teaching has increasingly linked access to this merciful love and forgiveness even for lesser sin with the person of the confessor. Clearly, if there is a role for the confessor it is vital that he is accessible, knows something of God and his mercy, and is as well skilled as possible in the knowledge of human beings. He should also be a man of prayer.

Training

When someone comes to submit himself to the authority of the Church, asking to 'try his vocation' in the ordained ministry, he may or may not have any knowledge – intellectual or practical – of confession. If he does have any knowledge or experience, he will understand that confession is only one part in thinking, training and living for the priesthood. Some indeed among the Free Churches and even in the Church of England may have no experience of confession and no teaching on it. For Roman Catholics the teaching and practice will be there and lived, or else questioned and perhaps in disuse. In the latter case, the disuse will almost certainly emerge in interviews before the candidate is accepted for training.

The training itself, quite rightly, is firmly based on the study of scripture, philosophy, theology, Church history and so on. It has always been stressed in the main Christian Churches that those who are to be priests, teachers and leaders must be grounded in the Old and New Testaments and in theological development which has been going on down the centuries. This grounding explores the Christian churches' understanding of God from revelation, and especially the knowledge of the life and teaching of Jesus Christ. Between the different denominations and churches there have been varying emphases in training according to the outlook on what a priest is and is for.

The content and ethos of particular training colleges and centres varies therefore quite considerably. What is important is that there should be a balance in this grounding and growing of the potential priest or minister. It is not easy to get the right mixture between the intellectual and the practical. Of course, there is also a great variety of ministry to which the trainee will eventually emerge. Without in any way wanting to undervalue the importance of the academic and the intellectual, I think there is room for the colleges of the various churches to be as alert as possible to the importance of trying to offer the emerging pastors an all-round set of tools for the job. Of course, the training is not complete when the new deacon, priest or minister first presents himself to the people of God whom he has been sent to serve. Much can only come from experience. At the same time it is essential in this very delicate area of training for work with souls that there is sufficient time and importance given to pastoral studies alongside the more academic. Some reasons for a possible imbalance within theological colleges which may still exist today in some places are set out by Frank Wright:

> In the academic hierarchy, pastoral theology is seen to be the 'practical bit' at the end of other theological studies, but with a considerable gap existing between it and those other studies. Perhaps the truth may some day dawn that other forms of theology cannot be wrought in isolation from pastoral theology; if dogmatic and systematic theology does not come alive in the 'care of persons' and if pastoral theologians cannot ask themselves pertinent questions about the meaning for human beings of statements made by dogmatic and systematic theologians all the way along then there is deservedly little hope for theology in the

future. Of course, as with all attempts at integrated studies, there is a legitimate fear that one aspect of those studies will dominate the rest, and there is some truth in the contention that 'the context of theological inquiry' has been a very pale and self-effacing context for many attempts at the writing of pastoral theology. In the U.S.A. there has been such a harnessing of psychological insights and techniques to church-based ministry that ministers often seem to have simply taken over secular counselling roles on weekdays. But if that situation is undesirable, it is less so than the poverty-stricken spectacle of pastoral theology shelves in the religious bookshops on this side of the Atlantic, treating as pastoral theology manuals of 'preaching at Parish Communion' in the absence of much else.[4]

Frank Wright has his own ideas as to why this atmosphere which he senses exists. He feels that proper weight and seriousness is not given in the Church to pastoral theology because of fear and mistrust of psychology as a godless discipline. He also sees a professionalism in two fields as taking away the accent from the pastoral, namely liturgy and management. Thirdly he suggests that the implication of the word 'pastor' is paternalistic and aligned with the worst of what is drawn from the Good Shepherd analogy. Yet, although someone caustically said: 'Who would want to be a sheep anyway?', there is much of value in the analogy, and the word pastoral in fact seems to be more and more in current use.

For me, the balance of the training remains in question, though there is development all the time. Dr. R. S. Lee, in his well known and much used *Principles of Pastoral Counselling,* points out the lack of specific training for priests in pastoral counselling, and emphasises that where it is given, it is often inadequate and leaves many questions as to its use by the ordinary parish priest. While he raises the whole question of developing specialised ministry either by training individuals to work in different areas or placing trained personnel at special centres, he is very clear that this is not enough:

> We may accept that there is a strong case in favour of setting up a specialised ministry in one form or another and, as a corollary, of developing courses of training to equip men for this ministry, but this does not rule out the question of training all clergy and social workers of the church. Admitted that the full training cannot be given to all and that perhaps some are not suited to receive it, there is still need for some training to be given to all. Such training need not be considered as second class and inferior to the fuller training. It should be aimed to produce better pastors, not specialised pastoral counsellors. It is possible to be a good pastor without being a pastoral counsellor in the technical sense.[5]

It is essential that we take his point about the difference between pastoral care and pastoral counselling in the strict sense. If we take the latter first, the point at issue is that there should be specialised training for the pastoral counsellor which is over and above, deeper and more specialised than that which is necessary for the ordinary parish clergy to exercise valid pastoral care. If some would-be clergy are trained in this specialised way, it is to be hoped that they will be used as full-time counsellors, which moves their role away from that of the run-of-the-mill pastor. The specialised role is important; it is in a field where the Church should have a place, making available personnel who combine the training which is acceptable and respectable among other trained counsellors with their own Christian commitment as men and women of faith and prayer. This particular ministry is not confined to the ordained, but should be a work of non-ordained Christian men and women, provided that they have reasonable training, and are dedicated christians.

Some would argue that, in today's world, the role of pastoral counsellor, bordering on or continuing into the role of the psycho-therapist, is more suitable for the profession of those who are not ordained. In general I agree with that. But I would stress heavily and with years of stumbling pastoral work behind me that there is space and reason for a number of ordained or religious order men and women, whose full training and competence places them on a level footing with trained members of the laity. It has always been characteristic of those who came forward for ordination that they had a wide spectrum of ability and competence. There have, over the years, been those associated with the sciences, the arts, teaching and the law, to say nothing of administration and even government. To pursue this is outside the scope of this book, except to point out at this time that there is, or should be, space for the specialist in the ranks of the clergy. This is a far remove from taking the line that psychology, psychotherapy and psychiatry are ungodly and should be shunned by anyone believing in God, especially priests and ministers.

But, in regard to the non-specialist, the ordinary pastor, it is essential that the training of all who are going forward to ordination should include an introduction to the study of human behaviour. (This introduction should equally apply to religious and lay church workers). The weight and the time given to this study should be on a par and interlocking with the main lines of theology. All of those who are responsible for training and for setting up and staffing seminaries should ensure that those who will instruct the would-be ordinands are themselves more than simply academic brains. Pastoral experience of involvement at the street or field level cannot be replaced by any other competence or innate goodness in those who are training others to be fitted for a pastoral role in the care of human beings. The ideal teacher should be highly theologically qualified but also pastorally experienced and aware. The course should be not only scriptural and theological but also geared to have teachers well trained in the growth of the human person, in behavioural sciences, in the background and development of the main lines of psychology and counselling.

There is no intention here of belittling the value of academic study and the deepening of knowledge of the things of God through theology. What I am trying to say is that quite a number of those who have been trained for work in the pastoral field seem to have been less than well served in their training, because they have not been taught how to communicate all the depth of their understanding of the mystery of God. They lack the psychological knowledge and awareness which would enable them to get across to the ordinary person in the pew or the street.

In order to be able to convey all the knowledge which has been acquired in the years of training, the individual must also have been led to discover who and what he or she is, and how people react and respond.

Unless an ordained person has already come to know that he must try to relate to all that he finds in himself, the good and bad, the potential and the inadequacy, the fears and the joys, there is much danger in letting him loose on other people. Indeed, it would be fatal if he came out thinking he knew everything, as some have in the past. He is to come out still in the learning process which hopefully will continue until he dies. But if he does not know that he is developing, that maturity develops by stages, that he can be still at the spiritual or physical age of fifteen when he is twenty-five, forty or more – then he will not seek to grow, and he may enter into fear. Nor will he be so well able to listen to others and learn from them, or to listen and share his own growth with them.

From this knowledge of himself, there must be opportunity of learning to relate in all sorts of conditions to others of both sexes and differing ages, varied racial backgrounds and political, religious or non-religious attitudes. This may sound idealistic. Well, at least the principle should be taken and the extent and demand acknowledged, so that the future pastor will himself be challenged to go out and meet people, to risk something of himself instead of playing safe, to share the depth of his belief, his doubt, his desire and his frustration.

I write this with some assurance. I have been through it myself. I know the danger of not being given the basic training necessary both for my own development and for helping others. Church authorities and pastors can escape into abstract theology and administration rather than sharing the insights of theology in the costly discipline and vocation of knowing and being known by the ones Jesus came to save. Some of my experience was harrowing to myself and to 'clients' when I failed to understand the intricacies of human nature. I was personally very fortunate. I was thrown in at the deep end with war service after university life. Later, and considerably later, I realised more and more deeply my lack when I had the privilege of working some eleven years close to Dr. R. S. Lee in Oxford University. At the same time, there were those trained and practising in the psychiatric field who were prepared to listen to my questions, and to assist my amateur work where it bordered on or indeed obtruded into the psychiatric field. I did learn. But I have always been aware that at no time in the priesthood have I had or made time to do any in-depth study in psychology, the behavioural sciences and so on.

At this point I want to try to set out various aspects of the priestly/ministerial character and calling, hoping gradually to build up an over-all sense of the qualities and tensions which are part and parcel of the ordinary confessor. This is a collage; it is not a finished picture, there are other facets which can be added. Not each individual will be a whole picture. However, at least some of the essential ingredients are here.

A teacher

The style and content of priestly training is the background from which the ordained person will draw material for the function of teacher. Teaching, preaching, spreading the Good News are all ingredients. Because this is so, the priest has to come to terms with the difficulty of bringing out different facets at different times. It is very necessary that he teaches with authority, standing in, as it were, for Christ in his teaching role. However, the mantle of teacher can be difficult to wear at the same time as the mantle of counsellor, if counselling is largely non-directive, while the confessor may need to be directive.

As confessor, alongside listening it may be necessary for the priest to do some positive teaching within the rite of confession. This may occur when a person is doubtful about some act or omission – is it sinful or not? He may also have occasion to give a teaching line on the way to avoid some kind of failure confessed, or give positive teaching guidance on prayer, the use of the sacraments or service of neighbours. Sometimes a penitent can be positively wrong about a 'sin', which is in fact no sin. Here the priest may need to set the person right, guiding his general attitude to and recognition of sin along the lines of the teaching of the Church. Within this role there is a temptation for some of us to become too didactic and even authoritarian in approach.

Teaching in confession should therefore be compatible with the situation. If the confessional accommodation is open and the penitent at ease – that is, seated and ready for a lengthy encounter, the priest may be in a position to expand and clarify as necessary. But the accent is on helping the penitent to understand and come to terms with the doctrine of the Church in regard to a particular aspect of morality which is unclear or at variance with the conscience of the penitent. The confessor needs to have a sound basic knowledge of moral theology, together with a sensitivity in teaching the individual who is there. It is at this point, especially if in the confines of an enclosed confessional, that teaching can become heavy and done in a kind of 'shorthand' which may be less than helpful.

The value of the teaching role of the priest is that it should be behind all that he is in relation to the community. Teaching should come through his sermons, his talks to individuals or groups, his attitude to families, to marriage, sickness, death, crime, violence, practice or non-practice of religion, and so on. The more he is known and his mind and heart are known, the more easy it is for him to put across teaching in the confessional situation. It is therefore very important indeed that the preaching and teaching at the parochial or community level are *relevant* at that level, and not desiccated and abstract expositions.

It is the responsibility of the priest as teacher that he keeps abreast of the developments of thought which are current at the time, so that he can assist those who come for advice and not simply have recourse to what he remembers from his days in the theological college. Probably insufficient emphasis is put upon the in-service courses which are or might be available for the ordinary pastor. The flexibility of mind and the openness to new ideas is of very real value in the teacher who is meeting people of so many differing origins and outlooks. Fossilisation implies petrification! Rock hardness in the confessional is too often destructive.

One aspect of teaching is being able to listen to the person who is wanting or needing to learn, and making available for him or her the possibility of development. Sometimes the real importance is to be able to point an individual to another teacher, whether this is a human person, a group or a book which goes beyond where you have gone and helps further growth in the penitent. The general principle is that which I have mentioned before, namely that God, who made each of us out of love, wants each of us to grow more and more into union with him in love.

Prepared to share

The priest has the duty of relating to the people whose priest or minister he is. His reaction to this duty will depend upon his own personality and upon the training and experience he has. It is disconcerting for a parishioner if the priest is over shy or sensitive, a person who cannot mix and is not approachable, who almost hides away from the congregation, is aloof or distant. Those who choose, train and ordain have a responsibility for summing up the potential that a candidate has for developing along the lines necessary to spread and share the Gospel. Mistakes can be made, and then the ordained person may find real difficulties from shyness. It is not too easy for us to work upon ourselves for change. But there are things we can do to help ourselves to be more available for others. Our efforts to become approachable people may be hard work, but we should not feel hopeless if there are difficulties. There is always room for development.

Many of us have been brought up in an atmosphere where it really wasn't done to talk about oneself, especially in regard to the intimacies of life – spiritual life, sex life and so on. Without doubt this was generally inhibiting, but it could easily come to be regarded as a matter of good taste and breeding. I know in my own case that it was very possible to be shot down for being pious or a show-off if there was any serious God-talk started from my side. It was a wonderful breakthrough when I was first able to discover my mother as a person who was open to talking about God. Even before that, I had found in a Jesuit spiritual director at school a man who would not only let me express things I thought and felt, but shared with me some of his own life with its doubts and sorrows and vision. This was a tremendous experience for me. Although it did not prevent a complete loss of faith on my part at a later stage, it probably had an underlying influence when I believed again, and made speaking to a priest much more possible.

However, in my experience there are large numbers of ordained and non-ordained who are spiritually shy. Sometimes this comes from deep within their own natural shyness, sometimes from pride which fears to appear a fool, to be looked down upon or to be sneered at. It is not at all infrequent to have an inbuilt or environmental attitude which quite simply says to mind and heart that this is a private matter between me and God. It is wiser and safer to keep it all to myself.

Once a person has been able to break through the barrier of reticence, much can happen. How then, to break through? The priest or would-be ordained, the religious sister or church helper, needs a helper – not only in training but during and after training . . . and then for the whole of life. It is all too easy to be forever on the receiving end of life stories, problems and sorrows, with the demand for a word of assurance or kindness, love or assistance. It is perilous for the helper if he is not open to be helped. If I am never on the pouring out end, with someone listening and sharing and giving me the word of comfort or encouragement, I am the more likely to withdraw further, to become simply superficial or even to get near to a breakdown.

Who will help the helpers, if the helpers all the time try to help others and never seek or expect or get help themselves? There are various possibilities ranging from trained psychiatric help, through different forms of counselling, to the ordinary set-up within the Church of priest and ministers and others having a soul-friend or someone equivalent who can be rung up or visited, who can shoulder some of the burden, and ease tension. Those responsible for training and those leading the clergy through dioceses or circuits or whatever kind of organisation there may be should be aware of clerical isolation. In this they can do well to begin by looking at themselves. A leader is naturally isolated to some degree. He is subject on one side to adulation and over-protection, on the other to attack, loneliness, misrepresentation and a sense of failure.

For me, an experience of great benefit has been a group of clergy, religious sisters, trained lay counsellors and psychiatric social workers meeting regularly for sharing. We simply opened our experience to each other in an exchange of concern and on an interdisciplinary basis. We all felt a great measure of benefit, felt the support of others who were on the same endeavour, yet differently founded and differently patterned. It was equally useful to discover the possible overlap between us in our work, and also the strengths and limitations which each of us had in ourselves and in our method of working.

Many dioceses and church groupings are now beginning to develop means by which the clergy can come together to discuss among themselves and with others, opening up some of the areas which they may not have been specifically trained in, such as spiritual direction, behavioural sciences, working with conflict situations and so on.

Such opening in a group or on a one-to-one basis can be a great help. The difficulty will remain however, if the ordinary pastor remains shy and withdrawn, and refuses to accept that he personally will ever be competent to guide anyone else, especially among his peer group. There must be very many ordained ministers who would curl up at the thought of giving 'spiritual direction'. They would feel this was for the monks and friars – the religious, not for the mere ordinary priest. So a vital part of the pastoral care of the local minister is immediately put out of his sights or turned away by himself, to be done by a member of a religious order ... or perhaps by a member of the laity, perhaps a trained counsellor ... perhaps one with no basic theology or belief.

Yet, there is a very real need for more clergy and others to feel the trust which enables them to share of themselves and their spiritual life with others. It is particularly a need today between priest and people. Rather than running away into meetings and administration and such like, each of us should learn to be available, not to be afraid.

At very least we can be listeners, not always in a hurry, not putting people off because we are scared. In my estimation, except for a very small minority of clergy who may never have the confidence to be available for guidance – though gifted in other ways – the ordinary run of the clergy should take it for granted that hearing confessions is part of the priestly ministry, together with giving a listening ear and pastoral care within the local setting. This is one purpose of ordination, and one not to be neglected. In humility and truth, each of us as ministers must be open to the corollary that, in beginning to be open and trying to assist or even guide someone else, none of us is the last word. What is more, a specially trained and qualified professional counsellor will be needed by some people. We can help the person to identify the need. We may also be able to suggest an approach to the right kind of qualified person.

For an ordained person or a religious or church worker who has never really opened up to anyone, there may at this point be a danger. That danger is the temptation to say to oneself that it is too late now; if I had done all this before . . . and so on. Well, fight that temptation. There is always time, and the opportunity which may be opening up now could make all the difference to your own happiness and growth, as well as to the people who are given to you by God and the Church. Do not be ashamed. It is never too late. Even at the eleventh or twelfth hour, God can work on us.

I myself have found earlier in life the difficulty of initially opening up to anyone at all. Then at different times, people have come into my life, and it has been both possible and productive to open up. Sometimes this has been to an understanding confessor, who was not particularly directing me, because somewhere else I already had such a director. For myself, I would say that the distinction can easily become blurred, and indeed I do not see that there are necessarily two separate functions of confessor and director. I shall expand on this point later. I do not find it easy to talk about myself much. To have to tell more than one person the whole story is even harder. When my soul-friend dies or goes away and it is incumbent on me to begin again, it becomes harder again.

Unfortunately, the years pass by and not only is there movement of clergy round the face of the earth, so that the sheer distance can be a limiting factor, but also death can intervene. This may mean a period of emptiness and loneliness because it has to be admitted that not all priests are available and even if each one was, we are different individuals, and one person suits one person, another suits another. You may just not be fortunate at any given time in having access to anyone at all on a regular basis. However, ask around, keep your eyes open. God can bring people into our lives most unexpectedly.

Another point which is worth considering is that you may possibly get the help you need from someone who is not a member of the denomination to which you belong. There can be complications here if you are seeking sacramental absolution. But this line of investigation should not be eliminated. I suppose it is possible that a particular individual might not feel free or willing to be present for you to open up, but in my experience this could be true for a member of one's own denomination as for one from another church. It should also be mentioned in the same context that there is much value even for the ordained person in being able to share with a non-ordained the depth of soul and spiritual life. In the past, a non-ordained person has been acceptable as someone to whom confession could be made, both in the pre-Reformation Church in the West and among the Orthodox.

Confessor, counsellor or both?

The combination of roles in the one person of the priest can prove difficult. As teacher he must be able to give definite guidance; as counsellor he is less so or even non-directive. He is the one who leads the eucharist, consoles at death beds, tries to help with marriage problems and a hundred and one things.

There has been a certain question mark over the exact role of the priest or minister in the rite of penance or reconciliation. We shall come back to this later. Suffice it to say here that there are those who hold that confession is to be strictly held apart from counselling. For them, any degree of intervention by the priest by way of advice or counselling really blurs the reality of the presence and power of God in the sacrament. There are others, and I come among them, who do not feel the need for a total divorce of the absolution and counsel.

The division of opinion is partly in regard to the view of 'purity' of the work of God on the human soul, when a penitent comes in open and honest humility. We enter the region of the mystery of God who can touch, melt and heal without any human ministry. Those disliking or dismissing the priestly role argue that the 'chemistry' of the encounter between God and his individual human beings is not to be disturbed by advice or direction given by the human minister, who could appear to be speaking for God. This is particularly so when the priest sees it as his role to underline the gravity of something which has been confessed, to seek an assurance of a purpose of amendment of life, or to admonish the penitent in regard to any injury his wrong action may have caused to another person.

Confession brings the penitent to the presence of God and charges the Church's ministry with the responsibility of making available a priest as a human presence which can facilitate and assure the penitent. Sometimes the penitent comes in doubt, but more usually he comes with an accusation against himself. He probably supposes that the priest will take his word for it that he is guilty in the terms of his self-accusation. He normally then comes in self-accepted guilt. By confessing, expressing sorrow for the wrong done, and by purposing to try to do better, he lays himself open to the merciful forgiveness of God. His attitude then is self-condemning before he starts. If the priest takes what he confesses as the truth, as a priest he has to assess intention, gravity, sorrow for the action committed, and the desire to do better in the future.

The priest is within his mandate if he simply listens to the matter confessed by the penitent, suggests a form of penance which is accepted by the penitent, and then says the words of absolution without any words of comfort or advice. After confession and absolution, he can say: Go in peace and sin no more – or he can say simply: Go in peace.

Until recently, the ordinary local priest in the Roman Catholic Church has not really been encouraged to give any guidance. Some have done so because to them it seemed right on some occasions to offer guidelines. But many have simply given a penance and the words of absolution. The 'feel' of the situation has now changed, where confession takes place in an open situation, face to face. And the formula or rite of the sacrament of penance has also explicitly opened up the possibility and indeed rightness of giving some advice.

It is, therefore, necessary and important that the priest should come to terms with what he understands his role to be, thinking out what difference there is or may be when counselling is included and is accepted as integral to the rite of confession.

The counsellor in the more strictly psychological sense is one who has been trained for counselling, and may or may not be ordained. The counselling is the centre point. The very nature of this training is different from the training of the confessor. Though the confessor is to be a listener, he is also trained to a teaching role, and he is at liberty to teach the penitent directively if he sees fit. Thus he can distinguish right and wrong; he can put clearly what the law of God or of the Church is; he can even go so far as to refuse absolution if he thinks the disposition of the penitent is not right.

Speaking generally, it is not for the counsellor to be judgemental, to lay stress on faults, sins or omissions. He is there to receive the other person as he or she is. He is there to allow that person, his client, to work through the difficulties which he already knows, so that he can come gradually to the disclosure and personal realisation of unconscious motivations. Hopefully, this will uncover the sources and roots of his overt behaviour.

The counsellor can and should come alongside the client, so that the client can understand that he is understood. The counsellor can, as it were, play back to the client the substance of what he has been saying, so that it is clear that the former is on the ball in regard to what is being revealed. This is helpful in that it gives encouragement to the client, but he is not actually being led forward anywhere, he is being affirmed where he has got to. Incidentally, a few such words of re-iteration may help the client by allowing him to re-phrase what he has said, or to elucidate it. The counsellor is there to be warm, accepting and listening. He has to have both time and patience for the person, without expecting that there will be any move forward, or indeed any sign of anything in one, two or more sessions. The counsellor is at the client's disposal. He is not there personally to achieve a breakthrough, to set the client right or to turn him away from a particular course of action which may be sinful. Indeed sin, moral judgement or rights and wrongs are at the client's disposition and discretion. In other words, the counsellor is essentially non-directive. To begin to lay down the law about sin could be prejudicial to the whole pattern.

I hope this makes it clear that the basic form of confession can be seen almost in contradiction to the basic form of counselling. Nevertheless, in many conditions, especially among the clergy or religious men and women leading more dedicated lives, there grew up the custom of having a 'spiritual director'. It was normally assumed that such a person would be seeing the particular penitent over an extended period, sometimes almost a lifetime. During this relationship the penitent would consider that the priest had the function of forgiving sin in the ordinary confessional way, but he also had a special function. He was in the situation of being the skilled and hopefully spiritual father who was to lead and guide his spiritual child to a greater maturity in his or her life. This would include advice on the seriousness of sins committed, suggestions on prayers and penances which might help to guard against further sinning; there could be guidance in ways of prayer, suggestions about a rule of life to be undertaken. The director might well advise on books for spiritual reading and might firmly lead in the particular way that he the confessor was living, be it Benedictine, Franciscan, Dominican, Jesuit or any other 'school'.

Because the director might not himself be very widely read or practised in any other way than that of his order or society, it could mean that the natural instincts or inclinations with which an individual might already be coming to God could be uprooted in favour of a different way. I remember, when I was chaplain at Oxford University, giving a considerable time to a young woman over some years. She wanted to pray, took to prayer, and over a period developed into a deep and wordless form of contemplative prayer which suited her, and was in my understanding a very good and true way of spending time with God. Subsequently, she decided to join a contemplative order of religious sisters, and was accepted. She soon ran into a crisis because the novice mistress, after seeing her at prayer, told her gently but firmly that she must use *a book* during the time set aside for meditation in chapel. Happily the crisis was resolved after a while, but it is clear that, within that context, the novice mistress was not prepared for a novice who would perhaps be advanced on a way of prayer which was not going to fit in with the ordinary way novices were expected to learn to be with God.

It has, of course, always been normal in the Orthodox Church for the priest hearing confession to expect to give advice. In the Church of England and the Roman Catholic Church, it was for a long time customary for the penitents to end their part of the confession of sins by saying something like: I am sorry and ask God's pardon for these and any other sins I may have committed, and ask of you, my spiritual father, penance, *counsel* and absolution.

It cannot, therefore, be said that there has been any clear-cut distinction in the earlier days between confession as a directive and judgmental action, and confession which led the penitent to examine himself and to grow from the examination aided by the careful and non-directive approach of the priest. Naturally, it was expected that the penitent should make a thorough examination of his conscience. But this was done before coming to confession. The priest was trained to assume that the penitent had thought out what had to be said, and only perhaps if the penitent explained that he did not know what to say or asked for help would the priest intervene.

This somewhat negative approach leans towards those who favour complete non-intervention on the part of the priest. However, it is not clear to me that this attitude grew up in the Roman Catholic Church as a policy with a sound theological rationale. Rather, as I see it, the more recent history of confession in this century before Vatican II had two main lines which influenced the ordinary clergy. Firstly, it was assumed that the parochial priest was hardly trained to be a 'spiritual director'. This tended to lead to the possibility of adopting a habit in the confessional of simply listening to the penitent, asking a question if necessary to clarify the sin or circumstances, and giving absolution. Very often, there was no question because clarification did not seem required. The penitent was given a penance to say and told to make an act of contrition, while at the same time the confessor gave absolution. Secondly, the effect of more frequent reception of holy communion 'necessitating' more frequent confession meant that there were queues outside the confessionals on Saturday evenings. The confessor often had his work cut out to 'get through' the numbers even with simply giving a penance and absolution; there was certainly no time for much questioning. To offer only a listening ear, a penance and absolution became a way of life for many priests. It could be said in addition that the pastoral guidance from some teachers of would-be confessors was positively not to give advice.

It was into this atmosphere that I arrived as a priest. From early in my practice in the confessional I found a real need and gratitude for words of encouragement and advice during the course of confession. Some priests feel that a word dropped into the confession of an unknown person would be fairly useless, possibly trite and possibly harmful. My experience has been very different. From almost chance contacts, which may have been some working of the Spirit, the build-up of deeper relationship with individuals has been marked, and the development of a widespread counselling has continually increased over the years. I do not say that every confession must include counselling nor should each priest imagine that ordination itself makes a counsellor. But I do personally advocate an openness and sensitivity, with an inclination for the inclusion of counsel rather than against it. This attitude necessitates care, listening, concern and discretion. Especially in the face-to-face confession, for me the opportunity for developing the counselling role together with confession has been very productive. This has taken time, prayer and listening to older and wiser people.

My hope would be that confession itself becomes more regular but less frequent as individual people come to trust the individual priest. This hope is for the generality of ordinary people. Such people should know a priest who is a man of prayer, wise and a listener, and be able to get advice and be regular but not perhaps too frequent at the one-to-one encounter, relying day by day upon forgiveness within prayer and liturgy. However, a considerable number will require more frequent confession and counselling contact, some because of the style of life they have adopted, some because of personal search, depression or other psychological need. Within this latter category of more frequent need, I leave complete freedom to ask for confession only, counselling only or a combination. I do not see that it is necessary to adopt a hard and fast rule which divides confession totally from counselling. The old phrase is *sacramenta sunt propter homines* – the sacraments are for people rather than vice versa. If it is helpful to be a counsellor in confession for the sake of the penitent, well and good.

But, in summary, it is very important that each priest or minister brings himself to the situation and adjusts or modifies according to the needs he meets, providing always that he accepts and realises the utter dependence upon God and the very great variety of need in the individual human being.

A pastor

Ordination is geared towards a ministry, a life of caring, a pastoral involvement. The terminology can vary. What ordination means is that this particular person has taken on some share in the role of Jesus Christ. Jesus came as a friend and brother, he shared and he taught. He did not appear as a father figure, because he attributed fatherhood to his father in heaven. But he did, according to the fourth evangelist, take to himself the title of shepherd. Pastor and shepherd are really the same. Each has a guiding and supervising role over the sheep or the people who are his flock.

The newly ordained man finds himself appointed to a position where he is normally under an older cleric. He probably has a confined area of work. If he is assistant to a more elderly priest, he will largely depend for his training and understanding of pastoral needs upon the older man. If much is kept in his own hands by the senior cleric, the younger man will easily be frustrated. The established incumbent has a duty to make himself and the parish open to the enthusiasm and hard work of the young newly ordained person. For the latter is there to be opened to the preaching of the good news, to establish his potential, and to grow in confidence for his future mission. The present incumbent must not frustrate this growth by personal jealousy. He has a great opportunity for encouraging growth and development by sharing what expertise he has and realising the call we all have to follow John the Baptist: 'He must increase but I must decrease'. For the present incumbent the task he is asked to do may be personally self-effacing. But I can assure anyone who is upset or feels put down that over the years there will be wonderful refreshment as you witness the emergence of the younger priest into maturity.

The newly ordained priest immediately becomes involved with people – individuals and groups. Very quickly, I hope, he comes to know that not all he learned in college is immediately applicable now. He must continue learning not only from the older priest but from the parishioners. He is to work for and with them. He must listen and learn to integrate what they need and what he thinks he has come to provide. It takes time to know and be known, to build up the trust which does not come from wearing a collar or from having clerical status but from being about, being open, being a spiritual leader.

The young priest's training in a particular college may have put more emphasis on one angle than another – liturgy, preaching, administration, the social outreach of the Gospel, youth work, small groups or home visitation. In fact, he may find he is a jack of all trades, that his motor cycle is the best way into youth work, that the pub is a good discussion group, that hospital and prison provide the better one-to-one contacts. He may get pulled by the locality to look into unemployment, racial tension or housing problems. Within all this, he has to maintain his centre in God, his life of prayer and his commitment to the care of souls.

The extent and purpose of the priest as pastor has not been sufficiently studied by the churches. Training has not always covered this aspect sufficiently deeply or scientifically. The ordained individual has been left to make what he can of pastoral care, providing that he is covering the main services and sacraments. In preaching and teaching he is vested with some authority and is expected to use it. But he will use it better if he is in close relationship to the people, is a man of prayer, and lives out his theological grounding in the experience of life.

When the priest is called, or feels called, to be 'father', the very title brings into relief some of the problems which the priest has in relationship with people. He lives with them, he is pastorally responsible to God and the Church for them. At the same time they in their way are responsible for him.

The ordinary, human father or mother has relationships up and down the age range. There are parents on both sides of the family, the equality of husband and wife, the relationships at work or in the neighbourhood, the central position of father or mother to the children. I never really know how all this fits in with the psychology of an individual, but in many ways what the priest has to be in relation to his parish is no more nor less difficult or complex. Because he is not normally a blood relation of those to whom he is pastor, he has one advantage – a certain distance. He has the disadvantage that, because he is not a blood relation, there may not be anyone with whom he can really share enough of his care even if he is married.

The father or mother of a family can and should be able to speak of at least all family matters intimately. It may be more difficult when speaking of friends, relations or neighbours, and even more so if there are business or professional secrets. But for the priest anyone could corner him within the seal of the confessional.

He therefore has the wider relation of 'father' and he has to keep himself aware of his responsibility to each and every one of his 'family'. Here he has to grow a very large heart, because there is a real danger of not being open to all, of having favourites, of allowing some of those who may be most in need of help to feel unloved. I know in my own life I have been told that I have no time for my fellow clergy, no time for the poor, no time for the rich, no time for the Irish, no time for politics, no time for the Jesuits, no time for nuns. I have also been told I spend too much time with the rich, too much with the poor, too much with religious sisters, too much dabbling in politics, too much praying. So where am I?

If he is to be father, the priest must be approachable and he must be trustworthy – a person to whom anyone can confide a secret and know it will not be gossiped about. He must not be hedged off by battlements of relations, housekeepers, or secretaries who defend him from the approach, importunate or otherwise, of those who want him and his time. And so he has to have time to give without always seeming to be busy.

But, as father, he needs to know when he has to lay down the law, when he has to be lenient, when he has to be deaf, when he has to be blind, when he has to keep silent. One of the difficult aspects of parenthood must be the effort to keep abreast of the growing child. Parental qualities include the understanding of childhood trauma with the patience and skill needed to allow a young person to grow into personhood with all the awkward angles, the rebellions, the assertions of independence and the sudden regressions into childhood. These are parallelled in the fatherly side of the priest, when he has to manage all at the same time with so many differing age groups, social classes, educational and home backgrounds. For him, children come into knowledge and love of God and church or fail to do so; young people get bored with church, rebel against God and his law, want to be independent in their thinking and way of life. They want to be free from binding religious duties like church attendance. Sometimes then as a father he needs to be firm and even stern when there is violence or disruption, when there is flouting of morality and contempt of the home family. Yet, he can turn young people or older people off and away by severity, lack of understanding, narrow-mindedness or irrelevance. He therefore has to be patient to the last degree, while not allowing one person or set of persons to take up all his time.

He has to listen and listen in order to hear and understand what is being said on the surface and what is coming through unspoken from beneath what is being said. He needs to stand firm where it is necessary and yet be open to change as he comes to know and love the goodness and the difference of younger people in their growing enthusiasm. He has to be fatherly and yet not paternalistic, and all this is quite a catalogue which scarcely begins to cover all the nuances of feeling and behaviour required of the priest as father.

Of course, as with a human father-in-blood, there are easy ways out, which are not satisfactory in human or in spiritual terms. The heavy, so-called Victorian father can be taken as a caricature. Yet unfortunately I have known priests who could adopt that attitude; in times past, especially in the training of the Roman Catholic ministers, there has been a lot of authoritarian behaviour by clergy. Often parishioners were expected to listen to what was said from the pulpit, to take what was said in the confessional, and to be silent contributors of their presence and their money, not of their ideas. This tough style of discipline and authority contributed to large and stable congregations, to orderly church services and to a static conservatism, which to some extent suited the time and the people, but which is now outmoded.

With the severe or Victorian father attitude there is the danger that the penitent or parishioner will always be a spiritual and moral child. He will never be able to take possession of himself, own himself and be responsible for himself. There are always those in a parish who want all decisions to be made for them. This is not necessarily only in spiritual matters. Some can want direction on everything from flower arrangements to investments, from marriage to making a will.

However, I personally have no doubt at all that, though God wants us to be childlike in some ways of trust and even belief, he also wants us to grow in maturity, to be our own selves, to be adult in relation to him and to the world, to be full men and women. The father figure of the priest and the mother figure of the Church can breed a club of Peter Pans – far removed from the growth which Jesus obviously encouraged in his disciples, and which was very evident in emancipation of the early Church through the gift of the Holy Spirit.

This means that the priest, in being father, especially in the spiritual growth of his flock, must be prepared for those he is fathering to outgrow him. He will find them growing past him in wisdom, in worldly knowledge, in spirituality. Never must he hold them back, but in humility and joy be happy to let them go higher and further than he. Often they will come back to him again, and from them he can gain in his turn. But, first of all, he must let them go.

In this it can be said that the ordinary father and mother find it hard when their children move away to get advice and even human love from those outside the family ... teachers, peer group, counsellors, youth workers, clergy. Well, spiritual fathers should be aware that they will have their 'children' moving away to different teachers and preachers and spiritual fathers. It can be galling when this happens. The human tendency is to try to stop the move. But if we are truly fathers and truly interested in the growth of the family of God, then we must allow our pride to be pricked, and a new joy to be released in the growth of one we have come to know and love under the care of someone other than ourselves.

There may, sadly, also be those whom we alienate or with whom we apparently fail. The alienation is a real problem, because it is very possible for the spiritual father to make a mistake, to be over harsh or to misunderstand. Here the danger lies in getting depressed by failure, feeling guilt over a sharp word or a lack of feeling, and even losing the confidence to continue with others who have not been alienated, for fear that they, too, may be turned off. This is a time to re-emphasise the importance of a supporter, helper, guide, soul-friend for the priest himself.

He may be being challenged by his penitent, and though he cannot discuss the confessional matter with his own confessor, he can get help for sorting himself out. In the doctor-analyst context, C. G. Jung wrote:

> As a doctor I constantly have to ask myself what kind of message the patient is bringing me. What does he mean to me? If he means nothing I have no point of attack. The doctor is effective only when he himself is affected. 'Only the wounded physician heals'. But when the doctor wears his personality like a coat of armour, he has no effect. I take my patients seriously. Perhaps I am confronted with a problem just as much as they. It often happens that the patient is exactly the right plaster for the doctor's sore spot. Because this is so, difficult situations can arise for the doctor too – or rather especially for the doctor.

Every therapist ought to have a control by some third person, so that he remains open to another point of view. Even the Pope has a confessor. I always advise analysts: 'Have a father confessor, or a mother confessor!' Women are particularly gifted for playing such a part. They often have excellent intuition and a trenchant critical insight, and can see what men have up their sleeves, at times also see into man's animal intrigues. They see aspects that man does not see. That is why no woman has ever been convinced that her husband is a superman![6]

Man of hope and humility

Because the priest is the bearer of the Good News of Jesus Christ, he should always be a man of hope. He himself gains this hope from his close personal relationship with Jesus Christ. He is to be a person who gradually lives more and more in the presence of God, so that his own hope is fed constantly not by himself but by the power of the Spirit of God who leads us into all truth. Therefore, as he grows he tends to see more clearly his own shortcomings. Far from feeling proud that he is able to lead others to God, he feels his own state so closely that it seems unlikely, if not impossible, that he should be of any use to anyone.

Yet the person outside will feel the hope, the faith and the love which radiate from him. He may feel utterly empty and useless, and may want to lay himself down under a bush and say with Elijah: 'Let me die, Lord, I have had enough'.[7] But for other people, in a quiet and persuasive way, he will be a strength and a guide. Because he realises that he is a failure at the deepest point of love, that he has to struggle on in relationship and make mistakes, and because he does so, he can be an inspiration without knowing it. Going forward in hope he is going forward in love, being touched by love and touching others, even when he realises how much he himself is lacking in love. Indeed, this is an essential ingredient because he has to throw himself in his own inadequacy upon the power of God. Like Elijah, he then can go on to the mountain of God, on the strength of the Lord. But it may not feel like that to him.

It is also true of him that all he knows builds a humility as another aspect of hope, because it is based on poverty and truth – poverty in spirit and truth to which the Spirit leads. He is open to learn from those who come to him for guidance, and he grows from knowledge and love of them in the continual hope of their growth. In this he is dependent upon the love of God, the good news he is preaching.

It is by hope and humility that he becomes a healer as all priests should be, following the steps of Jesus Christ. He has hope for every sinner, because as a sinner himself he knows the hope of forgiveness which is his. Knowing that any and everyone can be healed and reconciled to God whose will it is that this should be so, he can also go ahead with tranquillity and assurance to the reconciliation of man with himself and man with his neighbour. No situation for the priest of hope is ever too chaotic, too prone to disaster. Out of the depth of the desolation of the cross, Jesus Christ brought the light of hope in the resurrection. The priest of hope knows the cross, knows frustration, knows pain and continues therefore as a reconciler, himself being continually reconciled. He is aware of sin in himself, so he is not surprised by sin in others; he is aware of his own need to be reassured in hope so that he is prepared to assure others.

Priest of prayer

Running through all that has been said about the priest, or at least underlying it, is the sense that the priest must be a man of prayer. To some extent he will be led to this perhaps before and during his training. But the growth is a continuous one and the best preparation for a priest to be a pastor and a confessor is to spend time in prayer.

The true path to union with God along which every single person must go is the path of prayer. Therefore, if the pastor is to be a true pastor he must continue himself on the path to God every day, because his work for God is that he should come to know God's will and do it, for God's sake and for his own growth. He also walks the path of prayer for the sake of those the Church in God's name has given him. There is no way out of this, only the way on.

Normally speaking, the people can tell pretty quickly if their pastor is a man of prayer or not. Sometimes they are wrong, but as a generalisation it is true to say that no priest can go on long without praying and this omission remain undiscovered. If he is not a man of prayer, he will not be asked about prayer by his flock. If he is a man of prayer, people will come to him, will expect him to pray for them and with them, will ask about prayer and will want guidance, probably inside the confessional as well as out.

Being a man of prayer does not mean simply doing the set offices of the Church and a little Bible reading. It means also the gift of time to God with an expectation of personal growth. It means being prepared to read, to ask, to listen and to share. It means a generosity with self, firstly to God in whatever comes through as his word and his will, then to those God has entrusted to him. It means coming to know himself in prayer, whether this is through joy, delight, praise and thanksgiving, or through darkness, boredom, suffering, dryness and desolation. At different times it will mean both. It means praying for the parish and the parishioners, for friends and relations, for all included in his pastoral concern, and for the cares and sorrows of the world. It means getting to know 'his' people through prayer as well as by the daily contact in the streets or homes or church.

Because 'his' people will be varied, being a prayerful priest entails that the priest's gift of time to God is extended into the gift of time to individuals in many different ways, conveniently and inconveniently. Moreover, through listening to them, as well as speaking to them, it means being open to the necessity to study further, especially about the various ways of approaching God in prayer. It will open wider fields of study as it becomes more and more clear that the whole person is involved. This way of living and learning will bring into relief aspects of personality which draw upon background, age, state of health, mental capacity, childhood or adolescent problems. In other words, the life of prayer lived by the priest every day in every situation and especially in the situation of time free for God will deepen, broaden and mature him. The life of prayer more than any other way will fit him for the work of confessor, pastor of souls, leader and guide. Prayer will form him into a director who can be non-directive, a counsellor who can allow the individual to be and grow into himself, discovering God in his own time and his own way.

It is not essential that every priest grows through prayer into contemplation. Develop he should, but how far he is led by God is only partially dependent upon the priest's disposition. However, prayer is an ingredient of a good confession. The penitent comes to the priest in a spirit of prayerful humility, placing himself before God in what is through and through an acknowledgement of God's power and merciful love. Unless the priest is himself living within the web of prayer and finds some value in the use of confession, it is difficult for him to lead others in this way. But it is important, because God works through human agents. The prayerful agent is a better channel of God's grace.

NOTES

1 Rom. 11.30-34.
2 Hab. 2.4; Rom. 1.17.
3 1 Pet. 2.9.
4 Frank Wright: *The Pastoral Nature of Ministry,* SCM Press Ltd.1981. p.3.
5 R. S. Lee: *Principles of Pastoral Counselling,* SPCK. 1980. p.3.
6 C. J. Jung: *Memories, Dreams, Reflections.* Fount paperbacks, Collins. p.155.
7 1 Kings 19.4.

Priestly Availability and People's Needs

WHEN a human being begins a relationship with another human being, he or she is setting out on a voyage of discovery the end of which neither can foresee. The covenant between God and man is symbolised in Genesis as the rainbow. We can see the same symbol for the covenant that should be set up between individuals as they meet each other and grow in relationship. We know only too well that the covenant between God and man has often been broken from man's side, but the covenant remains. The rainbow covenant between human beings is all the more easily broken, indeed sometimes is never even forged, and is possibly broken at either side of the covenant. Although death sometimes comes to seem to end a covenant between two people or a person and a community, those who believe in God and in life after death know that in this world we never come to where the rainbow ends.

In this chapter I want to look at some of the colours of the rainbow which emerge in the relationship between a human being and God, a human being and himself and his neighbourhood, and a human being and his confessor or counsellor. In this it is basic to any understanding that we are in an intimate, vital and mysterious relationship which we can glimpse but cannot comprehend, because we never meet the finished work. As the letter to the Ephesians puts it:

> We are God's work of art, created in Christ Jesus to live the good life as from the beginning he had meant us to live it.[1]

The only permanent relationship in the development of this work of art is the relationship between the artist, God, and the 'work', a human being. I, then, am God's work of art; he has been busy with me from the time of creation until the moment I was conceived in my mother's womb, in a remote preparation of the canvas. For over sixty years since my conception he has been working more intensively with the material which is intimately me, allowing the environment, people, the shape of history and my own freedom to have a part with him in the artistry. In thousands of ways I have been influenced and moulded as the days and years have gone by. Apparently there is still more to be done, though in his design it could have been cut short at any point if that had been enough. I am well aware that I can look back in hindsight and see something of how externally and internally there have been workings which have brought me to where I am now. God knows it could have been different, especially in my response, in the people who have come into my life, in the situations which have arisen partly from free choice and partly from circumstances.

When I come to sit back and think about myself in this way, I am also deeply conscious of the possible influence which I have had in relation to many other people with whom I have been positively, indifferently or negatively in contact. If this is true for me, it is equally true for any and every person in this world where we rub shoulders with each other as part of God's unfathomable plan. But it is particularly true for those of us who in any way seem to have been called to or fallen into a position of responsibility, teaching, counselling and so on. It is very easy to sit and pontificate about the importance of the influence and the care each of us should exercise. Truly, we are all human beings . . . but what a variety, what a glorious and beautiful and sometimes also horrifying variety: which comes through in Christian belief to the fact that you are the unique you in God's creation, and I am the unique I in God's creation, whatever category or group or classification or stereotype either of us has been placed in.

This uniqueness is something to remember each time a confessor is in a one-to-one relationship with a client; any time a parent or teacher is in relationship one-to-one with a child of the family or school. Having said that, it may seem ridiculous to proceed to discuss in a broader and rather classified way some of the different kinds of individual who may come to an individual priest or minister and say: 'Father, I have sinned'; or 'Please can you help me?'; or 'I'm in despair; I'm suicidal'; or 'I'm so happy; I'm in love!'.

It is important for the 'client' that the counsellor receives the other person as he or she is, listens attentively to the story, is open to hearing what the other person is saying and does not label the individual from the start. There is no doubt at all that there are certain skills and there is certain knowledge which are helpful in assessing what point of personal development the 'client' has reached. Here a basic training in psychology and the behavioural sciences can clarify what otherwise might be misunderstood in some of the apparent discrepancies between biological age, personal (im)maturity, and so on. Some of this is taught, some is picked up, some is a matter of living and experiencing. For the Christian there are additional sources from which to draw enlightenment. Scripture and the personal study of the life and teaching of Jesus Christ are obvious examples. There are also the insights of prayer, the centuries of spiritual writings, the lives of saints and well known directors of souls.

What follows is a very simple series of hints which I have culled from my own experience. They are not definitive. I expect they are open to disagreement and contradiction. I am well aware of the limitation of shortness. However, these thumbnail sketches may help some readers by an insight. In this I ask myself how possible it is to say, other than tentatively, that there is a correct line of approach to any individual? It is essential to meet him or her. If I am forewarned that a person is deaf or blind or unconscious, these are 'handicaps' I know before the meeting. Much, if not everything else depends on me taking myself to meet him or her, without presuppositions.

Children up to eleven

This itself is a poor category! But certainly among Roman Catholics it is an important one, because of the inclination to allow children to make their first Holy Communion at the age of seven or even earlier. Interestingly enough, this tendency to early Holy Communion is growing in certain sections of the Church of England and also among some Methodists.

The norm for a long time has been for children to make their first confession before their first Holy Communion. Clearly, the early development of a child is in the home. More and more it is seen that some modern conditions of parents at work, unsocial hours and so on make the parental influence uneven. There is much more incidence of one-parent families and social deprivation in a society which is not religious in atmosphere. Somehow, then, the beginning of the child's knowledge of good and bad, right and wrong, must be based somewhere. The home should be that place, but the awareness of problems in the home is part of the work of confessor, counsellor or church worker, as well as any helping agencies involved.

At a younger age than before, even pre-school children mix with their peers outside the home. Different values are met. It is important that there should be access for parents to continuing thought about good and bad, right and wrong, not only in their living experience, but in the visibility and approachability of living Christianity in the neighbourhood. This said, positive development is essential for the child in the home, in the Christian community and in relation to the experience of 'meeting' Jesus and his ministers. Hence, the newer emphasis on love and goodness and sharing with each other, rather than the older threatening of hell seems more in keeping with modern understanding. However, having said that, positive development has to stress the need for law, the fact that the law of love makes demands and can be broken. In other words, somehow it is essential to teach that there is bad as well as good; that evil can be present; that each of us is imperfect and has much to learn and much growth ahead. Also in teaching the love of Jesus for us and our love for him, while it is clear that a child can at an early age even come to kill, it must be pointed out that the general naughtinesses are hardly to be classed as *sinful.* There should be ways of helping a child to grow in understanding. This will necessitate reassessment by the Roman Catholic Church in particular and by the Church in general of the timing and method of helping children to be responsible at a level which is fitting for their age and mental, spiritual and physical development.

There is no doubt that some of the effects of an early stress on sin and guilt, the God who is judge and the priest who administers God's justice, have had serious and bad psychological effects on children. It is noticeable to me that many of those who truly appreciate confession and its healing and peacegiving strength are those who have not been involved with it at an early age, but have come to it later, either on gaining faith as adults after a non-religious upbringing, or by having their baptism come alive after only a desultory practice in youth. Our care in the present and future should be that we do not burden children with sin, that we do not make confession an ordeal or a 'nonsense of pernicketiness'. Their failures, and they will be many, are not unexpected or always punishable, but in a way to be rejoiced in as they stumble their first steps along the way of the cross, learning to walk with a loving father and mother. As far as God is concerned it is essential that he is not portrayed as an ogre who does not understand the children he has created out of love. Parents, priests and teachers have a wonderful but heavy responsibility to mirror God, who has a standard of love and wants us to live by it, realises we will not always succeed, and is always ready to help us up and on our journey, if we want to try.

One of the best ways for the confessor is to seek himself to have a relationship of easy friendship and interested care with and for parents and children alike. He must be *himself*, especially as the children grow through delightful stages of being all over him to the shyer and less easy developments. He must let them grow, and so change in their attitude to him. He may see many through long years but he must be patient and tolerant if they come and go. One medieval mystic is reputed to have said: 'Be kind; be kind; and you will be a saint'. Change saint to confessor or counsellor. But kindness does not mean letting things go. It means living out loving.

Personally, I do not advocate the age of seven for confession. I like early Holy Communion and think some simple form of penitential service should be adapted for children up to about the age of eleven, with a deprecative prayer for forgiveness – without recourse to the full confessional form of the sacrament of penance. Apart from an unhealthy emphasis on guilt, a wrong sense of the awfulness of sin – a break in love with God – is induced when petty items of every day imperfection are trotted out as *sinful.* In addition, if the young child is governed by frequent confession after an early first Communion, the beauty of Communion can be lost in the ritual of confession, making it either fear-filled or meaningless. For instance, once when I was stationed at Westminster Cathedral in the 1950s, there was a heavy persecution of Cardinal Mindzenty in Hungary, and we had all been asked specially to pray for him. At some point, there was a Mass laid on to be celebrated in the Cathedral and all the children from the local Catholic schools were to attend. The day before, a Tuesday, I was on morning confessional duty. A number of penitents came; then suddenly there was a scrabbling outside, and apparently a whole class of primary school kids began coming in for confession. One little girl of about seven came in, knelt down and was silent. I asked her gently when she had last been to confession. 'Last Saturday.' 'Oh', I said, trying to make her at ease, 'that is not long. Have you been very naughty since then?' 'No, Father', she said, 'Please, I've come for Cardinal Mindzenty!'

Young people growing up

What a world to grow up in! Yes, what a world! Yet it is the same world that Noah, Abraham, the prophets, Jesus Christ and all our ancestors grew up in. The difference is that the plan of God in our temporal sense is further on in discovery both of human nature and of the universe. It would be a happy thought that the world is now a better place to live in than it was at the beginning of man's evolution. Certainly a great deal of intelligence, sweat, love, hate, building and destruction has gone into the centuries past. We are in many, many ways the richer for all this, or we can be. In the ordinary run of each person's life, however, the availability of the richness is relative, and what each person *is* at any given point is all important to the creator, who made each one out of love, to be fulfilled in love.

It is possible to sit down and praise the past, condemn the past, praise the present, condemn the present, praise what may be the future prospects, or decry them. This is a waste of time. Especially with those who are growing up through the teens and beyond, there is a great deal to get on with now. As all through history, young people are a mixture of good and indifferent and bad. Some prospects are gloomy, some are as bright as they have ever been. Certainly, with nuclear armaments we are at a new point of possible self-destruction. But we are also at the edge of the universe of discovery.

As confessors, counsellors or simply friends of young people we are not to look down, but to look across. They are not only the future; they are the now. And it is good that in looking across we are open to meet them, to come alongside and share, because only in that way will they really meet us. In the art of relating, these years are not the easiest. Because of the pace of growing both physically and, especially, as a person in his or her own right, it is important to *help* each to grow. This needs a combination of authority and tact, freedom and interest, tolerance and love, warmth and understanding.

It is not surprising that the confessional is not the

most popular resort for the teenager! But that leads to the question, just how necessary may it be for someone during those years? It is a long period to cover and the individual development is of primary importance, but this is also within a community context. During these years it has to be accepted that not infrequently the parent or parents are not the first persons to whom recourse is made in time of tension, questioning or trouble. Happy the family where such a relationship does continue to prove growthful. But 'outside agencies' can be a source of strength. As far as the priest or minister is concerned the retention or the building up of trust is important. A growing and maturing age is not one in which rigidity and rules are paramount. To me this is a situation needing counselling more than confession. However, confession, its place and possible approaches to it must be taught at some time. Judging when to involve young people in the mechanics of confession is difficult. Probably there is no *right* time. But it could be that it is best to employ the end of junior school for this instruction, even if the use of confession does not emerge much until later in the teens. The teens are a period of testing out, trying out, experimentation. What is the idea or sense of sin during this period? At this time sex is emergent, alongside natural rebellion, inquisitiveness, energy, and frustration with rules. There is growing independence, a feeling that older people are out of touch and so on. Perhaps with groups and gangs and mates, the community aspect of the penitential service and general absolution would be better suited to their needs. But individual contact with a priest is invaluable.

The one phrase I would want to see at the head of the list of virtues for the parent, the priest and the teenager is the word 'trust'. How this is to be achieved is what we face in living. But one thing is certain. It does not mean that either the adults or the young people have everything their own way. We learn as we grow together. Yet, within this statement, it is very important for the adults to be themselves. That means the priest or counsellor does not play the teenager, but tries to understand the teenager; he does not necessarily approve what the teenager is doing, saying or believing. He maintains his own principles, explains his viewpoint if he has a listening public, but does not try to bulldoze any young person into his belief, let alone into the belief that damnation is round the corner. There is time, there is space, there is growth. Let there be joy and exploration and failure as well as success.

No one should minimise either the importance of this age of growth or the tensions and burdens that young people have in being part of that scene. There are pressures at school, at college, at university, at trying to get a job; pressures in becoming sexually aware and coping with one's sexuality and other people's; pressures at home, insecurity, inferiority, desire to be one's own person, breaking free; there are also pressures of the peer group – with competition, keeping up, dress, drink, drugs, relationships, violence and so on.

This period is a minefield, but it is meant to be a hopeful, encouraging, joyful, exciting and happy period, with support and love helping along the way. If God is here portrayed as the unfriendly policeman who is waiting to arrest on suspicion and is quite inflexibly demanding, we who portray him in this way are a danger to our calling, to those whom we counsel and especially to the true image of God.

It is important for a younger person to be able to find the confidence and courage to grow in openness with an adult. Sometimes this can be someone old enough to be grandfather or grandmother, sometimes elder brother or sister figure and so on. But this in itself means that the older person has to be available, must not rush the relationship but let it grow, must be prepared to be let down. He must be unshocked and unshockable, but not necessarily approving; he must always be ready, if the young person veers off, to let him go and, if he comes back, to welcome him. I personally find it is a constant thing of interest and even wonder when a now almost middle-aged man or woman tells me something about our previous meetings forgotten by me which were, they say, of great importance to them twenty, thirty or more years ago.

Never forget to keep these young people in your prayers. They are worth all our efforts; they are imperfect like us, but full of potential, of generosity, enthusiasm and love.

The ordinary person

Within this categorisation of 'ordinary person' I would like to make it clear that in a sense I do not know what 'ordinary' means. It is probably best to say that the vast majority of people are ordinary in a superficial view. It is in getting to know someone that the extraordinary begins to emerge, in both the strengths and weaknesses which may be part and parcel of the person here and now. Once again, then, it is a question of growing in trust. For such spiritual development, quick in-and-out confession, constant change from one confessor to another, or very infrequent confession to a different priest each time are not usually the best use of the sacrament. It is important that we preach and teach and lead people to the realisation that, in the words of St. Gregory the Great: 'The way to God is always a forward march.' Alas, too many of us ordinary people are content to mark time with God.

For the confessor with the ordinary person it is part of the personal awareness and care of the pastor to be able to 'feel' with sensitivity when all is not well with a particular person. This applies not just to a crisis which may arise, but to failure to grow. The approach of a change of life, not only in the physical sense, but when middle age comes along, when all the children leave home, can be traumatic or lead to depression. When a job is lost, when the financial position changes, when work is getting on top of someone, a helping ear and heart is invaluable. The confessor is not there to be poking and prying. He is there to be alert, aware and caring. Here, as much as anywhere, as he listens he may recognise some of the useful understandings of human growth patterns researched by the behavioural sciences. Some of these especially associated with middle life can lead individuals to guilt, loss of self-esteem, kicking over the traces and so on.

Sometimes, when a person comes with regularity to confession, more or less repeating the same failures each time, and is patiently going away and coming again, the confessor does not extend the warmth and encouragement which could make all the difference. Some people are day in and day out in very monotonous and boring jobs; some are coping daily with a sick relative, some have people in the flat upstairs who are constantly noisy, some have sons or daughters or brothers or sisters or dear friends who are simply a worry for some reason or other. Some have a real difficulty in believing, some have a difficult parish priest. The list, as I hope you know, is endless. But the confessor owes each person something of care, something of hope. This may or may not be in the actual confessional situation, but rather in a chat on the road, a home visit, a time when he or she calls casually about the church bazaar or the mothers' union meeting. At these and other times, we can miss so many opportunities; and these opportunities are an extension of sacramental confession and often a doorway to it. Especially if he can cultivate a spirit of prayer, the priest will be able to sense the opportunity for suggesting a moment or two of prayer with the person concerned, there and then on the spot. Though this can be shy-making, I have found that a discreet use of prayer coming from my own personal awareness of the power of the Holy Spirit calms, opens and gives the peace of a new hope to those in distress.

Because ordinary people are ordinary and extraordinary, I can do no more than say look out for, listen to and be available for the ordinary person. Many of them are living heroic lives in hidden ways. They need to have God's love and care expressed to them.

The list and the possible reactions and aids are as many as there are people in the world. But I remind you of the people of Nazareth and their failure to recognise Christ. Please ask yourself sometimes: Who or what am I failing to recognise among the local community?

The appearance of the ordinary person at confession and the importance placed on this will vary between churches and even within churches, according to the discipline and spiritual standing of the confessional practice in the mind of the individual pastors or church communities. The dangers are total neglect of confession on the one hand and over-emphasis on the obligation-sin-guilt syndrome on the other. It is here that those involved in pastoral care need themselves to have sorted out their own position. If they have never experienced confession, they may down-play or even pooh-pooh confession; if they have been in touch with the behavioural sciences they may say that confession has now been taken over totally by counselling skills and psychotherapy. If they personally or through others have suffered the effect of bad confessional skills and practice, this may be another reason why they could advise against confession.

However, confession has a sound and healthy basis – and its object is the building, growth and development of the human person in over-all relation to God's purpose. Each of us is imperfect in the most ordinary way. In building the person, it is encouragement and self-acceptance which are at the foundation of our need. The negative sense of sin and guilt which any wrongdoer will probably feel should be turned to positive to give the penitent hope and encouragement. This does not mean mimimising the wrongness of bad actions, but helping the individual to an understanding and acceptance of the goodness and possible growth in his person.

The good confessor can help to form an objective view of the spiritual state of the ordinary person. Each of us is different; the individual is not to be categorised – even though, for purposes of the present exercise, I am doing this very thing here and now.

The possibility of giving up trying rather than persevering is very close to the surface much of the time. How often the confessor hears the phrase: 'It's the same old story. However much I try, I just slip up again and have to confess the same things over and over'. One of the lines of suggestion I have used which has sometimes proved helpful for a period is to point out that at least what is being confessed is the same – there are no new excursions into previously untried fields of wrongdoing or neglect. When a penitent can come to realise the importance of this, and the continued love and acceptance of him by God, the basic imperfection becomes a source of wonder at God's merciful love. It is a reason for continuing in hope, for God's sake and not selfishly.

In the mind of a person tending to be disheartened is

often a picture of 'the perfect me', against which we erroneously put our imperfection and which causes us a constant guilt. Rather than this, we should learn to understand St. Paul's phrase: 'When I am weak, then I am strong'. We can admit our dependence upon God and his love, and we can with his grace pull ourselves up and go along further on the road to union with him. But often we could do with human help too. We are shy of asking for help, lacking the necessary encouragement. Without encouragement it is difficult to accept and live with ourselves in the continual hope of development. We need a boost to our morale in order to accept that there is a life-long process of growing in holiness. We are not there yet. God does not expect us to be already there. He wants us to grow.

Some might say that this sounds a bit bleak. Left on one's own this can be so. Many, I am sure, get lost, depressed or even hopeless. Regular contact with a priest can be very warming, and for some this will only be through the confession – at any rate at first. In this world there are too many negative forces which set about undermining our self-respect. The confessional is one place where that self-respect can and should always be guaranteed an injection of proper pride and hope. Here humility seeks truth in acknowledging wrong, but also seeks truth in the acceptance of forgiveness as the gift of God, whose love sends us out again into the world refreshed, buoyed up and enfolded in love.

Very many people *really* want to pour out their hearts, to find the listening ear and the kindly acceptance by another human being of themselves as they are. Perhaps it would be true to say that the ordinary person may well need more from confession than the big sinner – or should I say more from the confessor. Here the advice which accompanies the absolution may be effective in directing the penitent into deeper love of God. Without any direction or guidance, the penitent may simply mark time.

To the extent, then, that the ordinary person is one who has not penetrated very deeply – one for whom confession is more of a ritual observance than a real meeting with God's love – the confessor has the possibility of aiding and deepening the penitent's growth by his whole attitude, warmth and interest. I have known this to open a person up to contemplative prayer, to a life of great service of God and others, and to a development in holiness unprecedented previously in that person's life. It is easy to get stuck in the ordinary. The confessor has the duty and joy to take every person who comes to him as on the way to heaven. Sometimes there is a circuitous route, sometimes a definite marking-time, sometimes a loss of incentive to abandon oneself to the Holy Spirit. Yet such a person will ultimately only be full and happy when committed to present capacity on the way of the cross.

Married people

The joy of married life is made up of such a variety of ingredients that my few observations will be very superficial. Yet the married state is so general a way of life for men and women that the majority of those who make use of confession, apart from children and young people, may well be married. And there is no way of life, including marriage, which does not have sorrow and pain mingling with love and happiness. On the one hand, the confessor can rejoice with the deeply happy and loving family, who will perhaps come as a unit to the church to receive forgiveness for what they know have been the minor failures, irritations and worries of close relationship and inter-personal responsibility.

On the other hand, it is easy to put too much stress on the difficulties of marriage. One of the hopes that a confessor should have is that he may encourage and support and come close to many families so that, if there is a hiccup in their relationship which persists and seems likely to worsen, he may be a person liked and trusted enough to be of some use. The ordinary priest in a parish should be well-known and accessible to families. He is so often involved in the joyful times – marriage, baptism and so on – as well as in sickness and bereavement. But he is normally the 'GP' and not the specialist. His training may not have much concentration on marriage counselling courses. Nevertheless, from his frequent contacts in families he will be asked advice, in and out of the confessional.

The position of confessor, with its command to total secrecy on matters discussed 'under the seal', means that recourse to the other partner is impossible, unless it is agreed by the penitent that the confessor may follow up the matter outside the confessional. Generally speaking, one-sided counselling in marriage has its hazards and is inadequate. A special difficulty may occur where one partner is not a believer or even openly opposed to religion.

Marriage, of its nature, is so close and intimate that a considerable number who have marital problems are unwilling either immediately or in the long term to bring about a three-sided discussion. However, this does not necessarily mean that a priest listening to one side only is wasting his time. Even on that uneven basis progress can be made. But the priest may need to be as much a listening post as a person able to give much advice. If trust is established there may be possibilities of guiding at least one party to more professional advisory counsellors.

Marriage advice in my experience extends from pre-marital questions and sometimes guilts through the main phases of human life. Sadly, there appear to be increasing numbers of casualties in marriage and it is the casualties who need extra time and care and sympathy. I live in the inner city. Here we are perhaps more prone than elsewhere to violence, brutality, depression, mental breakdown, single-parent families, abortion and desertion. But even out of apparent chaos there can arise a new living: and recognition of a little ray of hope is of paramount importance in the sensitivity of a confessor.

To begin to cover the variety of questions in married life is a much bigger job than I have undertaken. However, there are many, many books dealing specifically with marriage in all aspects. What I would like to do here is to mention two areas which are especially difficult for pastoral care at this time. The first is when two Christians who are both desiring further growth in their own faith and practice are married and share their lives together *except* in religious practice. Such persons' state of life is now often referred to as a 'two-church marriage'. The main crux comes when the ecclesiastical discipline of one denomination refuses Holy Communion to the partner of the other denomination. Not all churches are equally insistent on this point. The Orthodox and Roman Catholic churches are most strict; but the Roman Catholic practice can vary from one country to another, or even from one district to another in the same country.

It is urgently necessary that attention be given to the possibility of inter-communion because this is a live marriage issue which faces such two-church families at least every weekend. The problem does not go away and loyalties are hard stretched. I realise that authorities can advocate patience, since inter-church conversations are going on, but the tension remains, and the fact that the actual application of the discipline varies so much enhances rather than lessens this tension. There have even been instances of permission being given officially for inter-communion on a special occasion such as a two-church baptism. But it could well be argued by married couples in this situation that every Sunday for them is a special occasion!

Presuming nothing will happen overnight, it is essential for pastors and such married couples alike to pursue ways of care, concern, discussion and possible development which can be lived out in the here and now. To further this, some couples have come together in a grouping of two-church families. Their work has already proved most constructive and anyone who is in this situation or advising couples so committed should be in touch with them. Meanwhile, the impact of the priest in or out of confession or another counsellor can be vital, either for development of a living relationship between the partners and the Church or, if negative, in the direction of a cut-off from practice and belief. The pastor/counsellor must welcome, listen, give time and try to develop understanding. Absolutism does not help.

The other area I want to mention is the growing occurrence of re-marriage after divorce, and the possibility of people in this situation being admitted to Holy Communion. The whole matter is under active consideration by the Church of England. Though in the Roman Catholic Church current official teaching seems clearly negative, there has over recent years been considerable movement both at a theological level and in actual practice. Changes at some future point in what is officially accepted are not inconceivable. The subject is too intricate for me to expand on in this book. But a pastor of any denomination who is faced with these couples would do well to read a careful exposition by Father Kevin T. Kelly, *Divorce and Second Marriage*, subtitled 'Facing the Challenge'.[2]

There has also been set up in the north of England, and is gradually spreading under Roman Catholic hierarchical approval, The Association of Separated and Divorced Catholics. They have regular meetings and support groups, reminding us that to be divorced, however difficult life as a married couple has been before, is akin to bereavement.

The scrupulous person

A very real affliction is the burden of scrupulosity. In essence this means a breakdown in the person concerned of a rational acceptance of human frailty or a failure to grasp the merciful forgiveness of God. This may develop as a neurosis in a person, for it is recognised as having a root in depression. Scruples have a very debilitating effect on that person's whole life, but especially on relationship to God.

The effect upon the person is to drive them to a perfectionsim which can never be satisfied. This perfectionism may be in relation to the content of what they are confessing: what they repeatedly feel is inability adequately to confess what they have done in terms of frequency, actual detail on the sin and surrounding circumstances. Another line of scrupulosity would be the conviction that no true act of contrition had been made – or no firm purpose of amendment. Any one of these worries tends to drive the person to a very frequent confession, a desire to repeat a former confession, and an intense concern with detail and minutiae.

Sometimes the onset of scruples can be detected by a confessor and the person gently led out of the trap. Perhaps more often, the person arrives for confession and faces the confessor with already rooted scrupulosity. For the scrupulous person the situation of doubt is very real indeed. What the confessor has to do is to enter into a normally slow involvement, seeking to effect a complete change in the outlook of the scrupulous individual. This requires a combination of sympathy, firmness, patience and a watch on length and frequency of recourse to confession. The underlying help that the confessor can bring to such a person is a growth of trust and respect, which will enable scrupulosity to be accepted by the penitent, but also taken into a new dimension.

If an attempt is made to change the person too rapidly, this will be taken as lack of understanding – as indeed it is. The normal reaction, especially if there is a solid refusal to listen to any more on the part of the confessor, is to go off and seek help elsewhere. It is a difficult tight-rope to walk so as to balance between dismissal and over-indulgence. Neither is good. But it is possible with trust to regulate both frequency and time-length, while retaining the necessary trust and gradually growing in respect and friendship. To allow the person to 'shop around' for an understanding priest is no good at all, but the cost to the confessor may be quite high in terms of time and patience.

Most of us resist change; and the need in the scrupulous person is to let go, to trust the judgement of another person and to accept that long enough for a new reality of values to grow up. In my experience, this is certainly not helped by a continual running in and out of confession. Yet the distancing of one confession from another can heighten tension and cut off the receiving of Holy Communion, the general enjoyment of worship, prayer and so on. It is not the easiest thing in the world to persuade someone that what he or she believes to be sinful is not sinful at all and to get acceptance of goodness and freedom. Scruples are a terrible imprisonment in a cell of doubt and self-recrimination. The world is an unreal world; the values untrue; the whole out of balance.

For some, there will be a lifetime of at least the tendency to scruples. But properly guided, this tendency can be held in balance, a periodic boost and reassessment can lead to a life of comparative freedom and real growth. For some, the change can be complete eventually, like a true conversion. During my life in the priesthood, which has carried me through thirty-three years, there have been individuals plagued by scruples with whom I have been in contact for as long as twenty years, others for a lesser time. Their state of evolution has varied – some have gone off out of my ken, and I do not know how they are faring; some have been totally emancipated, and my contact may be an occasional thanks by letter or in person, covering years of freedom. Some, however, do remain in close contact, either as it were to get a booster as they feel it necessary, or because they have not yet broken loose from their prison.

There is no doubt that part of the problem here is rooted in bad earlier upbringing and practice, either in the family or in the habits of the local church. The minister of confession, therefore, should be very alert to the tender conscience, the nervous disposition, the tendency to indecision in people. Prevention is far better than cure, especially if the illness was one which could have been detected in early stages and should never have been allowed to reach neurotic proportions.

The lapsed

So wide-ranging is this title, it could be valueless. I refer in a broad way to all those baptised people who have given up church-going for one reason or another. Often this may include a loss of belief, but not infrequently belief is quite strong underneath a veneer of busyness, a felt wrong in the past, a loss of sense of sin, a drifting, a re-assessment of the relevance or importance of religion or a negative reaction coming from the peer group. Church-going is not the only criterion, but its absence among individuals is a shorthand to assessing those who lose touch with the Church and the priest and often miss out on sacraments.

In the average parish area, it is today probably true that considerably more of the baptised are not going to church with any regularity, if at all, than those who are 'practising'. This means that the confessor has a very difficult division to make with his time. In one sense, all too much time is taken up with servicing those who are committed church people. They need confession, counselling, visiting, being listened to and so on. Yet, if I am right, among the lapsed, the majority are not touched by these activities, except peripherally through perhaps a church-minded member of the family.

There are two things to be said here. The first is that much of the priest's contact with ordinary parishioners is at church regularly or occasionally, in the street or at social occasions. Only a small minority are committed to 'good works', bible studies, etc. Without being oppressive and over-godly, the minister can preach to encourage those who are his regular congregation that they are wonderfully placed among caring though non-churchgoing people. Over and over again, I have come across and am today often coming across the remarkable network of care which exists among people. Through this network, the faith and love and concern of one person rubs off on another. In depression, in a crisis, it is to this kind friend that the distressed person turns for comfort and support. Frequently this network has no connection with the Church. However there is a store of vitality which the pastor can strengthen as he preaches and tries to practise the two great commandments, reminding his committed listeners that their effectiveness for God and for people depends upon their personal living of the message. The medium is the message. People are not out to 'convert'. They are to live the message, so that the message itself preaches through lived lives. 'Out of the abundance of the heart the mouth speaks.'[3] From such people the pastor knows that he has support. Not only will they do much spade work with those who cannot face him, but also the pastor can refer those in doubt or difficulty to such people, knowing that there will be a welcome and a listening and patient understanding.

The second thing to be said is that, if and when an individual of the local community who has 'lapsed' unearths his doubts, anxieties and so on, the pastor has to make the space to listen.

Given the size of the community in which he lives, the numbers are fearsome, and the time demand is very large, if the pastor is approachable and a listener. He therefore has to guard time, without appearing to do so. The process may be long, because the individual is bringing himself, sore, scarred, blank, bitter or whatever. So the would-be confessor may start a long way from the confession, and indeed he may hear many 'confessions' which are not brought explicitly to the sacrament. It is not at all uncommon for a person to unburden himself to a priest – the person may be of a denomination or none, but he has something burdening him which he must have off his conscience. Perhaps in some throw-back to previous attitudes or inherited folk-memories, the priest is approached. I suspect there is, too, a residue of underlying guilt-feeling which causes people to confess their lack of belief or practice. But there may also be more to it.

By no means always does this 'confession' lead any further. But there are times when a person will continue through a detailed account of all the wrong things he has done and all he has not done that he should have done. Finally, he will say: 'But I could never confess all that,' – having just done so! The way then lies open.

There are these people and others who are not ready to see any reason for confession; some who have to get straight on the idea of sin; others who are only selectively sorry. Each of the different kinds of people deserve our time and our listening. To my mind, though such talks and self-revelation are not in the strict sense sacramental absolution, they are humble, full and sincere and as such they reach straight to God. I can only be thankful for being an instrument or channel for their unloading. God's forgiveness is assured. Sacramental absolution may come later.

For some, the way back to God from the wilderness of unbelief or from the confusion of a full life taken up with wordly values may be a very slow and hesitant one. If they have background memories, there may be much updating to be done. Gentleness, time and patience are again essential, with the sense on the part of the priest that there are no limits to God's forgiving and merciful love. In my experience, the mending of the bruised reed comes in very many different forms and time scales. It is worked by God sometimes with miraculous swiftness and sometimes with painful slowness.

Heavy drinkers and alcoholics

One of the accusations which has been brought against Roman Catholics has been that it is possible for a person to get drunk, go to confession and then to Mass and Communion, and be drunk again the next evening. Of course it is! But that outside condemnation bears no relation to what the heavy drinker or alcoholic is battling against. Anyone who works along-side those who have taken to the bottle knows the continual urge to drink, and that the great hope, the only hope, is to build up a self-discipline against the urge.

And so, from outside this could be seen as a rather scandalous round of drunk, confession, drunk, confession. From inside the confessional, the assessment of the situation is often very different and often rather inspiring as one feels the struggle and the earnestness of the endeavour, even while realising the intense weakness and failure. From out of this, with the help of confession, absolution and counselling, I have frequently watched a growth into sobriety, with humility and a deeper prayer life.

Alcoholism is different from heavy drinking and more pernicious, being in the nature of a disease. Medical and psychiatric help are available and much used. However, doctors would accept that for one reason or another – often lack of perseverance and will – there is by no means a hundred per cent success rate. Many manage to gain not a full cure but a permanent alcohol-free way of living through membership of Alcoholics Anonynous. This organisation has done a very great deal for a large number of people and still works on. Alcoholics Anonymous also would agree that not everyone coming to them perseveres alcohol-free. There are other organisations, systems and attempts to cope with alcoholism and alcoholics, as well.

The confessor meets the alcoholic in the confessional or the church house or even in the street. In a confessional situation, the person may not know he is an alcoholic or may not want to recognise the fact. He may then simply confess to having drunk or drinking too much. The confessor needs a sensitive ear, great tact and an attitude of welcome. An alcoholic does not normally reveal the problem he has. This is a very private disease leading to secretiveness. The disease goes right back into and permeates the whole person. The confessor therefore has to gain the confidence of the individual. It may well be that the time will come when the confessor is so clear about the need the penitent has for medical or other help that he has to put such a suggestion to him. The latter can refuse, but if he agrees, the confessor must be absolutely certain that the facts of the situation are removed from the seal or secrecy of confession, so that with the full permission of the penitent he can refer him. The penitent is not then barred from confession. Indeed the continued and regular recourse to confession may be a considerable aid to any other support he is given in his fight against drink.

One of the central difficulties that an alcoholic has is in going it alone. There is really desperate need for sharing and support. Hence the value of Alcoholics Anonymous and other helping groups, with their system of regular groups and supportive members. Normally, the confessor cannot take on the intensity of commitment to support which an AA member can offer another. But he can and should be a considerable resource person, with the offer of regular counselling support. The priest may also find, as I have, that it is useful to recommend to the alcoholic that frequent Holy Communion, with the discipline of the Mass and regular confession, are strong supports in a difficult battle to get off and stay off drink.

Anyone, priest or lay person, who is concerned for and working with an alcoholic must realise and accept the continuing process which is involved. There are many varieties of battle which go on in different individuals but the likelihood is that the addiction factor remains through the rest of the person's life, with total abstention being the only day-to-day assurance of not regressing. Within that general statement, some people lapse back regularly, others manage to go for long periods, until a shock or depression or change of life's circumstances suddenly throws them, and they are set off again. Many manage to break clear by total abstention and live on as renewed members of their families and society. A slip-up is not the end, though temporarily it may seem so to the alcoholic. Support at this point is more than ever necessary, with accessibility and a strong measure of encouragement, which may mean an extra amount of time is needed. The discipline of religion building and relying upon the love of God and membership of the Church when lived day by day strongly encourage and foster the basic requirements of self-discipline. I have found that one form of help with a believer which is workable is to plan a small rule of life containing prayer and the sacraments, with the availability of the confessor as a checkpoint on these and other means the person is using in re-structuring a life which has seemed beyond repair.

It is easy for someone who is not touched by alcoholism to be totally unsympathetic. To live with someone who is afflicted by drink is indeed a trying experience. The patience, understanding and heroic support given by many a husband or wife is beyond admiration. But here, there is no doubt that friends can support by not ostracising, and the confessor needs to be aware that it is not only the alcoholic who needs support, but also his friends and relations. Patience, then, with a mirroring of the everlasting love of God in our relationships, are essential ingredients when working with the affliction of alcoholism. And hope must spring eternal.

Homosexuals

In moving about the country, talking to clergy of different denominations and listening, I am constantly struck by the number of people, clergy especially, who claim that they have never come across a person in their life or ministry who is homosexual. Now it is in fact unlikely that they have never met a man or woman who is homosexual. They may not have recognised the kind of sexuality, because still only a minority of men and women sexed in this way would announce publicly or even in individual conversation: I am a homosexual. But it should be of concern to a pastor, who is there for God's people, if he can sincerely say he has never knowingly met a homosexual person. Probably one in twenty, perhaps one in five of the population are homosexual. It is unlikely that any pastor involved in work in the community is not actually in contact with at least one man or woman who is homosexual, though by 'in contact', I mean living in the same village or town, not necessarily knowing or speaking to any such individual.

What does the 'never met' statement indicate? It may mean, speaking simply from the angle of the pastor, that he is not involved in confessional work or in counselling. It may mean that the priest in himself or in the aura of the Church is unapproachable as far as the homosexual is concerned. That may connote 'irrelevant', 'bound to be hostile', 'likely to reject', 'not sympathetic', 'will not understand'. It may again mean that the homosexual person is well adjusted to recognition and acceptance of his or her sexuality and sees no reason to ask advice or help from anyone, least of all a priest or minister. It may be that the person is in fact utterly shy, basically ashamed and fearful, terrified that anyone will find out what he or she keeps hidden as a 'guilty' secret. Even confession may be ruled out through fear. By and large, the general atmosphere of society is unreceptive, unwelcoming and frequently positively hostile, to the point of expressing disgust and rejection. This atmosphere is deeply resented and extremely painful for the homosexual person. There has been some difference since the Wolfenden report and the subsequent changes in the law, but there is still harassment and finger pointing. Periodically there are 'scandals' which are not necessarily scandalous until blown up by the media, after which the individual concerned may expect to lose his or her job, however well it has been filled, and even to become a social pariah. None of this atmosphere encourages the homosexual person to 'come out', as the phrase goes, to acknowledge to the public and live publicly a personal homosexual orientation.

There has been much research, much discussion, and even considerably more public awareness developed in the last few years. Most of the main religious groupings in the country have had working parties on homosexuality, which have subsequently reported back and their findings been published. There has been increased openness by homosexual groups through meetings, newspapers and campaigning. Television, radio and the press have all carried homosexual plays, discussions, stories and articles openly, and often much more fairly than before. There is a growing acceptance of couples living together and expressing affection in public.

Some younger homosexual people particularly now find it in themselves to be open with their parents about their sexuality, and certainly some parents have reacted much more positively.

However, there is still a widespread sense of rejection, exclusion and dscrimination which is keenly felt by homosexual individuals and groups. It is more difficult in smaller communities. Many live in a daily fear of discovery, become secret, shut-in people, find any positive relationship difficult to achieve, and not infrequently are niggled by well-meaning parents and friends for not marrying. Many move to the large conurbations where they can either be anonymous or at least find many more homosexuals who are openly frequenting pubs, clubs, discos and other places of meeting and entertainment. There are also organisations for contact, especially in a crisis.

In the midst of all this, the confessor should be aware of the good or bad effect that can be created by how he reacts to a person confessing a homosexual relationship. Abrupt or attacking attitudes by the priest can completely alienate, while increasing the tensions, crises and despairs which are among the hazards of being homosexual. It is one thing to admit being homosexual, to develop all the positive aspects of homosexual orientation: but living as a homosexual brings an assortment of difficulties and problems. These can come about through the breakdown of a particular relationship, through an upsurge of moral uncertainty, through the loss of a job or a landlord turning nasty. These are some of the anxieties, but it is worse for someone who knows he or she is homosexually orientated, or suspects and fears so, and is not very willing to accept this, sees it as a stigma, a horror to be put away, which it is impossible to share with anyone. There may be simply introversion, or a deepening melancholy and depression; there may be suicidal tendencies. There is probably an intense need to have someone to speak to; someone who will listen and understand and not be shocked. Will such a person ever turn to the clergy, church groups, church workers? Sadly, it is very doubtful indeed.

There is still considerable discussion in the churches and also in the medical profession. Opinions are deeply divided. Though the statements from some churches give a more liberal approach to understanding the homosexual, the overall attitude remains negative. What the priest or minister has to face up to is John or

Jean who is homosexually orientated, who wants to live a full, happy and generous life; who feels inhibited and cold-shouldered by the Church; who may be afraid of the sexing they have, or may accept or rejoice in it. John and Jean come or fail to come to the priest or the Church with a question – 'How can I be fully myself and at the same time be a full church member?' Within the Church, you or I the priest, minister or counsellor have to face this pastoral situation either in or out of confession. It is wrong to condemn and dismiss. There must be a welcome and an acceptance of the individual. But then what? I suggest that it is possible and fruitful within the Church to bring John and Jean to a full and fulfilled life as responsible adults living and working in the world, and respected, loved and admired by the local community. I believe this is one of the areas of pastoral concern within which the local priest or minister should be courageous enough to move and work. From my own experience, I can assure you that the response to Jesus Christ in life and work will surpass anything you would have imagined.

While saying this and expressing the pastoral care for the homosexual I must also make it clear that the homosexual must think out and be aware of responsibility, especially in relation to younger people. It is always possible for human beings to exploit others, especially when in a position of age or authority which can have undue influence. The individual human person must be respected, given freedom to grow and not used for personal satisfaction.

Religious Sisters

Not all Christian Churches have religious sisters, but where they do exist they are in a special position because they are vowed to poverty, chastity and obedience and often have a rule of life which includes regular, perhaps frequent confession. (It is right to include deaconesses in this section. They also have a special role and appointment which some would want to see included in the section below referring to priests and ministers).

In the past, religious sisters have led a life which varied from order to order, with different aims to the different societies, and rules which also varied according to the spirit of the founder or foundress. In some orders, especially I suppose in the Roman Catholic Church since Vatican II, there has been a considerable updating and renewal of constitutions. This has led to more openness, more flexibility and to an even greater variety of work, especially in the setting up of smaller communities.

For the confessor, then, it is important, in addition to having general knowledge of the church, the faith and pastoral practice, to be familiar with the spirit of the order. Though all are religious sisters, those vowed to be 'enclosed', given to prayer and contemplation within a particular convent and not moving out to work in the world, will have a very different atmosphere and rule from a convent teaching, doing parochial work, nursing or being geared to missionary activity.

The religious life is entered for the love of God and for the perseverance of the individual and community in holiness. Within the community, much of the day to day purification is not only in the canonical offices and works, but also in living together with the mixture of joys, sorrows, tensions, relationships, trials and frustrations which can seem magnified in the limits of community. Within this setting, this rule and this life-work, the sisters expect many things when they enter: a way of life tending to holiness, growth in prayer, love and service of each other. Needless to say, neither they, nor the other sisters nor perhaps the rule-as-lived fully come up to their expectations. Some get caught in a trap of self-guilt, some continue something of the old chapter of faults guaranteed to give a low self-esteem, some get filled with scruples, some find relationships in one direction or another intolerable. These negative aspects need to be treated seriously and sympathetically, not least because the confessor is often the only one external to the community in whom the sister finds it possible to confide. Naturally, much of what is confessed is really a form of imperfection and far from sin. This is all the more reason for the confessor in the convent setting to be a person able and suited for listening warmly and lovingly and giving sound advice.

In the contemporary climate, for one reason or another confession has ceased to be so frequent among the majority of people as it was before Vatican II. In some religious orders, this tendency to 'space' confession has been allowed to infiltrate, even where the rule laid down a weekly confession. I have spoken recently to a number of religious sisters. One, in particular, told me of the tension she felt. She used, under obedience to the rule, to go to confession each week. Following Vatican II she relaxed, went regularly but only occasionally, and found help through counsel at the same time. Now new constitutions have been promulgated which include confession every two weeks. She was anxious to obey the rule and at the same time clear that spiritually she had not been helped by her previous weekly confession.

Such a sincere spiritual problem between the individual soul and the rule he or she has chosen to follow is likely to come before the confessor. He has at heart the development of the sister spiritually. He needs patience and prayer and an understanding of the rule and of the sister so that he can guide her to growth in her love and service of God through the religious life.

Up to this point I have stressed negative aspects. There is also the very positive side of the life and growth of sisters who are ready to make progress or are already making progress in prayer and the spiritual life. For them, the confessor should have a personal background and experience of prayer and something of the spiritual classics. It is not good enough simply to hand on the way he prays, without finding the sister's way of prayer and opening her to other possibilities, as well as his own favoured way. It is God who calls.

Perhaps more than many penitents, the sisters need considerable affirmation. Running through as a general atmosphere in all confessions in the convent is the question of vocation – its rightness, the way the sister is feeling about it, whether there are doubts and difficulties – if so how serious are they? Give time to sisters; listen; be open; let them grow. God has called them; he loves them. They respond to love.

Priests, ministers and students for ministry

Anyone baptised is at once potentially a worker to share with Christ in his mission to the world of human beings. A particular ministry is laid upon priests at ordination. From that time on, they not only have the care of their own soul but also the God-given, Church-given care of others, more especially the spiritual care. This is a very beautiful calling, in which God is trusting to the priest the friendship, love and care of those whom God loves. It is therefore of special importance that the priest should himself be able to have the necessary assistance of a fellow priest to whom he can have recourse in matters of his own soul.

There can be immense loneliness and isolation in the life of a priest who has to share and bear the sins, grief and problems of others, if he does not have someone himself to whom he can unburden. This isolation is neither good for him in himself and in relation to God, nor is it fruitful in terms of his own pastoral work. To have a fellow priest as a confidant should be a must for a priest or minister.

Unfortunately, it is not always so easy to find such a person. It is strange that priests often do not see themselves in the role of confessor, especially to fellow priests. Though ordained to share with others the revelation of the mysteries of God in Jesus Christ, they do not see the commission as meaning this kind of spiritual guidance. But it really does. In deciding upon use of time in ministry, many a priest could with value allocate more to the spiritual care of souls. The souls of priests need care in order to care for others. A lot of time is taken up in endless committees and a lot of administration. Apart from deeper aspects of counselling for priests, the priest open to another priest has the opportunity of helping in orientation of his personal resources.

I have been fortunate to know a series of priests in my life and so from experience, I understand the value of having a ready ear, a sounding board and a relationship of trust. I have also had the experience of finding those who have become isolated and I know the cost of that isolation.

What is behind this tendency to isolation? Partly it is probably pride and additionally an inability to trust. This is a terrible accusation – not entrusting a fellow priest. Yet how true it is, and how inhibiting. While we expect trust from others, we distrust our fellows. You should think about this, and those in authority, especially during the early training period, should make sure that clear guidance is given to everyone who is to be ordained about the importance of trying to find someone trustworthy in whom to confide. This does not imply constant contact, but the regular knowledge of recourse available and a sharing relationship which goes deep in trust and friendship.

For the confessor, it is necessary to build a relationship if possible with the priest penitent. When trust and friendship are established, it adds a dimension, depth and easing of tension which it is strengthening and joyful to experience. There is the possibility of complete openness, of speaking not only of sin, but of worries, doubts, angers and attachments which we have never dared to voice before. From this comes the wonder of a listening ear and the comfort of sympathy, the encouragement of the reassertion of God's love, and the sound, friendly advice of a person experienced in the same field.

But the confessor has to give the time and expect there will be considerable need for sharing. Sometimes a priest feels he has no right to chide his fellow priest, to offer him good advice. Yet I can assure you, this is a most valuable and valued work. For who is going to help the helper? And there are manifold things which can become a matter of conscience for the pastor, where he needs help. Priests and ministers may break down through stress, take to drink, if married have family difficulties, find themselves at odds with the parochial church council. Some things may be a matter literally for confession, others may simply need clear thinking, warmth, encouragement and time to let go.

It may be difficult for priests, especially in the country, to find someone who is 'right' to take as confessor. This can be because there is really a shortage of priests suitable for this work – which is a sad and awesome charge to make, but probably true – or sometimes there is real fear of gossip among the parish or local community. I have known cases where parish clergy were literally scared of the reaction of their wives to close personal confidences being shared with anyone other than the wife herself. I am unmarried, but I would still not hesitate to say that there may be things which cannot be shared even with a wife – some pastoral and some in the very depth of the penitent's soul. It calls for patience and understanding and is a test of love, which can in turn lead on to deep love and deep sharing and a growth in holiness. Strangely, this can become a bond rather than a barrier and so intensify the bond of married love.

The elderly

In England at the time of writing we are an ageing population, not least among the clergy and religious sisters! The obvious result is that any pastor will have a considerable number of elderly, ageing and senior citizens in the parish or area in which he works. Many of these are young at heart and seem likely to outlive subsequent generations like myself, though I am rapidly approaching time for a free bus pass! For such as are hale and hearty into their eighties, nineties and even over the hundred mark, it is wonderful if those who are working with them pastorally can make sure that they can continue to fill a role and not feel put on the shelf. For instance, I am blessed by having an elderly religious sister in her seventies who comes with great regularity, drives me about, files papers, does civil marriage books, types for me and the parish, and takes her turn on house duty. An eighty-seven-year-old man in the area has recently joined the ranks of those commissioned to give Holy Communion – and so on. Contact with the elderly, whether it is through confession or pastoral visiting or meeting them at different church functions, is not always easy, but I find it is always rewarding in a lasting way.

It is especially true of anyone elderly who also becomes housebound, that there can be a feeling of emptiness, loneliness and isolation, which leads to a sense of uselessness. The fact is that being active, getting out, running our own lives and a variety of other things are important for our selfhood and self-respect. Being looked after, and sensing another person doing a 'charitable act' in calling or shopping or whatever, is not easily accepted. The elderly may get out of touch. But supposing they are in touch at all, the contact is often only through afternoon meetings with tea and socialising. While excellent in itself, this is not enough to make the most of old age. The church should be able to offer something more, so that the elderly can maintain their dignity as valuable members of society.

The confessor has a way into these lonely lives; many such people cannot find a listening ear. The elderly and the lonely need time. In confession there is an opportunity to open the heart, express emptiness and the feeling of being discarded. For many of those I have met over the years, regular confession in the church or heart to heart in the home is a valuable lighthouse flashing each week or month and proving very beneficial and therapeutic. Such contact may or may not look for absolution on each occasion, though until now many of the elderly have been brought up more according to a set pattern than have later generations. The expression of what is deep inside one, the verbalising of it, can have profound effect. Received by the priest, it can bring from him a warm word of reassurance, provided that the priest is sympathetic, patient, and does not appear in a hurry, off-hand or dismissive.

For the housebound, if numbers are large, the visit of the actual priest will have to be spaced out. This can be supplemented by the training and commissioning of lay people to give Holy Communion, as well as sharing a small Bible service in the home. Such contacts can become very close, can emphasise the union with those members able to worship in church, and can be used for involving the housebound in prayer for various local needs. You will surely see that the development of a relationship between a housebound person and a commissioned visitor may build up and develop, so that the deepest confidences can be exchanged.

Harking back to much earlier days when lay people sometimes heard the confession of other lay people, it is not totally beyond credibility that in the climate of these times, the Church might take a new look at history and come to extend confessional 'powers' to people not ordained to preside at Mass. As far as the deepening of prayer, closeness to the Lord and general involvement within the community of God is concerned, elderly persons are in special need of regular and perhaps extended contacts, which may be beyond the practical capability of the priest. The latter can remain as a regular but less frequent visitor, who can space himself round the parish, while others share more fully than now in apostolic work for the community.

The bereaved

There has been much new thought and practice in understanding and sharing with those who have been bereaved. It has become more evident that the bereaved person needs to express sorrow and emotion. Bottling-up is psychologically bad and can lead to complications later on. If the priest is in touch, he can act as a sponge for the depth of grief which frequently includes a sense of guilt. When someone we love dies, we tend to have regrets about what we have or have not done, the degree of our love, the actions we could have avoided. To be able to talk all this out of the person's system in the setting of confession and with the positive reassurance of forgiveness which is implicit in absolution can lift a desolate and guilt-ridden individual on to the first steps of their personal resurrection and new life.

But, the process of growing into new life is often slow and continues to be painful. The pastor needs both to be able to give some time as the weeks and months go by, and also to encourage neighbours in the same kind of service as is suggested for the housebound, but also more widely in helping to get the bereaved person back into life in this world.

The terminally ill and dying

It may seem odd to make a difference between the terminally ill and the dying. In fact, there can be a great difference in that a person, say, diagnosed as having a terminal cancer, may enjoy a respite which sometimes proves to be a 'cure' or at least sometimes lasts over a period of months or years – during which the person may or may not be an invalid, but can tend to live more in expectation of continued life rather than sudden death. With the terminally ill, there is much that a pastor should be open to learning. The main question and even confrontation is over allowing the patient to know the truth about his life expectation – long, short or really unknown. I am personally convinced that the general answer is to listen to the patient, assess the state he or she is in, and then as and when it seems appropriate, move simply into the facts, while bolstering the patient's morale by your presence, your personal faith, and your continued commitment to be with or alongside him or her as life begins again or draws to a close.

Much has been written and thought out recently in regard to the hospice movement, which specifically works with and for the terminally ill. The care and concern and closeness to the individual which can be offered by the committed priest is one aspect of what is seen today to be an area of growing concern. A priest can be – is not necessarily – a reassuring person. He, like others, can be a bridge between the patient and the consultant or doctor who sometimes fails to come across to the individual with either straight talk or warmth. The process of coming close to a terminal patient can be lengthy and fraught with difficulties but, while others have their part to play, I have no doubt whatsoever that burdens can be lifted, sorrows turned to joy and the path laid open for dying when the priest comes as a priest and gently leads the suffering/dying person onward. It is not an easy commitment, but many people, becoming conscious of approaching death, feel the need to confess. This opening up is very beautiful. And after it, divided families can be brought together for the first time in many years, and united families can be drawn even closer. It helps the sick person to die in peace.

Conclusion

I have put forward these thumbnail sketches of my personal attitudes and insights when as priest, and in particular as confessor or counsellor, I come across individuals with certain problems. In the space available I cannot enter these problems in depth, nor can I cover the whole range of human need. My hope in setting down these bare bones is that the reader will be able to get a sense of the pastoral style which has evolved during my thirty and more years of reading, prayer, work, contact and involvement. If you come to some 'feel' of what I am saying and attempting to do through these inadequate expressions, you will be able to reflect on Christian teaching and your own attitudes and practice. Like Jesus, we are here to do the will of God, meeting people of every kind, expressing the love and compassion of the Lord, and trying to be God's messenger of pardon, peace and hope. Through the history of God's revelation to man which in due time culminated in Jesus Christ there was change and development. Since Jesus, his followers have by no means all drawn identical lessons from his teaching and life. Popes, bishops, theologians and the whole range of clerical and lay workers among God's people have produced a multi-coloured variety of expression in word and in practice. Some of these expressions have subsequently been condemned, modified or accepted. The Church lives and life continues the rainbow image of God's covenant with his creation.

NOTES

1 Eph. 2.10.

2 *Divorce and Second Marriage*: Father Kevin T. Kelly, Collins 1982.

3 Matt. 12.34.

Rooted and Grounded in Love

THE preceding chapters have attempted to consider a wide view of sin, guilt, confession and reconciliation. In the line of thinking which I have been putting forward, repentance is Christ's call. The way his economy of salvation has developed in the history of the Church has included the part the Church has to play in reconciliation through confession. 'Confession' began as an isolated incident in the lives of some Christians, but then grew into an instrument in the more general growth of people who had accepted Christ's command: Follow me.

However, it may have emerged in what I have written so far that some of my thinking may not be one hundred per cent acceptable to members of all churches, possibly not even to members of one! I am a Roman Catholic, but despite what is sometimes imagined from outside about the monolithic structure of the Catholic Church, Roman Catholics live with tensions and considerable differences of opinion. This is healthy and leads to interchange of thought, vision and expression.

My object in this chapter is to try to draw together the strands of my thinking and practice, especially in regard to confession and counselling. The word 'confession' is subject to many interpretations, and so is counselling. For this reason I will sketch something of the background and attitude to confession of a select number of Churches in the second part of this book. However, there are very many other Churches or Christian associations which I have not been able to cover: the diversity and variation of teaching is so great I could never begin to go into every one here. The Churches which I have highlighted all have either a fundamentally clear and strong doctrine on penance or confession, or at least a remnant of it which has continued through reformation. If I have ignored or neglected others, I am sorry. But I hope it may be possible for members of such Churches to pick up something in what I am setting forth and use it either for correcting any wrong impression or for studying where their Churches stand, so that a dialogue may begin. We can all too easily be ignorant of each other, and can dismiss suggestions which are put forward by another party without due consideration.

In presentation, I have made use of my own personal experience and insights. The view I am giving I cannot claim as other than my own, here aided by what I have gathered from scripture, the Church and many people. Therefore, it may or may not be shared entirely by my fellow Roman Catholics, or again by other denominations, clerical or lay; and I do not know how these thoughts will be received by the caring professions, including psychiatrists, counsellors and social workers.

The world situation

It sometimes seems to me that the preacher like myself feels no sermon is complete unless it begins with Genesis and goes all through to the Revelation of John. I am not trying to do that, but I want to look at the place within the world situation of confession, penance, reconciliation or whatever we choose to call the long-standing Christian Church practice of entering a new relationship of forgiveness and love with God.

Church circles nowadays tend to talk in terms of the ordinary people of the world seeking almost desperately for peace. I believe human beings do seek peace fundamentally. But we are also caught up in ourselves, our ambitions, loves, jealousies and fears – all of which can form subject-matter for confession or counsel in the broad sense.

Part of such a suggested search for peace stems from a genuine personal desire to be at peace within ourselves. This desire is behind the spiritual process of reconciliation with God as the beginning of reconciliation with neighbours. Here the Christian approach through the Church would be based on personal conversion leading to the leavening of the world. But it has to be acknowledged that, both in the peace search and in some religious attitudes, there is liable to be a strong strand of fear – in the first, fear of a nuclear holocaust, in the latter, fear of God's 'anger'. Though there will probably continue to be the fear element, and in the case of religion this associated also with guilt, Christian teaching properly has strong emphasis upon God's forgiveness springing from his love: 'There is no fear in love, but perfect love casts out fear'.[1]

There can be no doubt that Jesus' message is of the reconciliation of the whole world to God, not just the reconciliation of the individual sinner, who may accept being himself forgiven, yet not go beyond himself to spread the good news. Forgiveness is the beginning of a process for the individual which should help to set off reaction well outside and beyond himself. For instance, after my own personal 'conversion' back to God from whom I had wandered, the impulse was to share. In my case, this took me into priesthood. I looked round at where I was, where the world seemed to be, and what I sensed as the immediate needs of those with whom I was working. But the forgiveness experience in me changed what I had been doing for people. From merely being a part of my job I came to realise that 'my people' were in fact God's people. I was touched by the pain of Christ in his suffering world near at hand and also far away. The new dimension of my work which brought in God extended my vision.

Since then, I have been conscious of the wider world purpose which is aiming for individual personal reconciliation and wholeness – but such a reconciliation as will lead individuals, groups and even whole societies to strive for justice and peace at all levels. Life has taken me to many parts of the world and I have been fortunate to have wide international contacts. In this way the world need for justice and the extent of deprivation and injustice are indelibly imprinted on me. At the same time I have been acutely conscious in run-of-the-mill confession encounters among literally thousands of members of the Roman Catholic Church, together with spiritual counselling of numbers of members of other denominations, that seldom does a self-accusation of failure to work for justice and peace enter an individual confession. The desire for peace, the search for peace seems too often to stop short of a sense that it is essential to work for peace. Undoubtedly, some are stirred by what they read in scripture or hear from those organisations which work for the Third World, or famine relief, or whatever. But I can say without breaking the seal of confession that consciences are often stirred by immediate disasters, but, apart from noticeable exceptions, seldom commit themselves to longterm action.

My stress on work for peace and reconciliation at this point is because Jesus Christ promised his peace. On one occasion according to the evangelist he linked this gift with forgiving sins:

> 'Peace be with you. As the Father has sent me, even so I send you'. And when he had said this, he breathed on them, and said to them, 'Receive the Holy Spirit. If you forgive the sins of any, they are forgiven; if you retain the sins of any, they are retained'.[2]

A counsellor, confessor or confidant who is working with individuals should be concerned with the possibility that the penitent's sensitivity to Christ's will for the reconciliation of the world may be extended and deepened through his own acceptance of forgiveness. Simply to accept forgiveness without the broader dimension can lead to a narrow emphasis on personal sanctification, which omits responsibility towards our neighbours and the world.

It is easy for me to be critical of what others may be aiming at or living out, when I am not much of a positive example myself. However, it seems to me that I must be rather forthright here if I am attempting to make suggestions for now and the future in regard to confession and reconciliation leading to peace. To my judgement in the limited areas in which I work and through the other contacts I have there is little sign of religious revival or renewal. The *word* renewal is used quite considerably. But I have not come across widespread evidence that there is much outcome in the ordinary life of the churches. In part this may be in the sense that the radical nature of Jesus' call is easily watered down. Official Church lead given in the British Isles is normally 'established', not in the sense that it always comes from the Established Church, but because overall it is good, worthy and not often controversial or disturbing. There is a lack of fire, drive and inspiration. Christ lived poorly, taught boldly, antagonised as well as converted, stood against the establishment of his time, and of course suffered for all this on the cross. Today, even work for the underprivileged in our affluent society can take on an acceptable decency which follows a middle and inoffensive path.

Certainly, one of the ways of stirring the smoking flax of our faith and practice into flame is through the use of examination of conscience and confession. Confession should include the forgiveness of God through the ministry of the Church and spiritual counsel enlightened by the Holy Spirit. The key word in the early writers on penance was *metanoia*, change of heart. The pursuit of peace and reconciliation needs change of heart in individuals in order to begin to change the world.

Confession, theology and psychology

God is central to the doctrine and practice of confession because he is acknowledged by Christians as the creator who is source of all life. The life, death, resurrection and teaching of Jesus Christ reconcile the human race to God, creator and father, in and through himself:

> If anyone is in Christ, he is a new creation; the old has passed away, behold the new has come. All this is from God, who through Christ reconciled us to himself and gave us the ministry of reconciliation; that is, God was in Christ reconciling the world to himself, not counting their trespasses against them, and entrusting to us the message of reconciliation. So we are ambassadors for Christ, God making his appeal through us. We beseech you on behalf of Christ, be reconciled to God. For our sake he made him to be sin who knew no sin, so that in him we might become the

righteousness of God.[3]

The preaching, teaching and encouragement to live a Christian life came through the infant Church into the growth and systemisation of the ensuing centuries. There were growing pains which showed in controversy about both doctrine and practice, but the main theme remained the work of reconciliation.

What I want to underline here is that the development of the sacrament of reconciliation, which is what confession or penance is now often called, was part of the evolution of doctrinal thinking and ecclesiastical practice. I will try to indicate some of this development in the chapter on the historical background. I hope this outline will make it clear that the availability and the considered need for reconciliation has varied a great deal. So, too, has the emphasis on the way into forgiveness, the frequency of confession, the role of the priest and so on. The process of evolution continues to our time. It is necessary for us to look at where we are and to re-assess how the work of reconcilation is to continue today in the Church.

The fundamental sacrament of reconciliation is baptism. Penance is the follow-through when it is believed that the relationship between God and man has been impaired by personal sin. This sin element has to be considered. My suggestion would be that there should be a renewed and serious study of sin, its nature and its implications in the light of modern scholarship and the pastoral experience of the present times. There has been a certain blurring of the distinction between right and wrong. There will always be a divergence of opinion and interpretation on sin, as well as on moral principles and all that flows from them. To some extent this is evident in the tension which can arise between the teaching that God is all merciful and forgiving and in confession meeting a hard priestly attitude on sin and forgiveness. A considerable amount of the disillusion with and fall away from confession stems from confusion among ordinary people about the nature and gravity of sin, together with a sense that there is no clarity of teaching in this sphere by the Church at the present time. This lack of clarity is not only between the exponents of the different Christian denominations but also within individual churches. I am by no means advocating that the ideal is a rigid attitude justified in terms of clarity. Rather, the very fundamentals of relationship between God and his will and the response of the human being should be spelled out afresh, with all the insights of both modern theological and spiritual writers and the work of those trained and skilled in psychology and behavioural sciences.

In elucidating right and wrong and the grey areas of morality, it remains true in Christian understanding that the human person has sufficient freedom to be responsible for his or her actions in a general sense, precluding special circumstances like severe mental handicap. The will of God is for the development of human beings so that they can individually and together stand up and be fully adult persons. The responsibility of the 'ambassadors of Christ',[4] in the sense of the leaders, teachers and priests/confessors/counsellors of the Church, or indeed any Christian, is to assist towards adulthood. Unfortunately, the ambassadors also have within their own freedom the possibility of stultifying growth, as and when they get the emphasis wrong. Fault and sin need to be recognised and acknowledged, but over-emphasis on guilt so that the individual becomes guilt-ridden kills growth. It is healthy and leads to wholeness to acknowledge guilt and failure where it is present, but also to accept God's forgiveness, and to try for the future to live more nearly according to his will.

What I have written so far in this section puts God at the heart of the reconciliation of the world, which we are now considering in the more limited area of confession. But one of the questions raised in recent times and needing re-examination is the possible link between what I dare to call 'the failure of confession' and the developing role of the psychiatrist and counsellor in our society today. The immediate and essential similarity between the work of the confessor and the psychiatrist is that both are clear that their aim is assistance into wholeness of a human person who in one way or another is wounded, incomplete or lost. The immediate and essential difference is that the work of the priest must be based upon belief in God, whereas the range of belief among psychiatrists varies through the whole spectrum from atheism to strict religious adherence. Psychology, psychiatry and counselling for the Christian involve God. But psychology, psychiatry and counselling do not in themselves include God, any more than medicine does. However, from the assistance to wholeness of the human person by any psychiatrist, a great deal can emerge and be very effective, including the religious dimension. Gerald Priestland, in a series of broadcasts which touched off something deep and wide in his very large audience, tells us:

> If ever I had anything like a Damascus Road conversion experience, it came to me on the psychiatrist's couch; for that was where I learnt to recognise the missing element of forgiveness.[5]

He does not tell us whether his psychiatrist was a Christian. I hazard that it does not necessarily matter, because the good practitioner helps a person to be in touch with the depth of his being, and from such depth can come the kind of experience which Gerald Priestland relates. Personally, both in theory and in practice I have long been open to the goodness, experience and expertise of many a psychiatrist who worked straightforwardly with clients, without particularly intruding his or her own attitude to religion. Time and again I have referred people who come to me and need to see a trained professional to the best psychiatrist or counsellor to hand I know, irrespective of the latter's religious beliefs. Subsequently I have been full of admiration for their work. Similarly, I have had referrals to myself by Christian psychiatrists and by psychiatrists of other faiths and of none at all. And their referrals have been clients whom they thought could be helped by me, even though, as I say, some of these practitioners did not believe in God and some held firmly to non-Christian faiths.

C. G. Jung asserted that mankind as a whole is God-seeking, but he himself did not have much time for belief as such, and put more stress upon experience. I do not want to enter into a discussion about what the notion 'God' for Jung means and whether Jung's 'God' is 'other' as Christians affirm or not. In the assertion mentioned we touch on Jung's concern with experiental knowledge rather than reliance simply on an intellectual faith. The Christian would include experience of the 'other' as well as faith in the wholeness of Christian living. My point in mentioning Jung here is that many believing psychiatrists have and do follow Jungian psychology. Pastors interested would need to read more deeply. One such pastor writes, in direct quotation from Jung:

> In a letter written in 1945 at the age of seventy he affirms, 'It is of the highest importance that the educated and "enlightened" should know religious truth as a thing living in the human soul and not an abstruse and unreasonable relic of the past'. With the growth of secularism and the weakening of the authority both of the Bible and of Christian tradition there is a growing recognition that faith

is much more than intellectual belief and must involve commitment of the whole person and should include at least some intuition of God.[6]

Those of us who are Christians should do all that we are able to understand and appreciate the great good which has come through psychiatry, psychotherapy, counselling and analysis. But we should also be aware that the average Christian may still prefer what he or she might consider the safety of becoming a client of someone who is a practising Christian, or at least is sympathetic to religious experience. In any case, if priests and others are asked for advice by parishioners or penitents about accepting psychiatric treatment, they should have enough knowledge to be helpful. There can be dangers in the uses of psychiatry, as of religion. The foundation for any recommendation should be the excellence of the practitioner. But the corollary to my argument is that recommendation of a Christian in need of both forgiveness and counsel through the ministry of the Church should likewise be to a confessor whose training, way of life and expertise in guiding souls to wholeness in God is assured.

There are, no doubt, many reasons for the 'failure of confession', but certainly among them I personally would want to put some blame upon both the teaching of moral theology and confessional practice in post-Tridentine times, leading to a lack of training which I have already touched upon. But rather than going over that again and into other factors, I now want to try to put before you for consideration – and I hope discussion – my ideas for the now and future of confession.

Confession today and tomorrow

In writing what has gone before and what will come now I want any reader of any of the Christian churches or congregations to take some time to consider their own individual understanding. What does confession mean to you? Should it be part of living Christianity or should it be rejected as unscriptural or irrelevant? For me and my thesis it is important that you should assess or re-assess where you personally stand in relation to the forgiveness of God in the first place, and the economy of God's forgiveness in the second. I take it that the vast majority of those who believe in God as manifested in Jesus Christ believe that he came to inaugurate a 'new creation' made one through his, Jesus Christ's incarnation, death and resurrection.

But the follow-through of Jesus, if I may so call it, has become in the exploration of human beings a very complex affair. At one extreme it seems entirely personal and personalised – Jesus is my saviour! At the other extreme it appears that salvation is some community or world redemption which leaves little or no space for personal responsibility.

The line of reasoning and teaching which I put forward here is that there is a twofold responsibility – that of the individual who is personally responsible for his or her soul, and also that of the followers of Jesus and their tradition which involves an authority for the care of those who wanted to follow in the steps of the master. It is the second area of responsibility which comes into question. Many of those who accept to proclaim the good news of Jesus will draw people to follow him through the mediation of their preaching and leadership, but when it comes to forgiveness get worried about any human being as it were 'intervening'.

While I accept that the individual can at any time call upon God for his forgiveness and accept his saving grace, to my understanding and the understanding of many Christians the Church has a significant role to play in God's economy of salvation. It is scripturally respectable to accept the Church as Christ's body. The Church down the centuries has had authority both in teaching and in discipline. The standpoints of the Roman Catholic Church and some others is that the role of the priest in confession is relevant. He is working as a member of Christ's body with the authority of the Church. In this, he is not interfering with access to God, but furthering God's plan that is centred in Jesus Christ, and stressing the way in which God seeks the co-operation of his creation in fulfilling his gracious purpose. This will, I hope, be made clearer in the chapter on Making a Confession, in Part Two.

I realise that this is not a line of thinking which will find favour with a number of Christians of various persuasions. But I want to ask each reader, whether immediately hostile, immediately in favour or hesitant about this thesis, to stop, sit and think. We all want to co-operate with God's purpose in Christ:

> You are fellow citizens with the saints and members of the household of God, built upon the foundation of the apostles and prophets, Christ Jesus himself being the cornerstone, in whom the structure is joined together and grows into a holy temple in the Lord, in whom you also are built into it for a dwelling place of God in the Spirit.[7]

Having accepted the role of the Church and the role of the priest, I want to sum up some personal suggestions on pastoral care in relation to the great variety of human beings who make up the people of God, the body of Christ.

Individual confession

A system of individual confession is currently available for Roman Catholic, Orthodox and Church of

England members. Since 1215, the western Church has had a rule of annual confession, which has not applied to the Orthodox, and which was dropped at the Reformation by the Church of England. This rule remains a requirement for Roman Catholics. In addition, even in recent documents from Rome, frequent confession has been advocated.

My personal experience in the Roman Catholic Church leads me to conclude that, in my lifetime and to the present day, there have always been those who did no more than an annual confession, those who came three or four times a year and those who had a regular routine of weekly, fortnightly or monthly confession. Today, this kind of spread still continues, but there has been a very definite fall away among the more frequent users. Those who come at present on a frequent and regular basis have varying motivations from long-standing habit to newfound profit, from adherence to a religious rule of life to support in attempting to control a particular weakness, from fear of being unworthy to receive Holy Communion to genuine love and peace in confessing and receiving absolution.

In my work as a priest I recognise all these approaches as I try to be open to all individuals. But I want to make some points here about the *purpose* of confession as it is seen and used. The forgiveness of God through confession, absolution and satisfaction – assuming sincerity and sorrow on the part of the penitent – covers all sins, serious or slight. Now, though a person is free to go to confession when he or she has done nothing grave, serious, mortal or whatever word is used, the Roman Catholic Church teaches that confession is only *necessary* following grave sin.

I think it is arguable that the later practice of people linking confession with the reception of Holy Communion, and so in more recent times going very frequently indeed, devalued absolution. By that I mean that serious sin was very often not involved, minor imperfections became the matter for confession and individuals came because an unwritten, but perhaps preached or taught rule led people to feel they could not go to Holy Communion unless they had been to confession. Among the various causes of fall away from the practice of confession this devaluation could certainly be numbered as a factor. My hope would be that a renewed understanding of confession would encourage a more general acceptance of the place of confession in the lives of individuals, but that for many the importance would not be to go every week with little to confess, out of a fear of being unworthy. In this sense I envisage individual confession more spaced out, but of course still available at any church, and preferably at any reasonable time. Properly understood and in concert with other suggestions I will make shortly, the use and beauty of this sacrament will again be seen. Of course there will, I am sure, always be those who are approaching the sacrament each week not from routine or from fear of otherwise having to stay away from Holy Communion as unworthy. Such regulars find the frequency spiritually enriching and very helpful on their journey to holiness. But not all do, so discretion and wisdom from the confessor may discern with different souls what is best.

What I have said so far here on individual confession I have intended to represent what I call 'basic' confession. I mean a confession to a priest who simply listens, asks a question if necessary, but otherwise gives absolution without anything further in the way of exhortation or counsel. There are many priests who think of this as the only true way of confession, leaving God entire freedom of working on the soul of the penitent without the confessor obtruding himself further.

Confession and counselling

I accept that 'basic' confession has its place, that many like this approach and grow through its practice. But I also want to lay stress upon my own experience, in going to confession myself, and in hearing the confessions of others. Though I have no wish to be absolute because I believe in variety, there is no doubt in my mind that incorporation of counselling into confession can be more than useful: over the years I have found it to be a vital ingredient along with the acceptance of forgiveness, if the individual penitent is going to be encouraged, helped and opened to development in truly Christian living.

I ask you to consider seriously my present point, namely that some counsel may be needed, and that the confessor is there for that purpose. His role is not necessarily simply to listen and give absolution, but also possibly to assist in a conversion which leads to deeper relationship with God. However, when I say this in regard to counselling, I must stress that this line of thought is putting considerable weight upon the confessor, and that is why I have found it necessary to emphasise some of the priestly qualities and also the training and growth of the priest in his ministry.

If the pastor accepts at his ordination the key nature of the confessor-role in what is to be his ministry with people, he must not only give time and space for the development of his availability for meeting individuals, but he must also give God what may seem an over-generous portion of each day in prayer. I am not suggesting that he withdraws from the ordinary humdrum tasks of parochial ministry or whatever is his assignment. He needs to be in the midst of where people are. But his cultivation of silence, stillness and solitary prayer must have a central place and a priority day by day, together with something which is more the gift of God than anything he can organise – an aura of approachability, a sense of emanating from him to others that he will listen, will be sympathetic and understanding. Above all, it is essential that he is to be trusted completely in guarding the privacy of the other person's shared self-revelation.

The older, more frequent and faster confession militated against the majority of penitents entering into the deeper exploration of their relationship with God, progress in prayer, and also relationship with others. Years ago I found the strands which came together to form fertile soil for growth included extended time, face to face dialogue, and consequently the openness of the penitent to be known by the confessor. Clearly, the frequency and the length of such confession-counselling sessions varies, and is largely the responsibility of the confessor, who has to be able to judge. Certain circumstances, such as new conversion, spiritual crisis, a personal fight against an addiction and so on, may for a time need greater frequency and length. But I find we can generally get into a pattern together. Quite a number of priests and religious like to come to confession as regularly as once every month or six weeks; some lay people like the same pattern. Other people prefer three or four times a year. And there are a group of those who have moved away, even overseas, and turn up perhaps once a year for a review of life, which ends with absolution. Some of this last group will also write during the year; frequently they have a policy of 'basic' confession periodically, wherever they may be.

An extended relationship

In this small section I want to put forward a line of practice which may not be for everybody, but which I have found spiritually rewarding both for myself and the other person. In some situations with certain individuals the growth of spiritual awareness, of desire for reconciliation at a deeper level, of learning more about the way of prayer, even perhaps of seeking out God's call, seems to require a wider context than that readily available in the ordinary line of confession and counselling.

The possibility for someone who is tight up inside to relax and be able to talk and share can be encouraged over a period of time. But how can this be achieved? One way which has worked is to accept a person into the living situation where I am. This gives something of a background security, opportunity to share and talk and even work together. There is by no means one hundred per cent success. Moreover, without going to quite such lengths, it is still possible to weigh up and decide that a completely different atmosphere from the confessor-penitent situation may be a way forward. This can take the form of going out into the country for a day, or going away for a few days, walking, eating, watching TV, praying and so on, in an unthreatening and undemanding atmosphere. Again, a lesser way is to visit the individual in his or her home, on their ground, or to share a meal out somewhere. Out of this I have rejoiced to find spiritual development springing up. Further, in the majority of such relationships, the bond has strengthened to friendship of a lasting quality which can withstand the test of long periods apart. Then the fruit makes me thank God as I watch the other persons really maturing, taking possession of themselves and striking out in marriage, priesthood, education, and many other directions.

Subsequent to these encounters and relationship patterns, some people remain in regular touch for a considerable time; others like to re-establish contact now and again. There is one man, for instance, whom I meet about twice a year. He lives in France and comes over for a week or two. Recently, as he is now getting older, he has decided to cut his visits down to one a year. Another person in the West Indies I now only know and talk to through letters, since I was last over there a couple of years ago. So for him confession in the strict sense no longer applies. But he pours everything out in his letters, and asks me to pray to the Lord to have mercy on him.

The reader may think this is stretching confession and counselling beyond the ordinary definitions. However, given God's desire to reconcile and the limits he went to in sending his Son to be about with us, it seems to me a Christlike extension of care, which has its tensions, dangers and heavy work load, but which can be borne if lived in the right balance of prayer, work, company and relaxation.

Community or communal confession and penitential services

As implied earlier, speaking of reconciliation in the dimension of neighbour, neighbourhood, social concern and world poverty and injustice, there is growing stress upon Christian people becoming aware of their responsibility beyond themselves. One of the ways of getting at this, as seems to be the tradition of Methodism, is through the meeting or service in which together the members of the congregation ask God's mercy and forgiveness for any and everything. I suppose it could be said that there was an element of this in the very early Church, when the working out of a penitential exercise and re-admission to the community were very much community rites.

But recently, in the Roman Catholic Church, the

sacrament of penance has taken on the community aspect, emphasising it most by two rites in addition to the normal rite for reconciling individuals. I think here it is worth seeing how these could be used, because by and large they are not employed extensively at the present time.

Rite B. Reconciliation of several penitents with individual confession and absolution

This form can be very effective as a medium for involving groups and larger congregations within parishes, etc. Much depends upon those who are organising the setting, music, content of the service and whole atmosphere of community friendship and sharing. Such an atmosphere is by no means common in congregations. Where it can be built up, the effect spreads both into the Eucharistic worship and into family and neighbourhood living. But Rite B is still unfamiliar to many and little used. I think that part of the difficulty where it has been used and discarded is that after the general togetherness of the service, including communal thinking about sin and forgiveness, the provision is that individuals move off to the confessionals or at least to a personal confession. For this, several priests are often called in to help and, with any big numbers, this stage can drag on, so that unless there is a keen and committed congregation, people drift away.

It is also true that queuing for individual absolution is rather public to the mind of the ordinary person, if the rest of the congregation is waiting for confessions to end so that the whole service may be concluded. I would want to suggest in practice that the litany or prayer which follows the communal examination of conscience and prayer of confession should be a deprecatory prayer for God's forgiveness. This should be explained to the congregation, not just at the service, but as an element built in to normal teaching about sin, forgiveness, the part of the Church and the different channels of forgiveness for individuals through the Church and in God's economy.

This means that in the use of penitential Rite B the prayer for forgiveness uttered by the priest leading the service – in the same form as that used at the Eucharist – when sincerely entered into by the congregation as penitents, covers all the lesser sins and failings. If a person is quite convinced of serious sin, is in doubt, or desires a confession of devotion, then he or she can have recourse to individual confession after the service. But the vast majority can gain great benefit and the deprecatory assurance of forgiveness, without the need specifically here to make an individual confession. From practice, I can say that this relieves many people who otherwise, though not in serious sin, feel the rite is incomplete if they have not been to receive individual absolution from the priest.

Further to this, I have come to realise the benefit there can be with children for the entry to the understanding and practice of the sacrament of reconciliation through the medium of a simple service of reconciliation. During this they can be led to look at themselves, at areas of fault and failure. Then they learn to confess to God silently in their hearts and, after saying together the general form of confession used in the Eucharist, they can accept the forgiveness of God prayed for by the priest. Young children seldom enter the realm of grave sin. Gradually, from this first reconciliation or penitential service, they can be introduced to individual confession in the confessional, or better, in an open face-to-face situation with a priest.

The method outlined above is one we have been

developing in our parish both with the children from the Catholic primary school and with those from different State schools who come in to the church each week for instruction. It has been greeted with joy and gratitude by parents, teachers and children alike. We now use the penitential services before Christmas and Easter. They take place at the end of a school day, and such parents as are free are invited to come along to share with the children. They come in good numbers and it is possible to make individual confession available for the adults if they wish it.

Rite C. Reconciliation of penitents with general confession and absolution

This rite makes provision for the occasion when it is appropriate and necessary to give sacramental absolution as it is given in the ordinary form to individuals – but here to an assembly of people, without prior individual confession to a priest. This rite was introduced into the Roman Catholic Church during the nineteen-seventies. Since then, however, there has been a gradual withdrawal by the Roman authorities, with stricter and stricter rules about the use of the rite.

During the autumn of 1983, there was a synod of bishops in Rome. The subject was Reconciliation, and the theme spread more widely than the sacrament, into world peace, justice, poverty and so on. The section on penance and the penitential rites or rites of reconciliation, as reported so far appeared to be of a conservative nature, with the emphasis on individual confession renewed. The final document has not yet been issued at the time of my writing, but there have been further indications of the line emerging.

The first of these is contained in *The Code of Canon Law* (Collins, 1983) under Canons 960–963. The most pertinent is Canon 961:

1 General absolution, without prior individual confession, cannot be given to a number of penitents together, unless:

1° danger of death threatens and there is not time for the priest or priests to hear the confessions of the individual penitents;

2° there exists a grave necessity, that is, given the number of penitents, there are not enough confessors available properly to hear the individual confessions within an appropriate time, so that without fault of their own the penitents are deprived of the sacramental grace or of holy communion for a lengthy period of time. A sufficient necessity is not, however, considered to exist when confessors cannot be available merely because of a great gathering of penitents, such as can occur on some major feastday or pilgrimage.

2 It is for the diocesan Bishop to judge whether the conditions required in 1, n.2 are present; mindful of the criteria agreed with the other members of the Episcopal Conference, he can determine the cases of such necessity.

The second comes in a report by the Vatican's International Theological Commission (*Origins*. Vol. 13. No. 31. January 12 1984.) Fundamentally, the Commission re-asserts the need for the full and personal confession of all serious sins, underlines the very extraordinary circumstances which are necessary for the use of general absolution, and confirms that after receiving general absolution, the individual still must have recourse to individual confession and absolution before receiving general absolution again.

In outlining the alternative forms of reconciliation service, the Commission suggests that more appropriate than the general absolution would be a new understanding and use of contrition, or sorrow. This not only gives the opportunity for considering sinfulness in common with other people, but also has the effect of leading on to the use of individual sacramental confession and absolution:

> . . . the confession of grave sins, which after a careful examination of his conscience, the sinner remembers, must have in virtue of God's saving will (*iure divino*) an indispensable place in obtaining the absolution. If not, the church cannot accomplish the tasks assigned to it by Jesus Christ in the Holy Spirit (*iure divino*), viz., the service of a physician, direction of souls, the advocacy of justice and love in private as well as in public life, heralding the divine promises of forgiveness and peace in a world often dominated by sin and animosity, a judgment of the authenticity of the conversion to God and to the church.
>
> 6. The integral confession of mortal sins, therefore, necessarily belongs to the sacrament of penance (*iure divino*), and thus it is not left to the judgement of the individual, nor to the decision of the church. However, the Council of Trent does acknowledge the concept of a sacramental confession *in voto* (DS 1543). For this reason, in extraordinary emergency situations in which such an integral confession is not possible, the church can allow the postponement of the confession and grant the absolution individually or in a group (general absolution), without previous confession. In such a situation the church acts with the spiritual possibilities of the moment, but must see to it that mortal sins are confessed subsequently, and must instruct the faithful about this obligation by appropriate means. The Council of Trent

does not itself pronounce on the nature and extent of these emergency situations.

To solve difficult pastoral problems the extension, recommended by many, of the situations mentioned in the *Normae Pastorales* of 1972 and in the *Ordo Paenitentiae,* is not the only possible solution. For situations in which there is no *copia confessorum* (DS 1661) the council rather points to the efficacy of contrition for reconciliation, made perfect by love (*contritio*) which grants reconciliation with God when it includes the *votum sacramenti,* and hence the *votum confessionis.* (DS 1677). How the church should proceed in this matter concretely on the basis of the doctrine of the Council of Trent, is a question of pastoral prudence and love (cf. on this below C 11, 4). (p. 521)

The section referred to comes a little later:

II. Individual Confessions, Reconciliation Services, General Absolution

1. Awareness of the wealth and multiplicity of the forms of penance has often grown dim. It must therefore be made stronger and receive attention both in preaching and in the pastoral practice of penance. Isolating the sacrament of penance from the context of the entire Christian life, which is inspired by the spirit of reconciliation, leads to an atrophy of the sacrament itself. Narrowing down the ministry of reconciliation to only a few forms can make one co-responsible for the crisis in the sacrament of penance and the well-known dangers of ritualism, and of a reduction to the state of a private exercise of piety.

The various means of reconciliation should, therefore, not be placed in competition with each other. Rather, the intrinsic unity and dynamic relationship between the individual forms of penance should be explained and made visible. The forms mentioned above (cf. C1, 3) are shown above all to be useful for "venial sins." Forgiveness of sins can indeed be granted in many ways: Forgiveness of the sins of everyday life is always given when contrition informed by love is present, (*contritio*) (cf. DS 1677).

2. To the extent that the forms of penance mentioned above and the dimensions of reconciliation are practiced more clearly and in a more convincing way in the daily life of the Christian, the desire for sacramental private confession is also bound to increase. Above all grave sins must be expressed in the most individual and comprehensive way possible before the church and its official representatives. A general confession of sins is not sufficient, because the sinner must, inasmuch as possible, give concrete expression to the truth of his guilt and the nature of his sins, and also because such an individual-personal confession of guilt strengthens and deepens true contrition. Both anthropological (A II, 3) and theological considerations (B III, 4; B IV c, 2.5f) favour this thesis.

Sacramental power is needed to forgive such sins. It is true that today the authentic form of private confession needs to be profoundly renewed in its spiritual aspects, and this in connection with the revised *Ordo paenitentiae*. Without such a renewal the church will not be able to cope with the crisis of the sacrament of penance. For this a better spiritual and theological formation of priests is required, in order that they may be able to deal with what is now demanded from confession, viz., the latter should contain more elements of spiritual direction and of fraternal exchange. Under this aspect the so called confession of devotion retains its importance.

3. The term *celebrationes paenitentiales* is often understood in different ways. Among such penitential celebrations one thinks principally of the liturgical celebrations of a congregation in which the call to penance and the promise of reconciliation are given expression, and a general confession of sins takes place without individual confession or an individual or general absolution. This type of penitential celebration can help place the community aspects of sin and forgiveness more to the foreground. They can awaken and deepen the spirit of penance and reconciliation. However, they must not be placed on the same level as the sacrament of penance, much less replace it.

In their orientation these penitential celebrations are certainly directed toward sacramental private confession, but they do not merely have the function of inviting to conversion and creating the dispositions required for the sacrament: With regard to daily sins they can become a true occasion of pardon, provided there is a real spirit of conversion and sufficient contrition (*contritio*). In this way the *celebrationes paenitentiales* may acquire an efficacious significance for salvation, even if they are not a sacramental form of penance.

4. The *Ordo Paenitentiae* also mentions a common celebration of reconciliation with a general confession and general absolution. This presupposes ethically and juridically unambiguous norms which must be observed in pastoral work (cf. the *Normae pastorales circa absolutionem sacramentalem generali modo impertiendam* of 1972, and the *Ordo Paenitentiae,* Pastoral

Introduction, no. 35).

It follows from this that this form of sacramental reconciliation applies to extraordinary situations of emergency. As current praxis has occasionally shown, the granting of general absolution outside such extraordinary emergency situations easily leads to basic misunderstandings of a fundamental nature about the essence of the sacrament of penance, and in particular about the basic necessity of personal confession of sins, the efficacy of sacramental absolution which presupposes contrition, and at least the *votum confessionis*. This type of misunderstanding and the ensuing abuses damage the spirit of the sacrament of reconciliation.

The difficult and even somewhat dramatic pastoral situations in many parts of the church today mean that many faithful hardly have the possibility of receiving the sacrament of penance. In these critical situations it is indispensable to show the faithful concerned ways which will enable them to have access to the forgiveness of sins and to receiving the eucharist. In these cases the tradition of the church, confirmed by the Council of Trent, acknowledges the possibility of a Christian obtaining the forgiveness of grave sin by perfect contrition. According to the same tradition perfect contrition also always implies the desire (*votum*) of receiving the sacrament of penance as soon as possible (DS 1677).

Where there is no *copia confessorum*, such a perfect contrition is probably a sufficient disposition for receiving the eucharist, according to the doctrine of the Council of Trent (DS 1661; cf. above B IV, c, 6). In most situations of such pastoral emergency this possibility is more suitable than general absolution, because in this way the

> obligation to the later personal confession can be made psychologically more understandable to most of the faithful. The ecclesial dimension of such a perfect act of contrition can be expressed by the penitential celebrations we mentioned above.
>
> 3. The contemporary crisis of penance and of the sacrament of penance cannot be solved by stressing only one form of penance, but only by means of a view which takes into account the complex relationships between the different forms of penance and how they mutually complement each other. In this matter it will also be important to integrate in a better way the individual forms of penance into the administration of the sacrament of penance, in order to bring sacramental penance more forcefully into the consciousness of the faithful. (p. 522)

Despite the forceful message of the Theological Commission, I do not personally experience the danger which is envisaged of losing the sense of need for absolution. We are in a crisis in regard to confession. The teaching is that perfect contrition is a better alternative than the general absolution. I think this will have to be worked out and taught more fully if it is to be meaningful and useful to the 'ordinary' faithful. To some extent I think it is true that alienation from individual confession and the rejoicing in general absolution may not be fully realised by the theologians. The Commission stresses more than once the absolute need for expression of guilt to the Church through the priest in case of serious sin.

Because I am very concerned that the sacrament of reconciliation should come back into the effective life of the Church, I personally wonder whether the presentation at the time of writing will have any real impact on the faith and practice of the public in the

Church. A great deal was emphasised at the Council of Trent, but this came after a prolonged period of philosophising through the middle ages. The development into the essential elements of confession, contrition and satisfaction were long disputed and by no means elaborated from the beginning. I wonder whether, even given the latest teaching from the Theological Commission, it may be that there should still be some further exploration of the whole development of confession, the stress on the absolute need for individual confession, the place of contrition, the use of the deprecatory form – all this set out in view of the way in which the ordinary members of the Church are, when they are allowed to do do, rejoicing in the availability of general absolution. From my own experience, through the use of general absolution, individuals find their way back into practice of the faith, with confession, Mass and and Holy Communion becoming integral to their life's texture.

I have not found that this rite undermines the use of individual confession, but rather that it is spiritually rich and can prise open stubborn minds and hearts.

It should perhaps be added that, in the whole field of these different rites, the goal of supplying immediate theological lucidity and precision may not be altogether easily susceptible of harmonisation with the goal of doing what pastoral experience seems to indicate. To *some* extent, more analytical understandings may have to be allowed to develop over time.

The Eucharist and the deprecatory form of absolution

The main churches using the eucharistic form of worship include, at some point in preparation for joining the worship or for coming forward to receive Holy Communion, a penitential expression of sorrow and a prayer for God's forgiveness. The form of this prayer is identical with or similar to part of the full form of absolution used in the sacrament of penance in varying churches.

Pastorally, I would like instruction within the churches to emphasise the use and purpose of the deprecatory prayer for forgiveness used in the Eucharist. It is my experience, and firm belief from wider discussion, that the vast majority of those who come to the Eucharist to worship in love and service are not living lives involved in grave sin. If they understand that individual confession is primarily and essentially to cover absolution from grave sins, and only secondarily for lesser sins and out of devotion, lingering fears about Holy Communion without confessions should be cleared away. Many Roman Catholics already live by this understanding and it is largely for the Roman Catholic that this is written. Some of the wider views of other churches have been outlined previously. I believe it is pastorally sad when people are unnecessarily inhibited from coming to Holy Communion. The sacrament of God's love is the sacrament of unity. Properly understood and properly entered into by individual people forming congregation and sharing, the Eucharist builds us together in community and more widely builds up the Church, the body of Christ.

Further, if the acceptance and use of the deprecatory form of absolution was more widely agreed by the Roman Catholic Church, this could be one bit of bridge-building with other Churches. It might open the way also to a deeper discussion with those who fear the priestly or Church role in confession. It would also lead to the necessary ecumenical study of the relation between the merciful love of God, the nature of sin and forgiveness.

Towards Being More Deeply Rooted and Grounded in Love

ALL that I have written has attempted to throw light on the value of reconciliation, the sacrament of penance. There have, of necessity, been some criticisms and strictures about the past and even the present mode of presentation and practice.

I want to leave you with my personal and positive situation in regard to confession, counselling and growth in love. Confession as a practice has never fitted easily into my life-style. I don't like talking about myself – especially the nasty things about me. I was put off and frightened by my early experience of confession. But, having said that, I am still convinced – indeed more than ever convinced – that it is of very great importance for each one of us to be able to have recourse to the forgiveness of God in this concrete way. Moreover, it is humanly speaking most helpful to any individual to be able to speak with or open up to another human being who is kind, listening, sympathetic, wise and in some way skilled in counselling.

It sometimes seems to me that at no time in history have so many people wanted so much advice. We are in an age of counselling, as well as being in an age of alternative medicine and psychiatry, with a considerable present interest in relaxation, prayer and meditation. Surely, then, this should be a time to exploit all the wonder of what we have been given by God through Jesus Christ. He came to reconcile, and the basic hope of any psychiatrist or counsellor is some form of reconciliation between the client and God/Self, Family/Society, etc. Now, down the centuries, sometimes in a better way and sometimes with much failure, the sacrament of reconciliation has carried on the work of Christ who came to call sinners, who ate with publicans and sinners, who believed in and practised prayer, who said 'Follow me'.

At this late stage in history, it would be devastatingly sad if those who profess to follow 'the Lord Jesus' should fail to correspond with him in the full sense. He was *the* counsellor; he was *the* healer; he was *the* reconciler. It is for us to discover the places of forgiveness, the areas of pain and sin which need healing, the breakdown of family relationship . . . and the subsequent battles.

So much is hoped for by the Lord; let us rejoice and be happy that he has chosen us. If we are humble enough to accept his mediation through the sacrament and the priest we will move into a new relationship of trust and love. It should enrich and build up the work of Christ in breeding among and within his human creation the wonder of forgiveness, peace, reconciliation and love. Then each of us can hear the word of the one who listens to our outpourings and pleas for love. The word we shall hear will be:

Go in peace

NOTES

1 I Jn. 4. 18.
2 Jn. 20. 21-23.
3 2 Cor. 5. 17-21.
4 cf. 2 Cor. 5. 20.

5 Gerald Priestland, *Priestland's Progress.* British Broadcasting Corporation, 1981 p.60.
6 Christopher Bryant, *Jung and the Christian Way.* Darton Longman and Todd, 1983 p.2
7 Eph. 2. 19-22.

PART TWO

Confession – Some Historical Background

AS I asked various people of different denominations about their knowledge and understanding of confession I came to realise that there was considerable ignorance about. This ignorance was sometimes in regard to practice, but even more in regard to the history of confession. I was led in my own ignorance to do some research into the development of doctrine and use down the centuries. This in turn made me decide that it is important for the now and future of confession that there should be a chapter on history, although it may not seem directly relevant to confession and counselling in the pastoral care of people.

The development is long and complex, with an immense amount of detail. I have not attempted to portray it here in more than outline. However, I hope that this potted story from apostolic times until the present day is authentic and balanced. I have tried to cover the period in such a way as to clarify centuries of development so that we can see the reasons for past and present teaching and usage. At a time when there is much anxiety for peace and reconciliation about in the world, a better understanding will encourage us to go ahead into the future for further fulfilling of the reconciliation of human persons to God.

Prior to the Reformation, there was a wide diversity

of teaching and practice, especially between the Orthodox and the Western Churches. Since the Reformation and until the re-emergence of the Catholic strain in the Church of England, most of the teaching, writing and discussion on confession has been Roman Catholic based.

However, we must not ignore that there was some discussion and teaching, especially with individuals like Lancelot Andrewes (1555–1626) and Jeremy Taylor (1613–1667). Taylor, both in *Unum Necessarium* (1655) and *The Rule and Exercise of Holy Living* (1650), stressed the value of confession. He wanted to rid people of the bondage of the Roman command to confess, but he wanted to retain the value of 'laying open our wounds to cure', and of taking on the use of a spiritual guide (*Holy Living*. p. 208f). Taylor did not accept Rome's teaching that confession was judicial; for him it was remedial. He maintained that confession to God is sufficient, unless restitution to one's fellow is necessary (Cf. Works. vii. p. 438ff). Normally, confession was necessary in four circumstances – in sickness, for a scrupulous person who was unable to find pardon and peace of mind by recourse to God alone, or for notorious sinners who needed help and guidance to assist their true repentance. Finally, confession was useful for devout persons who wished to advance the growth of their spiritual lives.[1]

The legacy of Israel

By the end of the Old Testament era, when John the Baptist and Jesus Christ came into public in their teaching roles, much of the interpretation of the law and the prophets had become highly legalistic. The laws held still for Jews, even though the Roman domination meant that these only stood alongside the alien laws of the ruling power, as is instanced in the tussle with Pilate over the fate of Jesus.[2] Breaking the law was breaking the covenant between God and his people. The break could be individual or it could be so serious and widespread that it seemed to touch the whole people. Recognition of this came to be made annually on the Day of Atonement. The high priest stood for the people and made his own personal confession. He then laid the sins of the people before God and made the sin offering as prescribed.[3] There were also lists of personal sins for which the individual had to make confession and sacrifice through the priest – uncleanness, stealing, false testimony and so on.[4]

However, as sacrifice was only offered in Jerusalem, in practice it became necessary for the rabbis to allow certain other ways of confession and other signs of repentance. The rabbis themselves became responsible. They thought out penances which were not unlike those used in the early Christian Church, such as praying, fasting, giving alms, wearing penitential clothing. Idolatry was always the most heinous breaking of the covenant. An idolator was to be thrust away and even to be put to death. If a whole group went to another place to join in idolatry, they should be pursued to that place and destroyed.[5] This kind of penalty was still carried out in Jesus's time, as is seen in the incident at Nazareth,[6] – and was usually modified simply to expulsion from the community.

The local rabbis also became involved in dealing with notorious sinners, who were put out of the synagogue and so symbolically out of the community. But they were allowed back after a time of penance, when they were judged to have returned to a proper way of life.

It is clear from early writing[7] that, while the disciples carried on with many of the Jewish practices, they remained confused about such matters as the need for circumcision[8] and the dietary laws.[9] St. Paul, as we would expect, gives the clearest picture of the way rabbis continued to interpret the law by the expulsion of notorious sinners. Writing to the Corinthians, he deals with the growing slackness in the local church, especially in regard to immorality; but he also includes the admonition not to associate with and even to expel those who are covetous, idolators, revilers, drunkards and robbers.[10]

Later, Paul has to write in a different tone. Evidently the Corinthians had carried out at least one expulsion, and Paul now feels forgiveness is more appropriate.[11] Here Paul lends his own personal authority from Christ:

> Anyone whom you forgive, I also forgive. What I have forgiven, if I have forgiven anything, has been for your sake in the presence of Christ.[12]

Again, in another letter, Paul teaches that persistent sinners should be rebuked in the presence of everyone 'so that the rest may stand in fear'.[13] Later again, Paul teaches how to deal with a man who is factious: 'after admonishing him once or twice, have nothing more to do with him'.[14]

In Israel, among the rabbis, the exclusion of the notorious sinner from the community and the later allowance of his re-admission was known as 'binding and loosing'. For a Jew, to bind something was to declare it forbidden; to loose was to declare it allowed. This was an extension of the law. It seems that the writers of the Gospels picked up this idea and portrayed it on the basis of the authority of Jesus. Jesus is shown giving Peter the power of binding and loosing,[15] and the need to call in witnesses before the expulsion appears afterwards.[16] Paul again is the most explicit. Writing of it he says:

> Let him who has done this be removed from

among you. For though absent in body I am present in spirit, and as if present, I have already pronounced judgement in the name of the Lord Jesus on the man who has done such a thing. When you are assembled, and my spirit is present, with the power of our Lord Jesus, you are to deliver this man to Satan for the destruction of the flesh, that his spirit may be saved in the day of the Lord Jesus.[17]

I have said earlier that the main line of teaching in the Gospels is of forgiveness of sins, which would imply re-admission on repentance. However, Matthew has Jesus making a specific exclusion:

> Therefore I tell you, every sin and blasphemy will be forgiven men, but the blasphemy against the Spirit will not be forgiven. And whoever says a word against the Son of man will be forgiven; but whoever speaks against the Holy Spirit will not be forgiven, either in this age or in the age to come.[18]

This is echoed by John:

> If anyone sees his brother committing what is not a mortal sin, he will ask, and God will give him life for those whose sin is not mortal. There is sin which is mortal; I do not say that one is to pray for that. All wrongdoing is sin, but there is sin which is not mortal.[19]

The author of Hebrews, after speaking of the principle of Christ's doctrine on repentance, baptism and the laying on of hands continues:

> For it is impossible to restore again to repentance those who have once been enlightened, who have tasted the heavenly gift and become partakers of the Holy Spirit and have tasted the goodness of the word of God and the powers of the age to

come, if they then commit apostasy, since they crucify the Son of God on their own account and hold him up to contempt.[20]

The atmosphere of those times was set for the imminent return of Jesus; the feeling was that there was no time for a second conversion. Those who had committed 'mortal sin' turned their backs on the forgiveness of Christ through the Holy Spirit; in their final impenitence, by not asking for forgiveness they committed the unforgivable sin.

If this sin was indeed that of apostasy, prompting expulsion from the Christian community, this did not mean that in its individual members the Christian community was free from sin. Much in the way in which the sins of the people of Israel who were still within the community were taken up by the power of God in the community and through the priest, so in the Christian understanding. The ordinary sin which was not mortal could be forgiven within the community:

> If we say we have no sin, we deceive ourselves, and the truth is not in us. If we confess our sins, he is faithful and just, and will forgive our sins and cleanse us from all unrighteousness.[21]

James goes a step further than this in stressing the importance of the community members in supporting one another. After speaking of the work of the elders in praying for the sick and anointing them, he goes on:

> The prayer of faith will save the sick man, and the Lord will raise him up; and if he has committed sins, he will be forgiven. Therefore confess your sins to one another, and pray for one another, that you may be healed. The prayer of the righteous man has great power in its effects.[22]

The early centuries

Little is known of the Church's practice of penance in the first and second centuries. There was reference back to the New Testament 'binding and loosing' and also to the reported commissioning of the apostles by Jesus to forgive or retain sin.[23] But there was a considerable variation in the way of interpreting the teaching.

The difficulty arose because the second coming did not come. Some began to fall away from the community. What was their situation if they committed serious post-baptismal sin like apostasy, murder or adultery? These three were marked as particularly heinous because each in its way struck at the very roots of the community. Apostasy by an individual and even more by a group broke the wholeness of the community. Murder cut down the numbers of the community and made growth that much less possible. Adultery broke the smaller community of the family.

The rigorist view was that there was no forgiveness; the more lenient that there should be a 'second baptism', but only once. Hermas, who lived in Rome and wrote *The Shepherd*, was one of the more lenient. He suggested, perhaps with approval, that 'certain teachers' say the only penance for the three great sins which is open to Christians is the one undergone at baptism. But he also proclaimed a revelation from God through an angel of a second chance for sinners who repented. They could be received back into the community even if they had been apostates because of persecution. This lenience was because of the nearness of the second coming. But this was a once-for-all chance and equivalent to a second baptism. Hermas writes: 'If someone sins and repents repeatedly it will do him no good, for such a person is not likely to live'.

The variety and contradictory nature of what was

put forward is too great to go into here. Suffice it to say that Clement of Alexandria agreed with Hermas that the second baptism was once-for-all. Clement of Rome stressed God's mercy and the 'desirability of repentance and confession', without linking confession to a catechumenate similar to that for those who were about to be baptised.

By the third century there was a more general pattern emerging. The person who wanted to become a penitent had to make himself known to the bishop. The confession of sin was probably always private, but the person became known publicly as a sinner because he was excluded from the Eucharist – except for the first part of the prayers – like the catechumen. The penitent had to show reform in his life, undertaking whatever works were prescribed. Such penitential exercises often looked back to the penance imposed earlier by rabbis – prayer, fasting and the giving of alms. Penitents also had to wear penitential clothes.

The length of time during which the exercises had to be performed could extend from weeks to months or years, before there was re-admission. During this time, some of the public admission of guilt could include going unwashed, weeping and lamenting publicly at the beginning of the service, or prostrating in front of the bishop so that he walked over the penitent. Sometimes the penitent had to kneel or even roll in front of the faithful. When re-admission finally came, the bishop normally laid his hands on the penitent, alone or accompanied by priest. He could also delegate.

Many Christians of yesterday and today have received a background history picturing Christians of the early centuries going gladly to the lions or other forms of torture and martyrdom. However, this was not universally true. In 249–250 there was a short, sharp persecution under the Emperor Decius. Large numbers of Christians seem to have done what they were ordered, even to apostasy. They sacrificed to the gods and bribed their way to immunity. But some, when they had repented what they had done, went off to Christians who were about to be martyred. From them they begged letters. These letters would give the assurance that, after being put to death and passing to the new life of heaven, the martyr would pray for the apostate; they also asked compassion for the apostate from the Church on Earth. This led some bishops immediately to re-admit the apostate because they had such high regard for the martyrs. They even arranged the re-admission without any public penance, which brought an outcry from the more rigorist members of the Church, who wanted a full discipline imposed.

Some of the muddle and the contradictory approaches to the practice and doctrine of penance are highlighted in the testimony of Tertullian (160–220). He began as a Catholic and wrote *De paenitentia*, which uses arguments from scripture to assure all sinners without exception of the certainty of forgiveness, provided they do penance. Later he became a Montanist – that is, a follower of Montanus, who had quickly drawn support for stricter discipline set over against what was felt to be laxity, particularly in the practice of penance. The Paraclete was believed to speak in Montanus and is quoted by Tertullian: 'The Church can forgive sins, but I will not do so, lest others also commit sin'.[24] Here, then, there seems to be an admission that the Church *can* forgive sins and has used the power up to that time. From this time onwards, however, there is to be a new rigorism whereby there will be no forgiveness of sin by the Paraclete, because of the fear that such a mild attitude might encourage others to sin.

De pudicitia was written by Tertullian when he had joined the Montanist sect. In it he totally denies the power of the Church to forgive grave sins. Thus this later Tertullian *(De pudicitia)* is in opposition to the earlier Tertullian *De paenitentia.* And there is an important and basic difference between the Tertullian Montanist doctrine and the Catholic doctrine of the time. Tertullian takes grave or mortal sin out of the power of the Church but still allows the forgiveness of lesser sins. He seems to have been quite alone in this, as he was in his stress upon idolatry, murder and adultery, the three mortal sins in the practice of the early Church rather than a more extended list.

In most things, Tertullian continued to agree with Catholic doctrine about the part played by the Church in penance. But he went further, stating that the Church's prayer is the prayer of Christ, pleading before the Father, and pronounces forgiveness. This prayer of the Church had a kind of sacramental efficacy, and Tertullian's point of identifying it with Christ's prayer gives for the first time a dogmatic basis for the practice of public penance. The argument goes on that because Christ's prayer is always heard the Church can grant forgiveness to a sinner. Later, however, as has been mentioned above, he limits the intercession of the church and the bishop's forgiveness to lesser sins.

As there was a wide variance and even apparent contradiction in the practice of penance because of the relative independence of bishops, some bishops began to come together to work out area policies. The African bishops, for instance, in the middle of the third century drew up rules by which the punishment would suit the crime. Thus, if a person had actually offered idolatrous sacrifice, even though he could become a penitent, he could not be reconciled until death. If there was simply a letter of sacrifice, and no official act of sacrifice, penitential exercises over an extended period were sufficient for eventual re-admission. A letter from a martyr did not excuse from public penance, but helped reconciliation. However, those who put off asking to become a penitent until the time of dying – because of the public humiliation of confessing their sin – were to be left to God's mercy. It is probably against this fear of public humiliation that Tertullian wrote: 'Is it better to be damned in secret than to be absolved in public?'[25]

In Spain, the Council of Elvira in the fourth century made it clear that sacrifice to other gods would not be forgiven and there would be no re-admission to communion even at the end, because this action was considered the greatest of crimes. On the other hand, Cyprian of Carthage a little earlier took the opposite line, urging apostates to be reconciled 'while their confession can still be accepted, and while the satisfaction and forgiveness granted through the priests can be received by God'.[26] He was emphatic about the need for *metanoia*, for a change of heart, and he urged the need for ecclesiastical forgiveness even though it is God who forgives, because the change comes during the period of penance when the individual is working through repentance in himself and externally. The final act of re-admission, when the bishop imposed hands on the penitent's head, was a recognition of the completion of the change of heart and way of life which marked the forgiveness of God.

Constantine and after

The conversion of Constantine to Christian thought early in the fourth century brought the whole empire officially into Christianity. This was a watershed. No longer was there persecution under a particular emperor. It became more prudent to be a Christian than not. The step of conversion was neither a hazard nor a cause for persecution. Because it was all so much easier, those who came forward for baptism may not all have been so strongly motivated in their conversion as previous generations.

On the other hand, the Church they entered was more unified in approach, and liable to some leadership from the emperor, as for instance when he called the Council of Nicaea in 325. The general line of teaching on serious sin was that there was only one reconciliation after baptism, but on the other hand it was allowed that even apostates, adulterers and murderers could be reconciled after public penance. The biggest shift in thinking and practice came in the Council of Nicaea in canon 13. Here the bishop is told that if anyone who is dying asks to receive the Eucharist, the bishop should investigate and then grant permission – 'no matter who asks it'. Those lapsed who had not been publicly reconciled could be reconciled on their death beds, as also those who had not yet completed their penance. The only condition was that, should they recover, they enter the order of penitents if not already there, or complete the penance from where they left off.

It is difficult to assess how far this was a purely theological development and how much a reaction to the developments in the empire. It seems likely that the vast majority of ordinary Christians were not in touch with the major penalties and had no recourse to the order of penitents. The normal approach to sorrow for sin and forgiveness was through sharing in the worship of the local church. This form of unspecific acceptance of sinfulness within the congregation at the Eucharist was known by the Greek word *exomologesis*, meaning confession.

However, with the average Christian only using this approach to the forgiveness of God, there was a widespread mix-up in thinking and practice. A person like Constantine himself waited for baptism after his conversion until near his death. Many seldom if ever received communion. Very few became penitents.

There was one other aspect of the Constantine period. That was the rather greater emphasis on legalism. Much more was decided in council, bishops' decrees became more like legal documents, and church rules became laws, canons and so on. In the fourth century the bishop was given certain rights to act for the emperor in civil cases, and to some extent there was an overflow from the civil into the ecclesiastical. It was somewhat like the later Old Testament development of emphasis on the law. This can be stressed too much, but the danger was that for some it seemed that the penance imposed for reconciliation was the church counterpart to a sentence for a civil offence. It was liable to bring a move from the understanding of the need for change of heart to a picture of a simple penalty for breaking God's law.

However, the general stand in doctrine was still that there was only one repentance possible after baptism. The approach to baptism was long and quite arduous. The path to reconciliation had the same character. The two sacraments were seen in similar terms, and repentance was called the second baptism. But the penalties imposed continued long after re-admission to communion. Many were for life and included ending of all marital relationship, giving up certain professions like soldiering, and not entering into litigation.

My reason for spending this space on the early years of the Church's reconciliation of penitents is because of a possible parallel with today. When there is a confusion of discipline, with a dual approach of liberal and rigorist in the teaching and practice of morality, the average person is also confused. This is spiritually enervating. The result varies according to denomination. Some get disillusioned and lapse; some find it all too much, and go to church but never communicate.

Some believe utterly in the mercy of God, continue to communicate and see no need to use the Church's means of reconciliation. In many ways today the situation is, as it was in the first four centuries, that the more rigorous accuse the more liberal of watering down the holiness of the people of God. On the other hand the more liberal accuse the more rigorous of a rule of fear rather than a rule of love. Some of this is discussed at other points in the book. Here I simply want to note the importance of the background to present doctrine and practice.

St. John Chrysostom and the East

Penance once in a lifetime, the public nature of penitential exercises and their length were serious drawbacks for the generality of people as the Church grew older. What was upbuilding in a small and close Christian community and seen as a visible reminder of sinfulness became a source of sneering and contempt in a wider and more open society. The long hard path to re-admission was followed by the remainder of life with no further recourse to mercy. Human beings, it could be argued, would have to be very trusting to submit to this discipline, knowing their own weakness, especially perhaps in the sexual area. In the sixth century, a preacher called Caesarius of Arles posed the question in a sermon: 'If I am an officer in the army and have a wife, how can I possibly do penance?[27] A soldier doing public penance would probably be forbidden to carry arms again, a married man told to refrain for his lifetime from sexual relationship with his wife. It was this kind of result of entering the rank of the penitents which kept many away. They came to rely upon the unseen mercy of God, because they could not endure the public working out of God's mercy through the Church.

Among bishops, thinkers and writers who came to a more liberal view of the application of the 'second baptism' was John Chrysostom, in Antioch and Constantinople at the end of the fourth century. Antioch seems to have been a pretty grim place morally. Chrysostom was both a realist and a man pastorally concerned for his people. Many Christians were lukewarm, nominal or alienated entirely from the Church. They could not be brought to the long penitential process, nor could they face the subsequent almost monastic way of life expected of them.

For Chrysostom *metanoia,* change of heart, was all important. This change of heart was to be interior and not to depend upon long penitential exercises. He saw the change as possible for all after baptism. He cited the Lord's own prayer where he tells his followers to pray for their sins to be forgiven as they forgive others. He suggested various ways for the sinner to find forgiveness, including confession, contrition, humility, almsgiving, prayer and the forgiveness of others. These are alternatives and he would like them used daily.

In his fourth homily on 2 Corinthians he says that a contrite and humble heart fulfils the requirement of penitence: 'For he had a contrite and humble heart, which most of all wiped away his sins: for this is *exomologesis,* this is *metanoia'.* When later he moved to Constantinople, he continued to speak of the variety of ways of penance. After his death, his homilies on the Epistles to the Hebrews were published without his correction. The sixth homily adds a further means of reconciliation – recourse without reserve to a priest. It was said of Chrysostom that he stated that though a man should sin a thousand times he might repent a thousand times and still find forgiveness. When at the Synod of the Oak (the first of Chalcedon, 403) Chrysostom was charged, the main grievance was in regard to his teaching on penitence. This led to his being deposed, banished, recalled and banished again, to die in exile.

At Antioch, Chrysostom was working in with the system he found there. As we shall see later in reference to England and the Roman custom of public penance, Antioch was apparently an area which had never been involved in the more elaborate penitential rituals of other parts of the East. It is important to note that this kind of independence was possible both in the East and in the West.

One interesting figure in the development of confession was John Cassian. He was born in Syria in the middle of the fourth century and sent to be educated at Bethlehem. About 390 he and a friend called Germanus took a seven-year leave of absence. The purpose was to go to the Upper Nile, the Thebaid, to study by experience the life and spirituality of the ascetics who were known to Latin Christians as the *renuntiantes*.

Troubles which erupted at the beginning of the fifth century made Cassian and Germanus go with other religious to Constantinople. At Constantinople, Chrysostom ordained Cassian deacon. Cassian was much drawn to Chrysostom. When the decision of the Synod of the Oak deposed Chrysostom, it fell to Cassian and Germanus to take a protest to Rome on behalf of the clergy who had remained faithful to the archbishop. Cassian remained in Rome for ten years and became a friend of Pope Leo I. He is then discovered in the region of Marseilles where he founded two monasteries, one for men and one for women. Here, in addition to the foundations, he gave conferences and produced his *Institutions*. This is our centre of interest. In the fourth book of his *De coenobiorum institutis* which is sub-titled *De institutis renuntiantium*, Cassian brings in his experience from being with the Egyptian monks in the Thebaid. He tells us that the monks, in their pursuit of perfection and as a way to assist them, should not conceal through a sense of shame any bad thoughts of the heart. As soon as these arise, the monks are enjoined to open themselves in a kind of confession of faults to the senior monk.

Here Cassian seems to be urging confession as a part of the ordinary mode of a devout, monkly life. He does not make any reference to obtaining reconciliation in the form of the penitential system of the Church after the commission of grave sin. Monks at this time were not normally priests, though Cassian probably was, so the confession would not necessarily have been a 'sacrament' in the strict sense; but it would certainly have had a sacramental value in the healings of failings within the community.

It might be said that the shameful thoughts of the heart would not come within the scope of the major sins for which the once-only second baptism was envisaged in the broader Church. It is interesting that he lists in the same treatise (Book Five) the eight principal vices as distinguished by Evagrius, which later became known to us as the seven deadly sins – gluttony, fornication, avarice, anger, despondency (*tristitia*), moroseness (*acedia*), vainglory and pride, In the ninth century, this list became the common basis for clerical training.

Though he is slightly later in the century, it is worth while at this point noting that St. Benedict, who became known as the father of Western monasticism, drew upon Cassian and that in his own Rule he treats of habitual confession. Born in 480 he died somewhere round 540 and the passage important to us is: 'The fifth step in humility is when a monk by humble confession does not conceal from his abbot all the bad thoughts that come into his heart and the sins he has committed secretly'.[28] The rule draws upon the Cassian practice, which itself is based upon that of the monks of the Desert and the East. Frequent confession as an integral part of the life of the monk aspiring to holiness became a rule and an atmosphere which is fundamental to the development of the practice of confession. The new practice revolutionised the Church system of penance and reconciliation still largely taught in the West during these centuries. We shall see the impact as we speak of the Celtic influence.

The influence of Ireland

About the time that Cassian was in Constantinople with Chrysostom or moving on with his defence to Rome, a young lad whose Celtic name was Sucat was captured from his home by sea raiders. His home was probably somewhere on the coastline between the Clyde and the mouth of the river Severn. He was sold as a slave in Ireland, subsequently escaped, and found his way home and then to a newly founded monastery at Auxerre in France. His Latin name was Patrick. As a monk, he was ordained first priest and then bishop, and he was charged with returning to Ireland about the age of forty, to Christianize the island.

It is not known how much St. Patrick was influenced by the life of the monastery at Auxerre, or indeed what the rule was like there. Certainly Cassian would have had his monasteries well founded before St. Patrick left Auxerre in about 430. But in any case, the way of life in the monasteries was austere and given to penitential exercises, while the outside world had largely come away from the rigid and long exercises leading to forgiveness. Sadly, however, the relaxation which was largely made in an effort to draw more people to seek forgiveness in the Church really did not work. The majority still kept away and waited to a point near death before seeking reconciliation.

St. Patrick, in coming with other monks to Ireland, brought with him what he had learnt and lived in Auxerre, but the way in which Christianity developed in Ireland was local and must have been inspired by St. Patrick with his instinct of love for the people and his ability to be with them, as he had been in his time of slavery. As a result, the ordinary liturgy of the Church in Ireland grew from Celtic roots. It was celebrated in Latin, but was little like the celebration in the rest of the Western world. The other feature which was markedly different was the form taken in reconciling penitents. It must be remembered that Patrick and his monks were beginning from the beginning. His method was to set up monasteries in different parts of the country. It was a rural country throughout, with no cities. The background of the people was tribal and they had very different standards and moral codes from those which were brought in by the new religion. The Christian life as it was seeded and grew, flourished round the monasteries. The system seems to have been that the monks, many of whom were priests and some bishops, went out on expeditions from the monasteries preaching, baptising and celebrating the Eucharist. They met the people where they were and tried to give them a system which would meet their needs and bring them to Christ, first through the living of a Christian life which was possible within their society.

As far as penitential practice was concerned, the monks applied to the ordinary people the system which they knew as monks, namely private and repeatable confession, suitable penances which could be carried out within the people's way of life, and reconciliation available after a comparatively short period.

The system may have worked in this way. On one trip away from the monastery a monk could hear confession, assign penance, offer the Eucharist if he was a priest for those who were not seriously at odds with God's covenant. Then on the next visit, those who had been given a penance would be reconciled by the monk praying with the penitent and asking God for forgiveness. There had been no official excommunication and no recourse by the penitent to the bishop, and so, instead of the imposition of hands by the bishop as a sign of reconciliation, the monk, who may or may not have been a priest, showed the forgiveness with a blessing. As a further extension of this, for their lesser failings, the people were advised, as was the habit of the monks, to confess to each other and to undertake some form of mortification.

As time went on, in order to have some common practice when different monks went about to different places, there grew up a system of books with lists of appropriate penances for different faults. These became known as penitentials, and it is almost certain that they derived from similar Welsh lists. One of the best known of the Welsh penitentials is attributed to St. Gildas who died in 570. His *praefatio de penitentia* presupposes private confession and private penance. As in Ireland, there was no mention in Wales of public reconciliation.

The first known Irish penitential is one by St. Finian who visited France, and also stayed with St. David (d.c. 601) in Wales. St. Finian wrote that the penalties or penance which he considered appropriate for particular offences are 'in accordance with the sentence of the Scripture or with the opinion of very learned men'. It has been suggested, and probably correctly, that these 'learned men' were St. David and St. Gildas, the latter of whom had come from the Clyde and was settled in a Welsh monastery. At this period of time, there seemed to be much coming and going and sharing among the Christians of Celtic origin in the regions of West Britain, Wales and Ireland. It is also likely that the composers of the penitentials knew the writings of John Cassian, the practices of the Egyptian desert ascetics and the kind of confessional system used among the monks which was advocated by Cassian himself. The exact route of infiltration, whether it was through the monasteries of Marseilles and so through Europe, or even a more obscure route through North Africa and possibly Spain, is not known.

An important point about the tone of the penitentials is that the Irish penitentials were more concerned with the motives and intentions than with the simple acts of the offence. Confession of lesser sins directly to God was mostly concerned with the 'notions of the mind'. An authority on Irish private penance wrote recently: 'It accentuates a feeling in man that his relations with God can take the form of effective dialogue. Forgiveness is asked for in consideration of a conversion entailing sacrifice and God grants pardon'. Private penance is seen as an aid to bringing man closer to God.

Penitential exercises were often used as a medicine to cure the sickness of sin, as an aid to restoring moral health, and as a way leading to social as well as divine acceptance. The medical schools' principle of contraries was applied: for example, an over-talkative person could be given a penance to keep silent over a period of time, a glutton told to fast, and so on. The penitentials combined this sort of approach with morality drawn from the scriptures, while keeping an eye on the social and legal heritage of the local community. Some penitentials, for instance, made it possible to substitute money payments for bodily penances in much the same way as was practised in Celtic and Germanic civil society. Bodily penances were severe. St. Patrick himself had given an example of extreme ascetic practice, and the origins of fasting in Ireland go back to pre-Christian times; a penance could be to fast on bread and water for years rather than days. 'Condiments' such as cabbage could be used with bread by monks when fasting, so it is possible that these were allowed to those fasting as a penance on bread and water.

The toughest penalties were against those sins which the Church had held traditionally to be serious or mortal sins. The three especially emphasised were murder, adultery and apostasy. The wider list included fornication, sorcery and habitual theft. Perjury was considered to be a very great crime and hardly redeemable – 'but the mercy of God is great'. As in the general course of Christian history and moral teaching, the gravest sins were those which broke up the smooth running life of the community. A very tough penance could be exile or pilgrimage, because it was a very hard thing indeed for anyone to leave home and family. In every case, penance for serious sin included deprivation of communion. But it was clearly understood that it was a real spiritual hazard to keep people away from communion for too long a time, and so very long penances were frequently changed to short, intensive alternatives. At all times, the strictest secrecy was required with regard to confession.

In the monastery which St. Finian founded at Clonard there was an important departure from the ordinary run of monastic life. There were three types of persons living in and around the main monastery building. The first and closest were the full monks under their strict rule. Then there were others who came as clerks or would-be scholars, who really sought education, but underwent it within the monastic discipline. Finally there were the penitents, who came to work out their time of penance in the monastery, which was already geared to a penitential life. Here they could live away from temptation and from their normal life. Often they lived in small houses within the wall of the monastery, with chapel and grazing space and plots for growing food.

St. Finian's penitential does not include public penance in the context of the liturgy, or public reconciliation; nor does the bishop have a mention in the ritual of reconciliation. Of course, in the rural setting, bishops had less importance than they would have had in the cities of Italy and Europe. Because of the basically monastic set-up in Ireland, the abbot was normally the head and ruler of all who lived within his domain.

It was from St. Finian's handbook-penitential for the use of priests that other penitentials grew. Most notably there was the penitential of St. Columbanus (b. 563). This had much influence because Columbanus had been trained at the daughter house of Clonard at Bangor, and had subsequently become a pilgrim and exile for the love of God in 591. He went with other Irish monks and founded monasteries according to the Irish pattern on the Continent in the Vosges. Columbanus was not noted as a scholar, but he was enthusiastic for the love of God, and the monastic life of his followers drew people from all walks of life; bishops, nobles, ordinary folk all flocked to his monasteries. Some came for learning, but very many came for the Celtic form of penance. It was now, but it was also something which met the needs of the people of the time. Jonas of Elno, the biographer of St. Columbanus, wrote: 'From all sides the people flocked together to the medicaments of penance'.

Of course, the penitential of St. Columbanus was not merely catering for monastic persons and covering their sins. It was also concerned with the ordinary sins of ordinary people, but the monks only dealt with those who came to them. The common penance seemed to be fasting on bread and water, though there could be exile for perjury or murder.

It is notable that the office of the priest is more evident in the penitential of St. Columbanus than that of St. Finian.

Columbanus was driven from his Burgundy monastery in 610 and went to found a new monastery in Northern Italy. His followers founded other monasteries in Switzerland and Germany and also spread through France. More penitentials appeared. The influence was both great and widespread and no doubt led to the Council of Chalons (639-54) stating: 'The penance of sinners which is the medicine of the soul, we consider useful for all men'. This was a far cry from public penance and a once-only 'second baptism'.

The influence of England

There does not seem to have been any time when England was under the once-for-all second baptism doctrine and practice of so much of the Church. Hence it was that England was able to assist in the spread of the Celtic type of penitential system during the seventh and eighth centuries. In the north of England and south Scotland monks came in from Ireland, normally by way of Iona. They brought the Irish system of frequent confession made privately to a monk or priest. From our perspective today the actual penances appear very severe, but the clergy seem to have known their people and what they could take.

When Augustine was sent to England from Rome by Pope Gregory, he does not seem to have brought with him the Roman system which was so widely used in the Mediterranean. It appears that there were a number of missionaries in the area, perhaps not known even to the Pope, who would have been influenced in the main by the Celtic tradition or were themselves Celts. After Augustine, the new Archbishop of Canterbury was Theodore of Tarsus. He was a monk of the Eastern Church, and it seems strange that he was appointed to England. But he was! He quickly got to work to unify and organise the ecclesiastical system of the country. But he found that there had never been a system of public penance in England, and he did not try to impose it.

There is a penitential ascribed to him, and even though it is not from his hand, it contains according to its preface replies from Theodore 'to various persons who questioned him on the remedy of penance'. Theodore had Eastern background which would have given him knowledge of writings by Chrysostom and others. He seems also to have known the Celtic penitentials and made use of them. His penitential was accepted first in the north of England, where they may already have been familiar with Finian and Columbanus; it was not so readily received in the south.

This penitential is more comprehensive, fuller and more consistent than the previous Celtic books, which tended to be rather haphazard compilations. Theodore shows his personal knowledge of both Eastern and Roman custom, but accepts the customs prevalent in England – the Celtic system – and also the laws of the area. Some of these were: 'If *weregild* was being paid after killing a man, the time of penance is halved; if a fighting man kills in 'open' war, the time of penance he must do is forty days'. (The same period was given with similar penance after the Battle of Hastings!)

Theodore, following the way of Chrysostom, suggested that confession could be made to God alone, but the penances indicated in the penitential should nevertheless be carried out. More normally, though, the priest was part of the rite of penance, especially if the sin was serious. The penance remained severe both with Theodore and the Celtic penitentials. This was partly to act as a deterrent at a time when there was a mixture of population, and the tribal laws were breaking down. If there was a notorious public sinner, he would be stopped from receiving communion until his penance was concluded, as happened with the canonical system.

It would appear that the custom in England was for the devout lay people to confess before Christmas. *The Dialogue of Egbert* (eighth century) suggests that this was the practice from the time of Theodore, and this may be from his Eastern influence, as that was the custom there. Egbert, who was Archbishop of York, has a penitential attributed to him. Monks and nuns had rules for frequent confession, but this penitential is the first time that the frequent confession of lesser sins is seen as practised among lay people.

It may seem that all this is rather laboured, but the change to frequent confession as a habit was dramatic in the life of the Church, and the practice of confessing venial sins regularly was also to have considerable consequences in the future.

Once started, the spread of the Celtic system continued – fuelled all the time by more and more missionaries from England. It is important to realise that while this was happening there was strong opposition from some quarters. For instance, a regional council in Toledo in 589 declared: 'We have learned that in some of the churches of Spain the faithful are doing penance not in accordance with the canonical rule but in another detestable way, that is, they ask a priest to grant them pardon as many times as it pleases them to sin. We wish to put an end to their abominable presumption and accordingly this sacred council declares that penances should be given in the manner prescribed by the ancient canons'.

St. Boniface was among the most active in spreading the Gospel good news widely through Germany and the Low Countries (675-754). Then Charlemagne summoned Alcuin from Northumbria to his court to bring learning to his empire. Alcuin especially encouraged young students who flocked to learn from him to confess their sins to a priest of God; and he continued to stress the importance of confession to the members of religious orders to whom he wrote. Later, as abbot of Tours, he continued the same teaching. It was with the support of Charlemagne that the two systems of canonical and Celtic penitential systems were looked at, and the Celtic was preferred. Nevertheless, at another Council of Chalons (813) the penitential books were violently attacked.

However, by the tenth century opposition to the penintential books had died down and private confession to a priest with private reconciliation had become the custom. The priest was normally still guided by one or other of the penitentials, though there was always the danger of a penitential becoming a kind of legal code with the priest as judge administering the law. Nevertheless, the penitentials were constantly stressing the healing role of the sacrament.

By the Fourth Lateran Council (1215) the bishops of the whole Latin Church decreed that all Catholics had to confess to their pastors each year.

So it was that regular and repeated confession to a priest, which had been forbidden and denounced over a long period, more or less crept in by the back door of the Church and became – through the monks and the obvious need of the people – the accepted form of confession within the Church.

Once it became obligatory to confess periodically to a priest the serious sins committed, the confession of lesser or venial sins to a layman was the ordinary means for the remission of lesser or venial sins. Bede was very influential in arguing this case, basing it on the passage already quoted from the letter of James.[29]

There were still some sins and crimes which the bishops reserved in jurisdiction to themselves, and this persisted in its small way through into the twentieth century, when there was still a category of sins reserved to the bishops and the pope.

The Middle Ages and Scholastic period

The procedure for the use of penance from the eleventh century brought the act of confessing and the formerly delayed act of reconciliation together. Confession now consisted of the confession of sins, the penance given and accepted, and absolution. However, this did not gather together all the amount of varying materials which had resulted from centuries of thought about and practice of penance. There was no synthesis. However, with the advent of scholasticism, theology and system were brought to bear by a series of great thinkers. This was the time of the rediscovery of Aristotle, which had a dual effect of presenting tools for the work of clarification, and also uncovering the possibility of an almost endless number of theories.

This was a very important period for the development of thought on the subject of penance. Indeed, the effects went through the remainder of the middle ages, through the Reformation and post-Reformation periods, and are still current today. Unfortunately, there was such a vast output from the scholastic era that it is impossible to give even a fair summary in this book. Nevertheless, we need to get a bird's-eye view of various contributions to the debate.

Peter Abelard centred on the interior disposition of the penitent. God looked at the penitent, saw the state of mind and soul, and forgiveness followed from contrition. For Abelard, the important feature was that an act of the heart which could be called perfect contrition, a sorrow which had its basis in love for God, removed sin. The work of the priest for him was only about the amount of satisfaction due after God had forgiven the sin. Eventually this led Abelard to be accused of heresy for denying that the Church had the power of the keys, the power of binding and loosing.

Peter Lombard agreed with Abelard that contrition for sin based on love for God led God to forgive the sinner, but for him the confession of sin to the priest was part and parcel of the sacrament because it was for the sacrament the outward sign of the sorrow within. The role of the priest was to be there as the assurance to the penitent that all he had brought with him in the way of sin was forgiven by his confession and by the depth and sincerity of his contrition. It was important that the penitent should realise that God forgave even before the act of confessing because of this sorrowful disposition. The priest witnesses and has some part because he has the power to discern the correct disposition of the penitent, to impose a penance and to grant admission to the sacraments.

The tendency of Peter Abelard and Peter Lombard was to the old tradition of the status of the priest's absolution – that it was 'deprecative'. This term means in the penitential rite that the priest prays that God will forgive the penitent and does not assume that he himself has authority to forgive. It was a very widely held and popular view.

The school of St. Victor, however, disagreed, because they thought the deprecative theory almost if not entirely did away with the Church's power of the keys, of binding and loosing. The reasoning was that contrition removed the bond of sin and the obduracy of heart, but a further bond of being liable to future damnation was only removed by absolution. This tended to focus the power of absolution upon the priest, with scripture cited as a backing, namely Matthew 16 and 18, and John 20. The claim was that Christ himself had given the power to forgive sins. The reference to binding and loosing was not only in the community but even as far as heaven. There were various permutations as to how and from what the priest absolved, but the basic difference between the Abelard/Lombard position and the school of St. Victor was the stress by the one on contrition, by the other on maintaining somehow the power of the keys.

It was Thomas Aquinas who came nearest to making a synthesis which united the personal contrition factor with the ecclesiastical element of priestly absolution. The unity came through his clear concept of penance as a sacrament. He made the divisions in the sacrament which became the norm for centuries. The sacrament was in the power of God, because only he could accept the renunciation of sin and forgive it. St. Thomas distinguished the matter of the sacrament as confession by the penitent and the contrition which accompanied it. Added to this was the listening and acceptance by the priest, which included the words of absolution. Finally the penitent had to accept the penance and work it out. The form of the sacrament was the absolution: 'I absolve you from your sins in the name of the Father and of the Son and of the Holy Spirit'. This form was essential because it confirmed the hidden and divine element of forgiveness.

There was no doubt in St. Thomas' exposition that contrition was an essential part of the matter of confession. For the penitent to come and confess without contrition would be an empty mockery. But here he took up a distinction conceived earlier of two kinds of contrition – imperfect contrition or attrition and perfect contrition. Contrition was motivated solely by love for God in the penitent and covered forgiveness of all sin. But for Thomas, perfect contrition was no easy achievement. So Jesus Christ had set up the sacrament of penance. By coming even with only attrition to the priest, the confession, the act of humility, the assistance of the priest and the words of absolution as it were boosted the attrition of the penitent and assured him of God's complete forgiveness. Absolution does not compensate for a lack of contrition, but the seeds are there already in attrition. The complexity of the argument would need to be taken up more fully elsewhere.

Duns Scotus was the great opponent of St. Thomas, and his system matched that of St. Thomas in its clarity and consistency. His line of development was closer to the school of St. Victor, especially in the importance placed on the power of the keys. Contrition as a whole was somewhat blurred, in that he tended to upgrade attrition, allowing it as sufficient for absolution in confession, without any transformation into contrition. He maintained that it was not possible for anyone to know if their contrition was indeed perfect. Therefore the use of the sacrament was more reliable. There is an obligation on everyone to choose the more certain way. For this reason confession is an obligation enjoined by the Church, even though the way of perfect contrition is open to anyone, in theory at any rate.

The sacrament of penance given by Christ was then, to all intents and purposes, the only sure way of salvation. The promises of Christ would always be effective, however weak the contrition of the penitent, provided that the sacrament was the instrument and the absolution pronounced.

For Scotus everything really centred on the absolution. This was preceded by confession and contrition, and followed by making satisfaction through the penance. But the sacrament was absolution and even came to be called so. But some felt this was cutting out too many parts of the penitential rite, and so a mixture of the two teachings began. Aquinas' teaching was held on to for the importance of confession, contrition and satisfaction. Scotus' for the heart of the sacrament being effectively the priest's absolution.

Gradually the result in the lives of ordinary people was a growing regularity in going to confession, though perhaps in a sense ineffectively. Various sidelines grew up, like indulgences, which tended to devalue contrition. For Scotus the sacrament took on a more or less legalistic tone. To sin was to break God's law. God forgives in free love for the merits of Jesus Christ. He *could* forgive without the cooperation of the sinner. But the law of justice deriving from his will normally sets sins right through punishment. This punishment is either in full among the damned; or through penance here and now, through indulgences or through purgatory.

The Reformation, the Council of Trent and after

The Christian Church of the West was in need of reform prior to the efforts of Luther, Calvin, Zwingli and others. Some of this reform almost took place, but in the event the opportunity was missed. In the area of penance, one of the outstanding worries was the use and abuse of indulgences. But there was also considerable debate among theologians in various ways refining, defending or attacking the Thomist and Scotist positions.

Martin Luther led the attack on indulgences and other aspects of the doctrine and practice of confession current in the Church at the time. Later, Luther pared down the sacraments to two, baptism and communion. The attack on confession was not total, as far as

Luther was concerned. He objected strongly to the Scotist teaching of the absolute value of absolution, insisting on the need to *experience* contrition for true absolution. So, despite denying the sacramental character of penance, he urged his followers to use it: 'Christ placed absolution in the mouth of his Church and has commanded it to release us from our sins. Therefore when a heart feels the burden of its sins and aches for consolation, the Christian finds here a sure refuge when he hears the words of God and learns that God, through the ministry of a man, releases and absolves him from his sins'.[30] However, the contrition which needed to be experienced had to be founded on faith, but did not merit forgiveness, for this had been achieved once and for all by Christ on the cross. In other words, confession was the experience of God's mercy, a rejoining in the atonement already achieved, and a release from any fear of further punishment in this life or after. Everything in forgiveness for the individual in confession depended upon the faith of the individual. The priest was not effective in his absolution, so that a person could confess to another lay person and be assured of God's forgiveness.

In fact, because Luther did not accept penance as a sacrament, the practice of private confession gradually gave way simply to general admission of sinfulness at worship; though Luther himself protested against the trend, private confession fell into disuse.

John Calvin agreed with Luther that there was no scriptural basis for private confession. He believed binding and loosing referred to ecclesiastical sanctions. He accepted that there had been penitential practices in the early Church, but he strongly objected to obligatory confession and the detailing of sins, because he felt the bad psychological effects could lead to scruples and a kind of mental torture. So, while accepting the good of confession in the broad sense as emphasising God's merciful love, private confession went completely into disuse.

The immediate result of the English Reformation was to remove the obligation of confession, auricular and private. Confession, however, remained available. In the Book of Common Prayer it is largely recognised that the specific recommendation comes in the section on the visitation of the sick and dying. Here it is urged as a relief to the sick person's conscience and an act to be encouraged by the priest. A rather wider exhortation is provided before Holy Communion in the prayer books of 1549 , 1552, 1558 and 1662. Here the general exhortation is to receive Holy Communion worthily, by confession to almighty God and purposeful amendment of life, which will include reconciliation with anyone wronged. It is only if a person's conscience is not quieted by recourse to God that he is enjoined to seek out a priest.

General reading round the subject of confession and the life and devotion of the Church of England indicate that, though there was still some writing and some teaching at the beginning of the seventeenth century, it gradually became less effective. Books remained in circulation, the exhortation before Holy Communion was still to be said as deemed necessary, but the practice of auricular, private confession was less and less widespread.

The emphasis upon the presence and importance of this thread of teaching and practice varies according to the churchmanship of the writer, preacher or historian of the period. In actuality, the practice of private confession lessened as did the number of those advocating it. Though material and teaching were both extant, a considerable portion of the Church of England became less familiar with the guidance to personal auricular confession, or even ignorant of it. The presence of books and occasional advocates from the pulpit failed to stem the virtual death of confession in the Church of England; but renewed interest and an increased number of those considering the practice and advocating it grew with the Oxford Movement and the development of Anglo-Catholic churchmanship – a revival which has continued somewhat more strongly, at least in certain areas of the Church of England, to the present day.

The post-Tridentine period

The council of Trent followed the line of theological development in the Church up to the Reformation. Such dogmatic decisions as were made were really the reply to new principles emerging from the writing and teaching of the various reformers. The teaching of St. Thomas received the fullest backing. The sacrament of penance is the efficient cause of the forgiveness of sins. Scotus had centred the sacrament itself on the absolution. Trent took the sacrament as the only ordinary means of forgiveness, effected through the words of absolution. At the same time contrition, confession and satisfaction were also needed as an integral part to rid the penitent of the 'remnants of sin'.

Confession itself became even more solidly embedded in Catholic faith and practice than it had been after the Fourth Lateran Council. Trent stated: 'The universal Church has always understood that the Lord instituted the integral confession of sins, and that divine law makes it necessary for all those who lapse after their baptism' (ch. 5). The more legalistic aspect of the doctrine now increased. It was understood that each and every unconfessed mortal sin must be included, because the priest by the power of the keys is constituted judge: he cannot 'try' the case rightly unless he knows all mortal sins and the circumstances which may alter the character of the sin. Venial sins can be cleansed by other means, but even going to confession just to confess venial sins is salutary. So the ministry of the priest is a judicial one and absolution a judicial act. There is now no room for the interpretation of the words of absolution as simply being deprecative. In addition, the importance of the acceptance and fulfilment of the penance imposed upon the penitent as satisfaction is stressed.

As a lot of doctrine had been laid down at Trent, much of the subsequent theological debate was of less importance than what had gone on before the Reformation. There was intense discussion on contrition and attrition, but virtually nothing of importance emerged.

In the seventeenth century, the Jansenist heresy grew, and continued as a potent force until the nineteenth century, with aftermath effects lasting until today. Its propositions led to extreme rigorism. The result was that confession once again became linked to a long period of prayer and penance as a build-up of personal conversion and purification before the actual confession was made. Often ordinary people only made their holy communion once a year, spending the rest of the year in preparation for confession.

After this confession and holy communion – usually at Easter – the ordinary person would begin again to work penitentially towards the next Easter, without receiving holy communion again. From this rigorism, there later emerged a system of slightly more frequent holy communion, say once a month, but always preceded on the day before by confession. This immediate connection of confession to holy communion caused a real difficulty when, early in the twentieth century, the then reigning pope, St. Pius X, urged more frequent reception of holy communion. Confession and holy communion continued to be inextricably linked in the minds of both priests and people. When it became more usual to go to holy communion each Sunday or even each day, the emphasis pastorally tended to stress that it would therefore be appropriate to go to confession each week. Long confession queues emerged. Confession was often very short and sharp and almost routine as a result, because the priest in confession had to get through the queue.

In turn, this frequency and possibility of superficiality of approach to confession led some people to question the whole purpose. By the nineteen-sixties both the teaching and the practice of the sacrament of penance in the Roman Catholic Church was in disarray.

NOTES

1 Ref. also: *The Piety of Jeremy Taylor*, H. Trevor Hughes, Macmillan and Co., 1960.
2 Lk. 23.1-25.
3 Lev. 9.1-24.
4 Lev. 5 and 6.
5 Deut. 13.
6 Lk. 4.16-30.
7 cf. Acts 2.46-3.1.
8 Acts 15.
9 Acts 15.29.
10 1 Cor. 5, especially 11-13.
11 2 Cor. 2.7-10.
12 2 Cor. 2.10.
13 1 Tim. 5.20.
14 Tit. 3.10.
15 Mt. 16.19.
16 Mt. 18.15-18.
17 1 Cor. 5.2-5.
18 Mt. 12.31-32.
19 1 Jn. 5.10-17.
20 Heb. 6.4-6.

21 1 Jn. 1.8-9.
22 Jas. 5.15-16.
23 Jn. 20.
24 Tertullian. *De pudicitia,* 21.7.
25 Tertullian. *De paenitentia,* 10.8.
26 Cyprian of Carthage. *De lapsis,* 29.
27 Caesarius of Arles. *Sermons,* 258.
28 St. Benedict. Rule. c.7.
29 Jas. 5.16.
30 Luther. *Grosser Katechismus,* 1529. Short exhortation on confession.

Making a Confession – a Guide

IN this section I want to open up to those who do not have a clear idea of the practices of various denominations the 'how' of making your confession. I hope this will widen the knowledge of those already involved and interested from their own practice; and I hope it will be useful for those who are puzzled and seeking. It is the purpose of God that we all come daily more and more fully into knowledge, love and service of him. If, as I believe, penance, reconciliation or confession (call it what you will) is a powerful contribution to this process of knowledge, love and service, then it should be widely familiar and appreciated and used.

The general comments at the beginning of this chapter are clearly mine. When I am trying to say something about the practice in the Church of England, and in the Orthodox and Methodist Churches, I am doing my best to expound what I have learnt from my researches. I have read round the subject and also spoken to 'practitioners' who are, as it were, both sides of the confessional grill. Only in referring to Roman Catholic practice can I say that I have first hand experience, even though over the years I have listened to and counselled members of various denominations when I was asked to do so.

Many Christians throughout the world today do not go to confession, but think of themselves as passable or good Christians despite this. There are various reasons and backgrounds. Some have never really heard of confession; it was not in their upbringing, in their way of prayer and worship. It is no problem because for them it does not exist. Some have heard of confession, have seldom if ever practised it, and do not see the point. More definite are those who from the outset reject confession theologically and pastorally. They believe that to go to confession to a priest is putting an impediment to direct communication with God, and that it is not only unnecessary to have the 'mediation' of the priest, but positively wrong. Different again from these are the people who have practised confession at some period of life, but have had such bad experiences they have been turned away. Their reaction in some instances has been to denounce strongly the whole idea of confession for the harm it has done them.

The Roman Catholic and Orthodox Churches have always taught confession in one way or another, and it has been available for the faithful. These faithful tend to know about confession even when they may not themselves be using it in their own lives. With the Church of England there is greater variety. The availability and teaching of confession depends largely upon the local incumbent. If he understands and uses confession, he teaches and shares it; if he does not understand it, he does not teach or preach it.

As a Roman Catholic, I have listened to various arguments against the sacrament of penance or confession as it is taught and practised in the Church to which I belong. Let me here remark on two of the points at issue – though I must emphasise that my object is *not* a systematic theological treatise on confession.

At the Reformation, various reformers refused to accept the long-standing teaching that the sacrament of penance is a sacrament of Jesus Christ. Today we can see that a large part of the issue here is what is *meant* by the notion 'sacrament of Jesus Christ'. There have been some developments of understanding here.

The second point concerns how the function of the priest is theologically conceived. The Council of Trent maintained that the priest in confession plays a causative role. Now, over the years, a frequently held view has been that the situation involves three individuals – God, priest and penitent: such that the priest in a two-way mediating capacity constitutes an *obstacle* between the penitent and God. Some presentations within the Roman Catholic Church have had this flavour. Certainly, this is how things have often appeared to onlookers, who rightly rejected such a picture. However, this picture is *not* in fact entailed by Roman Catholic teaching. In an absolute sense, God alone forgives sins. But that is compatible with there being some human instrumental causality, some created causative mediation, in the area of confession as in other areas. Trent insisted on a causative role for the priest, but not a particular model of it. Contemporary theology stresses that there are different elements in the process of reconciliation; these elements are mediations of God's presence and action. The reconciliation in question is in a crucial and primary sense reconciliation with the Church – which is embodied in the presbyter(s) for the purpose of the sacrament. In the relevant act of reconciliation, since the Church is the Body of Christ, God in Christ forgives sins. So then, there is not the slightest doubt that anyone, at any time, can turn to God in sorrow, asking for forgiveness for their sins. All church members are urged to examine their consciences daily, as part of their ordinary life, and to make acts of sorrow in their personal prayer and during worship. But there is also a key place for confession to a minister of the Church.

We all need to reflect on and discuss further the complex, difficult, yet vital matters touched on in the preceding paragraph. And we must take care not to dissociate the role of the priest in confession from so much that goes on elsewhere, so far as God's ways of working in our Christian lives are concerned.

Another aspect of confession has to be faced. Because the priest is human, he is subject to human frailties. He administers the sacrament, but may not always be as good a guide and aid as he should be. By that I mean that he should be a listening ear, able when necessary to assist the penitent in expressing his faults and his sorrow and his purpose to do better: however, as a priest and as a human being, he can be less than perfect. He can get tired and irritable. He can fail himself to grow in spirituality and so fail to lead others further in the love of God after repentance. When he is doing his work positively and successfully, the priest may be able to clarify a mixed-up conscience, to centre a muddled person on important issues or ease the tortured conscience into less scrupulous paths. But if he is censorious or patronising, if he cuts a wordy penitent short or dismisses an issue in an offhand manner, he can leave an impression which has lasting bad effects. Gentleness and firmness are attributes which should go together. Authoritarianism and a kind of 'Godlike' decisiveness can crush and alienate. He is a listener and an enabler. He is not God.

This difficulty is one which is common to other helping professions, as are various other problems. Doctors, psychiatrists, lawyers, social workers, counsellors and teachers and the clergy are all imperfect, but become resource centres for individuals. Ideally, I suppose, none of the difficulties would arise. In actuality they do. For instance, for all too many reasons one may be short and sharp, fail to listen properly, be tired and cross, be too directive and decisive. The 'client' may become over-dependent, may become possessive, may fall in love with the helper or develop a hatred against him or her. It is possible that a sharp word or a seeming indifference may drive someone away forever, with accusations of rudeness, misunderstanding or condemnation. It is easy to wish such things did not happen. From personal experience on both sides of the confessional encounter I know that they do! I also know personally that they happen with lawyers, social workers, doctors and psychiatrists. Not every appointment ends in sweetness and light, with comfort and reassurance.

For some people it is fearsome to go to see a doctor; some shudder at the word 'psychiatrist' and imagine an appointment with one is a one-way exit to a 'loony bin'. Some others refuse to be in any way involved in receiving help from social services, social security benefits or indeed anything which makes them feel objects of charity. Similar attitudes affect the Church. Priests, workers, and in the present context the confessor, come in for a strange and strong mixture of praise and abuse. In this there is a fellow-feeling with all helping professions and organisations.

It is likely that the Churches play down problems in relation to confession, or somehow fail to realise the widespread alienation from the sacrament over the years. As a priest who normally works at different levels in the community, I am vividly aware of the joy and peace and growth which the use of confession develops in large numbers of people. This is irrespective of the frequency or the spaced-out pattern of individuals' practice. At the same time, I am vividly aware of the damage which has occurred to many souls. I know this as a reality, and hope there can be some new balance of thinking. The origin of varied viewpoints is important. There is a great difference between the stance of someone who has never encountered confession – but has picked up ideas about what happens and the effects – and those who have themselves experienced good or bad results.

Here, for instance, is the testimony of a psychiatrist, Pierre Solignac, who has had personal experience, and has taken the trouble to look into the disturbing features which he has found to be common in his clients:

> Christian education is based essentially on anxiety and fear, lack of confidence in human nature, and scorn for the body, sexuality, and woman as a sexual being. At a very early stage, it encourages a fear of sin, and more particularly the fear of mortal sin: a child of seven cried himself to sleep every night without his parents understanding why. One day, amidst his tears, he told his father, 'I've committed a mortal sin, I said fuck to God'. The explanation was simple. His sister, aged nine, was going to catechism classes and used her knowledge with very obvious intent. The image of a coercive God allowed her to dominate the situation and get whatever she wanted out of her small brother. Exasperated, the boy ended up by saying to her, 'Fuck God' . . .
>
> Preparation for confession was another agonising aspect of this education. We were taught to go over our consciences with a fine-tooth comb, to search out the least little sin. I went to the communion-table mulling over everything I had told the priest, looking for something that I might have forgotten which could transform this communion into a sin.[1]

Pierre Solignac gives a series of case histories which in his estimation bear out the generally warping nature of a Christian upbringing, especially in regard to the emphasis on sin, repentance and confession. The whole educational system of the Catholic Church comes under his condemnation with its ethos and guilt-stress in the upbringing of children. This he has experienced in his own life and found mirrored in the lives of many of his clients. I have certainly heard it said among psychiatrists and counsellors that they meet in their work a high proportion of Roman Catholics especially, but also other Christians, who have given up practice of their religion because of fears and hang-ups brought on by the stress put upon sin and guilt.

I personally have no doubt that the current fall-off in confessional practice at least in some measure derives from the kind of experience people have had in the confessional. And this has been accentuated more recently. There is a two-way pull within Roman Catholic teaching. For instance, there was the restatement in the late nineteen-sixties of the prohibition on artificial contraception. But, at the same time, Vatican II had put more stress on the decision of individuals. What Pierre Solignac is attacking is all that emerges from a negative and precept-ridden approach to Christian living. He is urging a fresh approach, which I believe is in fact the new post-Vatican II approach. This must be more open, more love-centred, putting more emphasis on human nature's potential in cooperation with God's grace. It must rely more upon the encouragement of forgiveness and resurrection than upon condemnation in hell!

> Anxiety, repression and guilt will never allow us to live at peace with ourselves, and unless we do that we shall never be able to live at peace with others and really love our neighbours.[2]

I am putting some of these problems, hesitations and condemnations at this point, before coming to the day-to-day methods of making a confession. My reason for doing this is that you can straight away be alert to, and weigh up, the good and bad possibilities which can attach to the use of confession. I strongly agree that bad effects can come from bad teaching and bad practice. But I strongly disagree that this is essential to all confessional practice. Rather, I see confession as positive and good when both penitent and priest work and pray and listen to God for the good and growth of the whole person.

I therefore hope that what is written here will set out or reinforce what is positive and good, while not minimising problems.

THE CHURCH OF ENGLAND

The background

One of the results of the Reformation in England was to remove confession or penance from the sacraments of Jesus Christ. In the newly reformed church which came to be known as the Church of England, confession was no longer obligatory, was less widely practised, and gradually less preached. The Book of Common Prayer retained, in an exhortation before Holy Communion, the admonition to repent and confess to almighty God before receiving the sacrament, and if necessary for peace of mind, to have recourse to the priest. But the main teaching on confession was in the section on the Visitation of the Sick:

> Here shall the sick person be moved to make a special confession of his sins, if he feels his conscience troubled with any weighty matter. After which confession, the priest shall absolve him (if he humbly and heartily desires it) after this sort:
> Our Lord Jesus Christ, who hath left power to his

> Church to absolve all sinners who truly repent and believe in him, of his great mercy forgive thee thine offences; and by his authority committed to me, I absolve thee from all thy sins. In the Name of the Father, and of the Son and of the Holy Ghost. Amen.[3]

It is important today that this presence in the Prayer Book is acknowledged, because to a very great degree, confession of sin fell into disuse except in a generalised way in the ordinary Church of England worship for the whole congregation. Confession was brought back into greater prominence with the emergence of the Anglo-Catholic developments of the nineteenth century. But it remains true at this time to say that there are various attitudes among ordained and lay members of the Church of England. Some do not believe it right to confess to God in the presence of a priest at all, some are not moved to use confession, but there are also some who want to use confession.

Considerable numbers of the Church of England have little or no knowledge of confession, no experience of its joys or difficulties or its practical meaning in the life of the individual. This is despite the fact that the ordination formula of the Church of England *seems* to hand on the power to forgive sins to each ordained person:

> Receive the Holy Ghost for the office and work of a priest in the Church of God, now committed unto thee by the imposition of our hands. Whose sins thou doest forgive, they are forgiven; and whose sins thou doest retain, they are retained. And be thou a faithful dispenser of the Word of God and of his Holy Sacraments: in the Name of the Father and of the Son and of the Holy Ghost. Amen.

The newly ordained priest is then given authority to

exercise the preaching of God's word and the ministry of the sacraments by the bishop. The bishop himself may limit this ministry as he sees fit, for instance to a confined area or for younger men to hearing only the confessions of children.

The practice

One of the difficulties of setting down anything helpful is that the practice varies a great deal in the Church of England. This is one of the Church's strengths. It can also prove to be a weakness. Individual incumbents in neighbouring parishes may approach confession quite differently. Those who are opposed to confession and never use it themselves tend not to offer either preaching on confession to a priest or the availability of a confessor in the church. Their parishioners, therefore, would not hear of confession in their ordinary attendance at church. If they did ask for confession, they might be refused. However, there are those who, both as persons and as pastors, know the value of confession and therefore do all they can to make use of it themselves and encourage those with whom they are working to discover confession and benefit from the practice.

A priest, deacon, religious or lay person who has been brought up to the personal use of confession should know how to set about finding his or her way to the actual making of a confession without my writing.

However, there are considerable numbers who do not know what to do and who may be held back from beginning by ignorance or fear, and so I set out here the kind of step by step progress of a member of the Church of England seeking confession. It is only a guide, to which you can bring your own freedom.

Availability. If you are not familiar with confession, look first at your church notice board. Some churches list times for confession or tell you how to get in touch with the priest. If there is no indication, do not be shy. Get in touch with the priest either by ringing him up, writing to him, or speaking to him after a service. If you happen to meet him in the street, speak to him then and there.

Place. A confession is normally heard in the church. The place is probably in a side chapel within view of the general body of the church, but discreetly withdrawn. Sometimes confessions are heard in the vestry. Normally, the priest sits in a chair, which is placed alongside a kneeler, for the use of the penitent. On the kneeler is a card giving the method of confession and words used, in case you do not know them or are liable to forget.

Though church is the ordinary place for confession, it is possible to arrange to have your confession heard in the priest's study, or a rectory waiting room. Farther afield, confession can be heard anywhere if there is an urgent reason for this. For instance, walking in a garden, from a hospital bed, on a battle field, at a railway station, in a café.

Preparation. It is important to prepare before going to make your confession, preferably before you come to the church at all. There are various ways of thinking over and collating what you want to say. There may be a particular issue which dominates everything else. In that case, try also to think of other problems in your life, but accept that for you *now* this issue is overriding. Other methods include people trying to form a narrative about their life for the past month or two since they went to confession, the writing out of a list which they bring with them, or a very simple statement which is probably not all inclusive, but covers a range of faults and failures. Certainly, the average confessor would urge simplicity rather than complicated explanation.

Confession in church. Supposing that confession is a regular pattern in the church to which you are going to make your confession and you go at the advertised time. You may find others there before you. Kneel or sit while you wait, stilling yourself and asking guidance from the Holy Spirit to disclose your soul to the priest. Renew your sorrow for your faults and failures, concentrating your mind and heart on the merciful love of God. At every stage of the confession it is vital that you remember you are in the presence of God and in direct relationship with him. You must not allow yourself to be side-tracked on to the presence and person of the priest.

The form of confession. Come to the place of confession, kneel down, and if it is your usual custom, make the sign of the cross. The following sort of dialogue and action then takes place, depending largely upon yourself, unless you specifically ask the priest directions for proceeding:

Yourself: Father, please give me your blessing for I have sinned.

Priest: The Lord be in your heart and on your lips, that you may truly and humbly confess your sins, in the Name of the Father, and of the Son, and of the Holy Ghost. Amen.

Yourself: I confess to Almighty God, the Father, the Son and the Holy Ghost, and before the whole company of heaven that I have sinned exceedingly in thought, word and deed, by my own grievous fault. My last confession was . . . (N.B. If you cannot remember or if you have not been to confession before, simply tell the priest so). You then continue to say what you want to confess, using any method, including those mentioned above, which you find convenient. If you are stuck for words, don't know where to begin, or are simply afraid, you will not be the first, so be simple and straightforward. You may have spoken to the priest beforehand about your newness to confession, but if you have had no contact, do not hesitate to ask him to help you through. Be simple and direct. Hopefully, you will find a listening ear, warmth, patience and understanding from the priest.

When you have finished all you want to say, it is helpful to the priest if you conclude by saying something like this: For these and all my other sins which I cannot now remember, I am truly sorry. I mean to amend my life, and I humbly ask pardon of God: and of you, Father, penance, counsel and absolution.

Priest: He may ask you a question, give you some words of counsel or simply suggest a penance for you to complete. This penance can be of different kinds. It is not a punishment, but a further exercise of humility and prayer to continue the healing process of confession into your new life. It may be a prayer. It may be that the priest thinks it will help to suggest some action directed to a particular sin you have confessed. For instance, if you say you have neglected all prayer, he may suggest you try to do something the day you confess and to do what you can to spend some time in prayer each day afterwards. Or, if you have been at loggerheads with your neighbours or with people at work, that you should make an effort to be more friendly.

After this, he gives the absolution using these words: Almighty God have mercy upon you, forgive you your sins and bring you to everlasting life. The Almighty and merciful God grant you pardon and remission of all your sins. Our Lord Jesus Christ, who has left the power to his Church to absolve all sinners who truly repent and believe in him, of his great mercy forgive you your offences; and by his authority committed to me, I absolve you from all your sins + In the Name of the Father and of the Son and of the Holy Ghost. Amen. The Passion of Our Lord Jesus Christ and his infinite merits be to you for the remission of sins, the increase of grace, and the rewards of eternal life. And the blessing of God Almighty, the Father, the Son, and the Holy Ghost be upon you and remain with you always. Go in peace. The Lord has put away your sins. And pray for me, a sinner.

Yourself: If you are in church, go back to a pew somewhere, and spend some time in thanksgiving prayers. Say anything you like, but some which are recommended are from the Book of Common Prayer or later orders of service, such as *Te Deum, Benedicite, Jubilate* from Morning Prayer; or *Magnificat, Cantate Domino,*

Nunc Dimittis or *Deus Misereator* from Evening Prayer. Any one of the Psalms could equally well be used.

It is well for you to remember that confession is for forgiveness in the first place. Advice or counsel is secondary. Indeed, it may not always be appreciated. However, you can seek advice directly by asking, or implicitly by the way you speak in confession. You may feel you do not want advice, but it is in some ways up to the priest to be sensitive to you, picking up the hidden request for help, or the feeling your words imply 'no advice please'.

It is important to note that a new form of service for confession put up for discussion to the General Synod of the Church of England was rejected in early 1983. The weight of evangelical opinion swayed the voting to the rejection, specifically the introduction of the words 'I absolve you'. There will, no doubt, be a continued use of some such form as that which I have quoted above in some parts of the Church of England. It is also true that a large number of those who appreciate the use of confession have different forms available, which they use. As with the eucharistic liturgy, there is now marked similarity to the Roman rite.

THE ORTHODOX CHURCH

The background

The practice of the Orthodox Churches has been consistent and not subject to so much change as have the rituals of the Western Churches, whether Anglican or Roman Catholic. Perhaps the basic difference which has its effect on the whole Orthodox way of thinking and living is the meaning and breadth of the sacrament of Baptism. Here, the child is normally baptised very soon after the birth. But the Baptism is not just baptism. It includes what the West has separated off, namely the sacrament of Confirmation. Moreover, the little child is ordinarily given Holy Communion at baptism. This means that there is no question of whether Confirmation should precede Holy Communion, as in the Church of England. Nor is there any question of whether Confession should precede Holy Communion as in the Roman Catholic Church.

A child is considered as beginning to understand right and wrong, and therefore entering into the possibility of deliberate sin, from the age of six or seven. This largely coincides with the Roman Catholic emphasis on the age of seven being the age of the use of reason for a child. Seven, then, can be generalised as a possible age for the beginning of confession.

As in the older history of confession, the Orthodox emphasis is upon the second baptism. But it is also a repeatable sacrament. In addition to the sin-cleansing purpose of confession (or penitence or repentance as it is sometimes called) confession is accepted as a healing sacrament, which strengthens the soul. This is because counsel is seen as being very much a part of the ritual, together with the absolution from sin.

This is brought out in the Slavonic or Russian rite, but not the Greek, in words addressed by the priest to the penitent immediately before the confession proper:

> Behold, my child, Christ stands here invisibly and receives your confession. Therefore do not be ashamed or afraid, and hide nothing from me; but tell me without hesitation all the things you have done, and so you will have pardon from Our Lord Jesus Christ. See, his holy image is before us; and

I am only a witness bearing testimony before him of all the things you have to say to me. But if you hide anything from me, you will have a greater sin. Take care, then, lest having come to a physician you depart unhealed.

The practice

In the Orthodox Church, there is no regulation stating how often or how regularly persons should make their confession. This is left to the wisdom of the individual spiritual father. Sometimes the frequency is linked to the receiving of Holy Communion. If the reception of Holy Communion is infrequent, that is once or twice a year for instance, it might be enjoined on you by the priest that confession *should* precede Communion. But if it is the practice of the penitent to receive Holy Communion frequently, it is unlikely that the penitent will be guided to confess before each individual Holy Communion.

Availability. Because of the emphasis upon the spiritual father, there is not likely to be a regular series of 'public' times for confession. The individual will have recourse to his or her own confessor/spiritual father, making an appointment at a time and place convenient to both of them.

Place. As with the Church of England, confession is normally heard in the church, but in the open, not in a confessional box or a separate room. In an Orthodox church there is a screen which blocks off the sanctuary from the nave. This is called the *iconostasis*, from the icons with which it is covered. A confession is usually heard in front of the *iconostasis*, in full view of the main body of the church. However, there can be a variation in some churches where the confession is heard either behind the *iconostasis* or even in a separate room.

Priest and penitent are together, with no grill or barrier between them but, unlike the Church of England, it is usual for the priest and penitent to stand. They can be seated, but whether standing or sitting, both are in the same posture, showing an equality which realizes that both are sinners. The priest is not principally in a judging role – the judge is God. The priest is simply the witness.

The penitent will face an icon, which is suitably placed, and there will be a cross in front of him. The priest will be to his side.

Preparation. As confession is very much an individual practice rather than a regular event in the weekly life of the church, the preparation is up to the individual, who may well be counselled by his spiritual guide as to the method and scope of personal examination.

The form of confession. You, the penitent, come to the priest as an equal, stand beside him and speak to God. It is emphasised that the confession is to be complete. However, as the priest is there in the role of a counsellor as well as a listening ear, you, the penitent must expect to be both questioned and given advice.

Following the full confession you, as penitent, bow your head or kneel down, in reverence to the icon which is in front of you. This icon is symbolising Christ/God, who is the forgiver of sins (not the priest). All the emphasis of your confession is upon the work of God. It is carried through and further stressed when the priest says the words of absolution over you. The ancient way common to both Greek and Russian was deprecative. That is to say that the priest called upon God to grant the forgiveness, and did not take to himself the authority for forgiving. Today there is some difference between the Greek and the Slavonic/ Russian wording, because the latter was subject to a Latin influence. The Greek wording then is:

> Whatever you have said to my humble person, and whatever you have failed to say, whether through ignorance or forgetfulness, whatever it may be, may God forgive you in this world and the next. Have no further anxiety; go in peace.

But the Russian formula has moved somewhat from the deprecative, appearing to give the priest the power to forgive sins. The priest lays his stole and his hand on your head and says:

> May Our Lord and God, Jesus Christ, through the grace and bounties of his love towards mankind, forgive you, my child (he inserts your name) and all your transgressions. And I, an unworthy priest, through the power given me by him, forgive and absolve you from all your sins.

The reality of what the priest is doing is clarified by Kallistos Ware:

> Entrusted with authority to bind and loose, to withhold or to confer absolution, enjoying a wise discretion as to the advice that he gives and the healing penance that he chooses, the confessor-priest has laid upon him heavy responsibility. And yet his role is limited. The confession, as we have already insisted, is made to God, not to the priest; and it is God who grants forgiveness. 'I am only a witness' says the priest; and still more explicitly in St. Thikhon's paraphrase, 'I am a sinner just like you'. If at the moment of absolution, when laying his hand on the penitent's head, the priest stands, to a certain degree, in God's place, yet during the

earlier part of the sacramental action he stands at the penitent's side, as himself a fellow penitent, 'a sinner just like you', who also needs divine forgiveness. There is indeed, a two-way relationship between the priest and the one who is making the confession: the spiritual father is helped by his children, as well as they by him. The confessor-priest has also to go in his turn to confession; and when he does so, it is usual for him to remove the priestly cross from his neck.[4]

You will see then that the part of the priest is markedly limited. He is an aid used by the Lord. Part of the healing process which he can further is the imposition of a penance. You must see this not as a punishment nor as a means of gaining merit. The strength of the Orthodox approach to penance is that the whole practice is involved with *metanoia,* that is change or conversion. The part which the priest plays is seen very much in his presence, his spiritual depth and maturity, his wisdom in binding as well as loosing. He is there to guide the soul further and deeper into the love of God and union with him. From the Orthodox understanding of the Old and New Testaments and their theology of sin and repentance, there is a close link between repentance, confession and spiritual direction. So there is great stress upon the priest himself, with a person going to a particular spiritual father.

The attitude described ties in with the whole Orthodox understanding of sin and the person. Rather than too much centring on individual acts as sins, the attitude reflects much more the fact of the human being as a sinner, whose entire being has to be transformed into the truer image and likeness of God.

THE ROMAN CATHOLIC CHURCH

The background

After the Council of Trent, there was little change in confessional practice in the Roman Catholic Church until the early twentieth century. The time from Trent had been in many ways a dry and difficult period, with the effect of Jansenism making the reception of Holy Communion much less frequent and confession before Holy Communion being heavily insisted upon. The first major shift was early in the twentieth century when Pope Pius X led the Church to a renewed drive for frequent and even daily Holy Communion. Some of the old adhered to the new, and the result was that more frequent Holy Communion led to more frequent confession. This in turn led to long queues outside the confessional boxes, and the priest doing a quick-in-quick-out job.

This situation in turn led to some superficiality in confession, a rather frequent repetition of the same sins week by week or month by month. Children would make their first confession at about the age of seven, proceeding pretty soon to their first Holy Communion. From that time on, there grew up for many a pattern which depended on age, family, personal practice and whether you belonged to a particular group or sodality. Thus there were the weekly, monthly and annual penitents.

The Church had a general law for all that they should go to confession once a year. Many sodalities and groups had Sunday Mass attendance as a group and all went to Holy Communion that day. But those who went weekly or daily to Holy Communion often felt tied still to confession at least weekly. Unfortunately, it also meant that if a person did not get to confession, they might well feel barred from Holy

Communion, even when they might not be conscious of any serious sin.

The teaching on sin was another minefield area. An over-elaborate moral theology which developed during and after the medieval scholastic period left the penitent with lists of possible sins on which to examine his conscience, with degrees of importance in which the two main categories were mortal and venial. Mortal was a category of such serious sin, it was seen to 'kill the soul', that is to cut it off from God by deliberate refusal to do his will and a significant entry of the individual into self-love and self-satisfaction. Such sins might include murder, blasphemy, idolatry, major theft and adultery. An important inclusion in this kind of list was that missing Mass on a Sunday counted apparently as a mortal sin. Venial sin was much less serious, was a kind of failure or fall which is common to us all and did not need a constant recourse to confession. If asked for examples of such sins, a teacher might list such things as lying, petty stealing, thinking and speaking uncharitably, being lazy, not praying, being selfish and an almost endless possibility of thought, word, deed or omission.

From this distinction there grew various discussions on the likelihood of ordinary people falling into mortal sin, and for many there developed the understanding that it was possible to go through life without constantly slipping into mortal sin. But at the same time, there was an encouragement to go frequently to confession, even when there was no special thing to confess, on the understanding that this 'confession of devotion' was health-giving and aiding the individual further into the love of God.

The approach to the sacrament in the older pattern was taught from childhood and has only recently, in the nineteen-seventies, been updated as a result of Vatican II. This means that much of the older practice still remains in the actual life of the Church, and only gradually has the newer understanding been penetrating, especially in the case of more elderly people.

The practice

The purpose of the new rite is to make the celebration of the sacrament more fully understandable to the faithful, both in regard to the nature of the sacrament and its effects. The rite places individual confession and absolution in the context of celebrating the word of God. This is to help to emphasise the relation of the sacrament to the community, and to bring people together in penitential celebrations as well as individual confession.

Availability. The set times for confession are normally noted outside the church or in the porch. In addition to those times, there is generally added: 'Or at call'. Thus in theory confession is easily available. Many parishes have now adopted penitential services, which after community prayer and reading conclude with individual confession.

Place. Church is the usual setting for individual confession, with the use of the confessional box still being retained in many places. In this case you wait outside kneeling or sitting while you make a preparation, and perhaps while others go to confession. The priest sits in one compartment, as it were, while you enter by a separate door and kneel behind a partition, into which is cut a grill.

The new rite makes provision for confessional rooms, in which the priest and penitent sit together, perhaps facing each other across a table, or in any less formal pattern. Here the penitent is often given the option of going behind a grill or being in the open, face-to-face situation.

When confession is requested individually, the church is not necessarily used. A room in the priest's house, the sacristy or in the church sitting on a bench are all possible. In addition, when there is urgency, confession is heard anywhere – the street, railway station, a hospital bed and so on.

Preparation. Ordinarily, the examination of your conscience or state of life is very important, because you are placing yourself before God in truth. The sacrament of penance includes the confession of sins, and this should come from a true knowledge of self, together with contrition or sorrow for the sins. All is set in relation to your whole self, with the desire for *metanoia* or conversion of life. Only in this way can you come closer to Christ and follow his command to repent and hear the Good News.

The form of confession. Whether in a confessional box, a reconciliation room or any other place, the new rite makes the following provisions, though shorter, simpler forms are often used.

Greeting. The priest welcomes you warmly and kindly. If not in a confessional box, he will invite you to sit or kneel, as you prefer.

Sign of the Cross and invitation to trust. You and the priest make the sign of the cross, saying: In the name of the Father, and of the Son, and of the Holy Spirit. The priest then uses a few words or a verse from a psalm, etc. inviting you to trust, for instance:

> May God, who has enlightened every heart, help you to know your sins and trust in his mercy. Amen.

Revelation of state of life. If the priest does not know you, you are encouraged to say if you are single, married, a priest, a religious, etc. Also, how long since your last confession, and any special difficulties in leading a Christian life, or anything which could help the priest.

Call to conversion. If there is time and the opportunity, the priest or yourself reads a passage from Scripture proclaiming God's mercy and calling for conversion. For instance: Let us listen to the Lord as he speaks to us:

> See, today I set before you life and prosperity, death and disaster. If you obey the commandments of the Lord your God, if you love the Lord your God and follow his ways, you will live and increase and the Lord your God will bless you. Choose life, then, so that you may live in the love of the Lord your God.[5]

Confession of sins and acceptance of satisfaction. Where it is the custom, you may say a general formula like 'I confess to almighty God' before confessing your sins, and then do so. The priest can help you to make a full confession, and can give you counsel. He urges sorrow and reminds you that through penance the Christian dies and rises with Christ. He proposes an act of penance, which you accept 'to make up for the past' in some sense and to help in your new life in Christ, while also strengthening against weakness. The penance varies according to the nature of the sins. It may be prayer or self-denial, and especially the service of neighbours and works of mercy. These latter help to connect the social and community aspects of sin, repentance and new living.

Penitent's prayer of sorrow. The priest asks you to express your sorrow either in an act of contrition you know, or by using some part of a psalm, etc., for instance: Father, I have sinned against you, and am not worthy to be called your son. Be merciful to me a sinner.[6]

Absolution. The priest extends his right hand over your head and says:

God, the Father of mercies,
through the death and resurrection of his Son
has reconciled the world to himself
and sent the Holy Spirit among us
for the forgiveness of sins;
through the ministry of the Church
may God give you pardon and peace,
and I absolve you from your sins
in the name of the Father, and of the Son,
and of the Holy Spirit.

You say: Amen.

Proclamation of Praise of God and Dismissal. There are various versions and possibilities for the ending. For instance:

The Lord has freed you from sin.
May he bring you safely to his kingdom in heaven.
Glory be to him for ever.

And you respond: Amen.

The priest then says goodbye in the same warm and friendly way in which he welcomed you.

Thanksgiving. The penance will often be something to be prayed after the end of confession. It is well, then, to go back into the church or some quiet place to give thanks for the forgiveness and mercy of God, and to get a view of the way ahead in union with Jesus Christ.

The community dimension. The new rite is there to put more emphasis upon the community aspect of the sacrament of penance. Thus Pope Paul VI:

> By the hidden and loving mystery of God's design men are joined together in the bonds of supernatural solidarity, so much so that the sin of one harms the others, just as the holiness of one benefits the others.[7]

Penance entails reconciliation with our brothers and sisters who are always harmed by our sins:

> In fact, men frequently join together to commit injustice. It is thus only fitting that they should help each other in doing penance so that freed from sin by the grace of Christ they may work with all men of good will for justice and peace in the world.[8]

This aspect is more than an aspect and more like a fundamental re-statement of the essence of the sacrament of penance. As Christ himself was 'sacrament' when he lived the life of this world, so the Church is sacrament in the continuance of his ministry for the rest of time. The older pattern of individual and very secret confession minimised the part of the Church, and to some extent also the effect upon the neighbour. Now, not only is there the broadening of the rite of reconciliation for the individual referred to above, but there is a new development of penitential celebrations normally conducted in church. Suitable readings, meditations and an examination of conscience can all be put into a prayerful expression of sorrow and a communal appeal to God for mercy and forgiveness. Various examples of these celebrations are given in the *Rite of Penance* approved for use in the dioceses of England, Wales and Scotland.[9]

The Rite also lays out the possibilities of general confession and absolution, with rather strict norms for use. When it was first issued by the Congregation of the Doctrine of the Faith in 1972, General Absolution was certainly celebrated in England, and possibly also in Wales and Scotland. It was much welcomed and advocated where it had been celebrated. Later, however, there was a restatement from Rome which underlined the confining rules as to the circumstances in which this rite can be used.

The result has been that bishops have by and large stood back from General Absolution, maintaining that the circumstances laid down are not applicable in our situation in these countries. However, it is true to say that, especially at Christmas and Easter, the General Sacramental Absolution is still celebrated in some areas. It is one of the best attended and most spiritual and moving of all celebrations throughout the year. As far as the people of God are concerned, they are voting with their feet and their heads and hearts for this very beautiful implementation of the mystery of reconciliation.

THE METHODIST CHURCH

Explanatory note

Methodism emerged from the Church of England at a time when the practice of confession had long since virtually disappeared in that Church. Though John Wesley, as we shall see, had definite ideas on sin and sinfulness, there has never been a system of individual confession. In order to give some picture of Methodist 'confession' I decided to give a brief background through John Wesley, and then to outline the structure of Methodist church life, and especially the covenant service. This latter could be said to be the nearest approach to confession, but is in the form of a public service and personal commitment, along with the grateful acceptance of God's forgiveness.

The background

John and Charles Wesley were both ordained ministers of the Church of England. The great conversion experience at Aldersgate Street came through the influence of the Moravians, but John was soon to be at odds with the 'German stillness', continuing to criticise the Moravians throughout his life. Around 1738-9 he began to have difficulties with the Church of England. But he relied upon the Church of England in all sacramental ways, not holding his services at a time which would clash with Holy Communion in the local parish church. However, later, his followers began to make the Methodist preaching service an alternative to Holy Communion. In 1787 Wesley re-issued a sermon which he had preached on the Eucharist fifty-five years before at Lincoln College, Oxford.

In this sermon we get an idea of Wesley's mind on sin and the Eucharist. He urges reception of the Eucharist, for the first reason that this was Christ's own command. He goes on:

> The second reason why every Christian should do this as often as he can is because the benefits of doing it are so great to all that do it in obedience to him – namely, the forgiveness of past sins, the present strengthening and refreshing of our souls. Whatever way of life we are in, whatever our condition be, whether we are sick or well, in trouble or at ease, the enemies of our soul are watching to lead us into sin. And too often they prevail over us. Now, when we are convinced of having sinned against God, what surer way have we of procuring pardon from him than the 'showing forth the Lord's death',[10] and beseeching him, for the sake of his Son's sufferings, to blot out all our sins?
>
> The third reason. The grace of God given herein confirms to us the pardon of our sins, and

enables us to leave them. As our bodies are strengthened by bread and wine, so are our souls by these tokens of the body and blood of Christ. This is the food of our souls; this gives strength to perform our duty and leads us to perfection. If, therefore, we desire the pardon of our sins, if we wish for strength to believe, to love and obey God, then we should neglect no opportunity of receiving the Lord's Supper.[11]

Wesley professed that his purpose was 'to beget, preserve and increase the life of God in the souls of men'. As the system evolved, the preaching service became dominant and was considered a conscientious reason for not going to the parish church for Holy Communion. But there grew up the annual Covenant Service, which became the focal point for the now infrequent reception of Holy Communion.

A system of 'classes' was started. These were to work throughout the year. Each class was traditionally made up of twelve people with a leader. The leaders themselves were supported by a class leaders' meeting. Each class met once a week. The purpose was fellowship, study, prayer, testimony and discipline. The testimony was a witnessing to an experience of being saved, rescued or liberated from some sin or temptation. This sin or temptation was acknowledged explicitly in a form of public 'confession', and regretted. The actual testimony was strictly confined to the period since the last class meeting and it was customary to use one of Wesley's hymns during the class. One such hymn which is still today used annually at the Methodist Conference says:

And are we yet alive and see each other's face?
Glory and praise to Jesus give, for his redeeming grace!
What troubles have we seen; what conflicts have

we passed –
Fightings without and fears within, since we assembled last!
But out of all the Lord has brought us by his grace.

There were even smaller groups called bands. A question was asked at every band meeting: Are you ready to be told your faults and that plainly? This was more like a monastic chapter of faults than a confession, but the bands kept the discipline among themselves by telling each other's faults.

The covenant service, including quite a long declaration, follows the traditional theology of Methodism, in that a prayer of thanksgiving precedes the confession. It is always argued that grace precedes and creates repentance. So Wesley argued in his own way and wording that receiving Holy Communion could be a 'converting ordinance' – communion could be a *means* of evangelism leading to the covenant, and not just the *goal*.

The practice

Today both classes and bands have fallen into general disuse. But in reference to confession it is interesting that the phrase 'in band' is still used from time to time meaning 'in strict confidence'. Though derived from the Methodist band, the derivation is also traced to Lancashire cotton mills. The band of people who worked a loom were in close proximity. The general level of noise in the mill was such that only those in the band could hear each other speak. So that everything said 'in band' was confidential to the group. The trust which this built up is similar to the trust between priest and penitent under the seal of the confessional.

Availability and place. With the disappearance of bands and classes, the emphasis now focuses upon the covenant service. This is held once a year only. It is a congregational meeting with a long history and could be said to be, apart from the ordinary weekly worship, the most important and solemn occasion for a local congregation in the course of the year.

The form of service. The old form of service as mentioned above included a lengthy declaration of sorrow and purpose by God's grace to live in covenant with him. This was within the setting of thanksgiving to God for the mercy of forgiveness. However, a newer and shorter form was devised some ten years ago.

Opening prayer

M. Let us rejoice in the fellowship of the Holy Spirit, the Lord, the Giver of life.
By him, we are born into the family of God, and made members of the Body of Christ.
His witness confirms us;
his wisdom teaches us;
he will do for us more than we ask or think.

P. All praise to you, Holy Spirit.
There follows a period of silence.

Confession of sin

M. Let us humbly confess our sins to God.
God our Father, you have set forth the way of life for us in your beloved Son: we confess with shame our slowness to learn of him, our failure to follow him, our reluctance to hear the cross.

P. Have mercy on us, Lord, and forgive us.

M. We confess the poverty of our worship, our neglect of fellowship and of the means of grace, our hesitating witness of Christ, our evasion of responsibilities in your service, our imperfect stewardship of your gifts.

P. Have mercy on us, Lord, and forgive us.
There follows a period of silence.

M. Let each of us in silence make his own confession to God.
Have mercy on me, O God, according to your steadfast love; according to your abundant mercy blot out my transgressions. Wash me thoroughly from my iniquity, and cleanse me from my sin.
Create in me a clean heart, and put a new and right spirit witin me.
Minister stands.

M. This is the message we have heard from him and proclaim to you, that God is light and in him is no darkness at all. If we walk in the light, as he is in the light, we have fellowship with one another, and the blood of Jesus his Son cleanses us from all sin. If we say we have no sin, we deceive ourselves, and the truth is not in us. If we confess our sins he is faithful and just, and will forgive our sins and cleanse us from all unrighteousness.

P. Amen. Thanks be to God.

The collect

M. Father, you have appointed our Lord Jesus Christ as mediator of a new covenant; give us grace to draw near with fulness of faith and join ourselves in a perpetual covenant with you, through Jesus Christ our Lord.

P. Amen.

An alternative form of service. Some congregations were not happy at the changes, and have been forming up-dated versions of the older rite which was fuller. One such version which I know retains a thanksgiving section before the confession including:

Thanksgiving

M. Let us give thanks to God.
God our Father: all goodness flows from you. You have been with us not only in this past year, but through all our lives. We thank you for your love and kindness, which have filled our days, and brought us to this time and place:
Lord we praise your name!
You remembered us when we forgot you;
you followed us, even when we ran away from you:
you met us with forgiveness when we turned back to you:
For your patience and amazing grace:

P. Lord, we praise your name.

The confession itself covers areas of Christian life, many of them corporate in which confession is a necessary discipline, for instance:

Prayer for forgiveness

M. Forgive us that so little of your love has reached others through us, and that we have thought so little of the injustices and sufferings inflicted on others:
Forgive us for being proud of things which are divisive, and for making it hard for other people to live with us:
Forgive us: we have been thoughtless in our judgements, hasty in condemnation, grudging in forgiveness:

P. Be merciful to us, Lord, and forgive us.

M. If we have made no ventures in friendship:
If we have kept in our hearts a grievance against another;

If we have not sought reconciliation; if we have been eager for the punishment of wrongdoers, and slow to seek their fulfilment:

P. Be merciful to us, Lord, and forgive us.

NOTES

1 Pierre Solignac, *Christian Neurosis*, p. 52.
2 Pierre Solignac.
3 *Book of Common Prayer*, Visitation of the Sick.
4 Kallistos Ware, 'The Orthodox Experience', *Sobornost*, Vol. 2:1 (1980).
5 Deut. 30. 15-16, 19.
6 Lk. 15.18; 18.13.
7 Apostolic Constitution: *Indulgentiarus doctrina*, 1 Jan. 1967.
8 *The Rite of Penance*, Introduction No. 6.
9 Collins: Goodliffe Neale, 1976.
10 cf. I Cor. 11.26.
11 *Sermons on Several Occasions*, 1788. Vol. VIII, pp. 133-152.

FURTHER READING

This list is not in any order and must be rationalised.

The Forgiveness of Sins. Edward Matthews. Collins 1978.

Priestland's Progress. Gerald Priestland. BBC. 1981.

The Rite of Penance. Liturgy Commission, Bishop's Conference of England and Wales. Collins: Goodliffe Neale. 1976.

Soul Friend. Kenneth Leech. Sheldon Press. 1977.

The Great Acquittal. Tom Wright, John Tiller, George Carey and Tony Baker. Fount Paperbacks. 1980.

Sourozh. Journal of Orthodox Life and Thought. Parchment (Oxford) Ltd.

Memories, Dreams, Reflections. C. G. Jung. Fount Paperbacks, Collins.

Summons to Life. Martin Israel. A. R. Mowbray and Co. Ltd. 1977.

Rediscovering Pastoral Care. Alastair V. Campbell. Darton, Longman and Todd. 1981.

The Joy of Being Forgiven. St. Paul Publications. 1975.

The Pastoral Nature of Ministry. Frank Wright. SCM Press. 1980.

Pastoral Care for Lay People. Frank Wright. SCM Press Ltd. 1982.

Doors to the Sacred. Joseph Martos. SCM Press. 1981.

The Courage to Be. Paul Tillich. Fontana. Twelfth impression 1980.

How to Make your Confession. P. D. Butterfield. SPCK 1978.

Jung and the Christian Way. Christopher Bryant, SSJE. Darton, Longman and Todd. 1983.

A Handbook of Pastoral Counselling. Peter Liddell. Mowbray and Co. Ltd. 1983.

Principles of Pastoral Counselling. R. S. Lee. SPCK. 1978.

Tight Corners in Pastoral Counselling. Frank Lake. Darton, Longman and Todd. 1981.
Basic Christianity. John Stott. Inter-Varsity Press. 1958.
The Wounded Healer. Henri J. M. Nouwen. Image Books. 1979.
The Cloud of Unknowing. Newly edited: William Johnston. Image Books. 1973.
A Catechism of Christian Doctrine. Revised 1978. Catholic Truth Society.
Divorce and Second Marriage. Kevin T. Kelly. Collins. 1982.
Hearing Confessions. Kenneth Ross. SPCK. 1974.
The Double Cure. Canon Eric James. 2nd Edition, 1980. Christian Action Publications.
Has Sin Changed? Sean Fagan, S.M. Gill and Macmillan. 1978.
The Mystery of Sin and Forgiveness. Michael Taylor, Editor. Society of St. Paul. 1970.
The Psyche as Sacrament. C. G. Jung and Paul Tillich. John P. Dourley. Inner City Books. 1981.
The Christian Counsellor's Pocket Guide. Selwyn Hughes. Kingsway Publications. 1982.
Tensions. H. A. Williams. Michael Beazley. 1976.
A Sense of Life and a Sense of Sin. Eugene Kennedy. Image Books. 1976.
Declaration on Certain Questions concerning Sexual Ethics. Sacred Congregation for the Doctrine of the Faith. CTS.
Reconciliation and Penance in the Mission of the Church. Lineamenta for the Synod of Bishops. Vatican City. 1982.
Statement Concerning Moral Questions. Bishops' Conference of England and Wales. 1970. CTS.
Penance and the Anointing of the Sick. Poschmann. Herder/Burns Oates. 1964.
Depression. Jack Dominian. Fontana. 1976.
Evil and the God of Love. John Hick. Collins/Fount. 1979.
Care of the Dying. Richard Lamerton. Pelican.
Bereavement. Colin Murray Parkes. Penguin.

Marital Breakdown. Jack Dominian. Pelican.
Homosexuality. D. J. West. Pelican. 1965.
Time for Consent. Norman Pittenger. SCM. 1976.
I'm O.K., You're O.K. T. Harris. Pan Books. 1973.
On Becoming a Person. Carl Rogers. Constable. 1974.
Client-Centred Therapy. Houghton Mifflin. Boston. 1951.
Crisis Counselling. Eugene Kennedy. Gill and Macmillan. Dublin. 1981.
The Pastor as Counsellor. A. Godin. Gill and Macmillan. 1966.
Alcoholism. N. Kessel and H. Walton. Penguin. 1979.
God and the Unconscious. Victor White, O.P. Fontana. 1960.
Psychology, Religion and Healing. Leslie Weatherhead. Hodder and Stoughton. 1963.
Words of Counsel. Louis Marteau. T. Shand Publications. 1978.
A History of Penance. Oscar D. Watkins. Longmans, Green and Co. 1920.
Vatican Council II: The Conciliar and Post-Conciliar Documents. A. Flannery (Ed) Dominican Publications. Dublin. 1975.
The Oxford Dictionary of the Christian Church. F. L. Cross (ed). Oxford University Press. 1957.

ACKNOWLEDGEMENTS

The author and the publisher with to express their gratitude to the following for permission to include copyright material in this book:

BBC Publications, 35 Marylebone High Street, London W1M 4AA, for an extract from *Priestland's Progress* by Gerald Priestland.

Catholic Truth Society, 40 Eccleston Square, London SW1, for an extract from *Apostolic Constitution: Indulgentiarum doctrina* (1 Jan 1967).

Collins Liturgical Publications, 187 Piccadilly, London W1V 9DA, for extracts from *The Code of Canon Law,* English translation © 1983 The Canon Law Society Trust, and *Memories, Dreams Reflections* by C.J.Jung, used by the permission of the publishers.

Darton, Longman & Todd Ltd, 89 Lillie Road, London SW6 1UD, for quotations taken from *Jung and the Christian Way* by Christopher Bryant, published and copyright 1983 by Darton, Longman & Todd Ltd, London, and used by the permission of the publishers.

Fellowship of St Alban and St Sergius, St Basil's House, 52 Ladbroke Grove, London W11 2PB, for an extract from *The Orthodox Experience* — Sobornost Vol 2:1 (1980 Kallistos Ware).

ICEL Inc, 1234 Massachusetts Ave NW, Washington DC 20005, USA, for excerpts from the English translation of *Rite of Penance* © 1977 International Committee on English in the Liturgy Inc, ICEL, all rights reserved.

National Catholic News Service, 1312 Massachusetts Ave NW, Washington DC, USA 20005, for extracts from the report by the Vatican's International Theological Commission ('Origins' Vol 13 No 31, Jan 12, 1984).

Oxford University Press, Walton Street, Oxford OX2 6DP, for an extract from *The Oxford Dictionary of the Christian Church,* 2nd edition published 1974, edited by F.L.Cross.

SCM Press Ltd, 26-30 Tottenham Court Road, London N1 4BZ, for an extract from *The Pastoral Nature of the Ministry* by Frank Wright, SCM Press 1981.

SPCK, Holy Trinity Church, Marylebone Road, London NW1 4DU, for an extract from R.S.Lee's *Principles of Pastoral Counselling.*
Every effort has been made to trace the owners of copyright material, and we hope that no copyright has been infringed. Pardon is sought and apology made if the contrary be the case, and a correction will be made in any reprint of this book.

A Penitent's Prayerbook

A Penitent's Prayerbook

Celebrating the Sacrament of Penance

compiled by
David Konstant

McCRIMMONS
Great Wakering Essex

First published in Great Britain in 1976 by
MAYHEW-McCRIMMON LTD
Great Wakering Essex England

Cum original concordat	John P. Dewis
Nihil obstat	Brian O'Higgins, D.D.
Imprimatur	Christopher Creede, V.G.
Brentwood November 20 1975	

Contents

Introduction

Michael Hollings has already given a brief outline of the rite of the Sacrament of Reconciliation (see pp.209–16 above). My task here is to help you in your preparation for the actual celebration of the sacrament.

A sacrament is a sign which effectively brings us into the presence of Christ. But how effective it is depends to a large extent on us. God has made a firm, unbreakable promise to us, sealed by his Son's life, death and resurrection. The promise is that we can break free from all that holds us back from leading a full life and so discover what it means to be like Jesus Christ.

God's promise is sure and sublime – but our co-operation is needed if it is to be fully effective. Consequently the celebration of any sacrament must always be a sign of something that is really happening in our lives. God is infinitely courteous with us: he invites us, and waits patiently for us to accept his invitation. So it is important that when we come to celebrate the sacrament of penance we should think carefully about what we are doing.

One sign we make in celebrating the sacrament of penance is that of conversion; there is a change of heart which leads us to declare our sorrow. We had turned away from God, or had not gone far enough in the right direction, but we have now come to our senses and, in admitting our sinfulness, weakness or foolishness, have turned back to him.

Secondly, we are making a sign that we forgive others in our daily life. Jesus taught us that we are forgiven insofar as we forgive others; he tells us not to take our gift to the altar until we have been reconciled with our brother. To put it simply, it just does not make sense for us to look for God's forgiving love unless we know what forgiveness means from our own experience.

Thirdly, whenever we celebrate the sacrament of penance, we are publicly accepting our responsibility for continuing Christ's forgiving and healing work. This is the work we were anointed (christened) for at our baptism and confirmation.

Finally, as with any of the sacraments, when we take part in the sacrament of penance we are publicly affirming that we are followers of Christ, that we belong to his Body, the Church, and that we need the support of Christ, his Church, and all our fellow men and women, if we are to grow in our relationship with God.

The Church has given us three ways of celebrating the sacrament of penance. The first is the traditional way, alone with a priest to whom we make an individual confession and from whom we receive absolution. This can be in a confessional or in some other suitable place. A second way is a Reconciliation Service of prayer, readings and reflection, followed by individual private confession. The third way, a service of General Absolution, is only allowed in special circumstances.

Even though you may not be about to celebrate the sacrament in a communal service, though, we should always remember that in a very real sense we belong to and need each other; we should see clearly the community nature of sin and forgiveness. In services of penance, moreover, we are helped to pray.

The pattern of the sacrament is very simple, and determines the pattern of this prayer book.

Preparation

The long term preparation has been indicated above. We prepare for this sacrament by becoming aware of the need we have for forgiveness and for God's supporting love. Before we come to make our confession we can prepare by praying for forgiveness (see pages 242 to 248), by examining our conscience (see pages 249 to 259), and by remembering that we are joining Christ in praising his Father.

Greetings

When we are with the priest we make the sign of the cross and say, 'In the name of the Father, and of the Son, and of the Holy Spirit. Amen'. The priest greets us in a friendly way, perhaps using one of the forms of greeting on pages 260 to 262. We may then tell him something about ourselves – just enough to let him know the circumstances of our life (for example, 'I'm married, with four young children'; or 'I work in a factory, on the night shift'). This is to help him understand us and any problems we might have. We should then say when we last celebrated the sacrament.

Liturgy of the Word

Either we or the priest may now read a short passage from scripture. There are a number of passages on pages 263 to 294. Many of them may appear too long, but there are two things to bear in mind. First of all, we should never feel hurried – if we need more time than is reasonably available on a Saturday evening, we are quite free to go at any other sensible time; the priest is the servant of his people. Secondly, we should choose a passage before going to the priest, and read it and pray about it. It may then be that just two or three sentences will be enough to recall the whole passage and its message for us – that is quite sufficient. There will sometimes be a temptation to leave out this optional part of the celebration; yet to omit the reading could be a great loss to priest and penitent alike.

Confession and Advice

We then make our confession in the best way we can. This is a question about our growth or lack of growth to holiness; about the difficulties of the daily grind; about our many failures and weaknesses; about our hopes and fears; about the things that really trouble us. To prepare a list may be fairly easy, but it may not mean very much. What we need to discover is the sickness, and not just the symptoms. The priest will help us make our confession well, and will try to give advice and counselling where necessary. The penance he gives will be a prayer, an act of self-denial, or especially the service of others. The purpose of the penance is to help us to overcome our weaknesses and to begin to live more generously. If we are asked to do something for others this reminds us that both sin and forgiveness are to do with other people as well as ourselves.

Prayer of Sorrow and Absolution

We then say a short prayer of sorrow (an act of contrition) in which we ask for God's forgiveness and healing power. Some prayers can be found on pages 295 to 300. Then the priest as a minister of the whole Church declares our forgiveness by God and our reconciliation with the Church in a prayer of absolution (page 301).

Thanksgiving and Dismissal

The priest now says a short prayer of thanks and, rather as at the end of Mass, tells us to go our way in peace. Some appropriate prayers are given on pages 302 to 304. Finally we can pray quietly ourselves in thanksgiving for God's forgiving love. Some prayers of thanks from the psalms can be found on pages 305 to 310.

Preparation

Psalms for Forgiveness

The psalms are Jewish prayers written more than 2500 years ago; they reflect almost every mood of man; joy and sadness; exultation and desolation; hope and despair; peace and anger. They are prayers known to and used by our Lord and his friends, and have always been familiar to Christians. In almost his last cry from the cross our Lord exclaimed 'My God, my God, why have you forsaken me?', which is the first line of Psalm 21(22)*. Before coming to celebrate the sacrament of penance we may be helped to express our desire for forgiveness in one of these simple prayers.

* There are two numberings of the psalms: the first follows the numbering found in translations from the Greek to Latin, while the second (in brackets) follows the Hebrew numbering.

Lord my God, I trust in your merciful love.
Let my heart rejoice in your saving help:
Let me sing to the Lord for his goodness to me,
singing psalms to the name of the Lord, the Most
High.

Psalm 12(13).6,7

I am here and I call, you will hear me, O God.
Turn your ear to me; hear my words.
Display your great love, you whose right hand
saves your friends
from those who rebel against them.

Psalm 16(17).6,7

You, O Lord, are my lamp,
my God who lightens my darkness.
With you I can break through any barrier,
with my God I can scale any wall.

Psalm 17(18).29,30

My God, my God,
Do not leave me alone in my distress;
come close, there is none else to help.

Psalm 21(22).12

The Lord is my shepherd;
there is nothing I shall want.
Fresh and green are the pastures
where he gives me repose.
Near restful waters he leads me,
to revive my drooping spirit.

Psalm 22(23).1–3

Remember your mercy, Lord,
and the love you have shown from of old.
Do not remember the sins of my youth.
In your love remember me.

Psalm 24(25).6,7

In you, O Lord, I take refuge.
Let me never be put to shame.
In your justice, set me free,
hear me and speedily rescue me.

Psalm 30(31).2–3

The Lord guides the steps of a man
and makes safe the path of one he loves.
Though he stumble he shall never fall
for the Lord holds him by the hand.

Then turn away from evil and do good
and you shall have a home for ever;
for the Lord loves justice
and will never forsake his friends.

Psalm 36(37).23–24,27–28

O Lord, you will not withhold
your compassion from me.
Your merciful love and your truth
will always guard me.

Psalm 39(40).12

Like the deer that yearns
for running streams,
so my soul is yearning
for you, my God.

Psalm 41(42).2

God is for us a refuge and strength,
a helper close at hand, in time of distress:
so we shall not fear though the earth should rock,
though the mountains fall into the depths of the
sea,
even though its waters rage and foam,
even though the mountains be shaken by its waves.

Psalm 45(46).2–4

Have mercy on me, God, in your kindness.
In your compassion blot out my offence.
O wash me more and more from my guilt
and cleanse me from my sin.

O rescue me, God, my helper,
and my tongue shall ring out your goodness.
O Lord, open my lips
and my mouth shall declare your praise.

Psalm 50 (51).3–4,16–17

O God, save me by your name;
by your power, uphold my cause.
O God, hear my prayer;
listen to the words of my mouth.

Psalm 53(54).3–4

O God, listen to my prayer,
do not hide from my pleading,
attend to me and reply;
with my cares, I cannot rest.

As for me, I will cry to God
and the Lord will save me.

Psalm 54(55).2–3,17

Save me, O God,
for the waters have risen to my neck.

This is my prayer to you,
my prayer for your favour.
In your great love, answer me, O God,
with your help that never fails.

Lord, answer, for your love is kind;
in your compassion, turn towards me.
Do not hide your face from your servant;
answer quickly for I am in distress.

Psalm 68(69).2,14,17–18

Let there be rejoicing and gladness
for all who seek you.
Let them say for ever: 'God is great,'
who love your saving help.

As for me, wretched and poor,
come to me, O God.
You are my rescuer, my help,
O Lord, do not delay.

Psalm 69(70).5–6

In you, O Lord, I take refuge;
let me never be put to shame.
In your justice rescue me, free me:
pay heed to me and save me.

It is you, O Lord, who are my hope,
my trust, O Lord, since my youth.

Psalm 70(71).1–2,5

O shepherd of your people, hear us.
O Lord, rouse up your might,
O Lord, come to our help.

O God of hosts, bring us back;
let your face shine on us and we shall be saved.

from *Psalm 79(80).2–4*

You are my God, have mercy on me, Lord,
for I cry to you all the day long.
Give joy to your servant, O Lord,
for to you I lift up my soul.

O Lord, you are good and forgiving,
full of love to all who call.
Give heed, O Lord, to my prayer
and attend to the sound of my voice.

Psalm 85(86).3–6

But you, God of mercy and compassion,
slow to anger, O Lord,
abounding in love and truth,
turn and take pity on me.

Psalm 85(86).15–16

Lord my God, I call for help by day;
I cry at night before you.
Let my prayer come into your presence.
O turn your ear to my cry.

Psalm 87(88).2–3

O Lord, listen to my prayer
and let my cry for help reach you.
Do not hide your face from me
in the day of my distress.
Turn your ear towards me
and answer me quickly when I call.

Psalm 101(102).2–3

O Lord, remember me
out of the love you have for your people.

Come to me, Lord, with your help
that I may see the joy of your chosen ones
and may rejoice in the gladness of your nation
and share the glory of your people.

Psalm 105(106).4–5

Help me, Lord my God;
save me because of your love.
Let them know that this is your work,
that this is your doing, O Lord.

Psalm 108(109).26

I called to the Lord in my distress;
he answered and freed me.
The Lord is at my side; I do not fear.

What can man do against me?
It is better to take refuge in the Lord
than to trust in men.

Give thanks to the Lord for he is good,
for his love endures for ever.

Psalm 117(118).5–6,8,1

With all my voice I cry to the Lord,
with all my voice I entreat the Lord.
I pour out my troubles before him;
I tell him all my distress
while my spirit faints within me.
But you, O Lord, know my path.

Listen, then, to my cry
for I am in the depths of distress.

Psalm 141(142).2–4,7

The Lord is faithful in all his words
and loving in all his deeds.
The Lord supports all who fall
and raises all who are bowed down.

Psalm 144(145).13–14

Examination of Conscience

Preparation for the sacrament of penance takes time. If we approach the sacrament without prayer and reflection there is the danger that it can become a merely routine or mechanical event. (There may, of course, be occasions when a penitent is moved on impulse to come to confession – such a desire may well be an urge of the Holy Spirit, and should certainly be followed even if this means that there is little time for detailed preparation.)

We may first of all think about the following:

* Do I come to this sacrament really prepared to change my way of life?
* Do I appreciate this sacrament as a means of deepening my friendship with God, or do I just think of it as an unpleasant necessity?
* Have I celebrated this sacrament sincerely in the past, with real sorrow, and have I tried to live more fully according to the gospel since then?
* Have I tried to make up for any damage or hurt I may have caused by my past sins?
* Do I come to this sacrament uncertain of what I am looking for?

In order to examine our conscience it is helpful, if not necessary, to think about our life in the light of God's word. Three possible frameworks for an examination of conscience are given below, but these can never be more than the vaguest of guides; their value is in pointing in directions that we might not think to look, rather than in asking all the questions that can be asked.

1. The Beatitudes (see p.273)

'Happy are the poor in spirit'

'What is my attitude to money?... am I honest in my handling of money?... do I share my goods with the poor on my doorstep, and abroad?... am I miserly?... or wasteful?... am I overanxious about money?... do I work honestly?... do I provide proper conditions for those who work for me?... do I look after my family properly – my husband or wife, my children, my parents?... do I use my own and other people's property with due care?... do I use the gifts of creation properly?... do I acknowledge my need for other people?... am I generous in sharing my time with others?... do I acknowledge my dependence on God?... do I pray?

'Happy the gentle'

Do I speak with gentleness to others?... am I harsh or abrasive in speech?... am I sarcastic towards others?... do I tell lies about others?... do I hurt others in any way by my words, or gestures, or actions?... do I treat my companions (and my children) with due respect?... do I use my authority wisely and gently?... do I treat those in authority with a proper respect?... do I listen to others with understanding?... do I act with feeling care towards others?...

'Happy those who mourn'

Is my sorrow for sin unselfish?... am I willing to accept discomfort, unpleasantness, and suffering?... am I sensitive to the sufferings of others?... do I turn a blind eye to problems for fear of being inconvenienced?... do I pride myself on being hard-headed?... am I in any way callous or indifferent to human suffering?... do I despise the weak?... am I inclined to write off the failures, the sinners, those who for any reason opt out of society?... do I accept friendship when it is offered?...

'Happy those who hunger and thirst for what is right'

Do I work for justice in my daily life and work?... is my desire for justice really deep?... am I more concerned that I should get my rights than that others should get theirs?... do I use the opportunities open to me to obtain a more just economy?... do I attend in a practical way to the needs of the Third World, or of other groups in need?... do I place a limit to my justice?... am I prejudiced towards any class or body of people – immigrants, employers, trade unionists, those of different religious beliefs or practices?...

'Happy the merciful'

Am I quick to forgive others?... am I ready to accept others?... am I generous in the way I treat others?... am I unselfish in my dealings with others?... do I profess to love my fellow men, but fail in any way to show my love for individual men, women and children?... do I harbour grudges or resentment?... am I ever secretly pleased at another's failure?... do I work for greater understanding and tolerance in the world?... do I hinder the growth of others by my hard-heartedness or by being a perfectionist?... am I able to forgive myself?...

'Happy the pure in heart'

Do I know God in prayer, or in my neighbour, or in creation?... am I blind or deaf to God's presence in my life?... do I put up barriers of pride, or laziness, or selfishness, or dishonesty, or intellectualism between myself and God?... do I allow my human weaknesses and instincts to cloud my vision?... do I respect my own dignity as a man or as a woman?... do I respect the dignity and worth of others?... do I consent in any way to the cheapening of human worth as often portrayed in the world?... do I practise self-control, in my life?...

'Happy the peacemakers'

Do I profess to love peace, but fail to make peace?... do I make peace in my own family, among friends, at work?... am I prepared to face difficult issues, to court unpopularity, to take trouble, to risk being laughed at so as to bring peace?... am I afraid to make a stand for peace?... do I fight or quarrel with others?... am I obstinate in my opinions?... do I listen to the other person's point of view?... am I at peace with myself?... do I treat all men as my brothers?... do I spread rumours, or run people down?...

'Happy those who are persecuted in the cause of right'

Am I prepared to be different because I believe and accept the gospel?... do I avoid the truth in case I may be hurt?... do I stand up for Christian principles?... do I support those who suffer in the cause of right?... do I condone persecution by my inaction or lack of interest?... do I discriminate against people who think differently from me?...

2. The Last Judgement *(Matthew 25.31–46)*

When the Son of Man comes in his glory, escorted by all the angels, then he will take his seat on his throne of glory... He will place the sheep on his right hand and the goats on his left. Then the King will say to those on his right hand, 'Come, you whom my Father has blessed, take for your heritage the kingdom prepared for you since the foundation of the world.'

'I was hungry and you gave me food; thirsty and you gave me drink'

Do I notice and attend to the needs of others?... do I give food and drink to those in need, or do I leave this to the State or to voluntary welfare services?... do I give life to people in my contact with them?... do I help others to grow?... do I encourage, praise and value other people?... do I give my time for others?... do I share my knowledge and expertise with others?... am I ready to give advice when it is necessary?... when I give to others, do I give willingly and pleasantly or grudgingly as a duty?... am I willing to give affection and love, without fear?... do I appreciate that Christ's food and drink was to do the will of his Father?... am I hungry and thirsty for justice, for truth, and for the Father's will?... do I try to live according to my baptism as a Christian?... when I receive communion do I promise to share my life with the whole of Christ's Body, the Church?...

'I was a stranger and you made me welcome; naked and you clothed me'

How do I welcome other people?... do I notice the person next to me at Mass?... do I find an excuse for not knowing my next door neighbour?... do I bother about the handicapped person?... do I ignore someone who doesn't belong to my particular group, who doesn't come from my part of the world, or who doesn't share my interests or beliefs?... do I try to understand those of other faiths or of other political opinions?... do I care for the defenceless – for the very young and the very old, for the ignorant, for the stupid, for the fearful?... do I accept people whatever their prejudices?... do I welcome the shy person?... do I show warmth to the lonely person?... do I try to encourage the dull person?... do I make room in my heart and in my prayers for the stranger?...

'I was sick and you visited me, in prison and you came to see me'

Do I visit the sick?... do I provide for the sick in any way?... do I try to strengthen those who are weak?... do I try to comfort the sad and depressed?... do I talk to those who are ignored?... do I listen to those who need to speak?... am I compassionate in the presence of suffering?... do I run away from someone else's suffering?... am I afraid to get involved with the hurt or the sick?... am I sensitive to another's sickness?... am I too selfish to give time for those in need?... do I realise how much the sick and suffering can give me?... do I try to release people from the prison of their fear, or their hatred, or their poverty, or their doubt?... do I bring the gospel to others, or am I too closed to the Spirit in my life?... do I try to bring freedom to the down-trodden?... do I, in fact, ever visit those in prison, and is this something I could do?... am I in any way sick or imprisoned?... if so, do I allow others to help me, or am I too proud or self-indulgent to look for help?... do I trust God as my Father?...

'I tell you solemnly, in so far as you did this to one of the least of these brothers of mine, you did it to me'

Have I recognised in my neighbour the image and likeness of God?... have I seen in my fellow-men the presence of the living Christ?... have I seen in the goodness of others the work of the Holy Spirit?... do I acknowledge that God lives in me?... do I truly see all men as my brothers?...

3. A Portrait of Love *(1 Corinthians 13.4–8,13; see p.287)*

'Love is always patient and kind'...

Am I patient with myself?... do I expect too much of myself?... do I rely on myself too much?... do I get angry with myself when I fail?... am I impatient in prayer?... do I give up if I don't get quick results?... am I patient with others?... do I get angry or irritable at other people's failures or weaknesses, or if they are less quick or clever than me?... am I patient with children?... am I patient with those who are very demanding?... am I patient and kind with the elderly and sick?... am I kind and gentle in my speech?... do I speak well of others?... do I act kindly to those in a less privileged position than me?...

... *'it is never jealous, boastful or conceited'*...

Am I jealous of someone else's good fortune, or success?... do I try to keep up with my next door neighbour?... do I drive my children (or others) so that I can boast about their success?... do I feel affronted if others don't live up to my expectations of them?... am I complacent about my success or goodness?... am I hypocritical in the way I live?... do I keep on comparing myself favourably with others?... do I look for praise from others?... am I slow to give praise to others?... do I bore others by talking about myself?... do I bother to listen to others?... am I grateful to God and to my fellow men for all they do for me?... do I show my thanks?... am I slow to apologise or to admit my faults?...

... 'it is never rude or selfish'...

Do I treat others with the respect due to them as persons?... do I behave courteously towards others?... do I bother about other people's feelings?... am I ever arrogant or overbearing?... do I annoy others by my bad language?... does my language reflect my human dignity and do justice to the gift of speech?... am I ever inconsiderate about other people's wishes?... do I press for my own wants to the exclusion of other people's?... do I inconvenience others by my selfish use of radio, TV or record player?... is my attitude in any way, 'I'm all right Jack'?... am I thoughtful toward my family?... do I consider the effect that my actions will have on others?... do I ever deliberately hurt others?... do I take a genuine interest in the needs of the Third World?... is my idea of justice limited by what I want for myself?... am I self-indulgent?... do I seek for personal pleasure at the expense of others?... does my selfishness lead me to ignore God?...

... 'it does not take offence, and is not resentful'...

Am I touchy about my rights?... am I prepared to accept criticism?... do I sense criticism where none is meant?... do I feel slighted if others are preferred to me?... how do I react to my failures?... how do I respond if I am unjustly treated, or misunderstood, or undervalued?... am I a proud person?... do I ever reflect on the humility and gentleness of Christ, who showed by his actions how to accept injustice?... do I forgive those who sin against me?... what is my attitude to law?... do I recognise that my freedom must be limited so that others can be free?... do I ignore the law if it inconveniences me?... do I keep the laws of the Church?... do I act on Christ's commandment, 'if you love me you will keep my commandments'?... do I impose laws on others that I am not prepared to keep myself?... do I drive others to resentment by harshness, unreasonableness, thoughtlessness, or selfishness?... do I unnecessarily give offence to others?... do I resent my dependence on others?... do I resent my dependence on God?...

... *'Love delights in truth'*...

Am I a truthful person?... do I value the truth?... do I hide or distort the truth by my speech, or by my actions, or by my silence?... do I exaggerate?... do I repeat what I hear without bothering to verify its truth or falsity?... do I spread rumours or scandal?... do I condone lies by my inaction or silence?... do I try to grow in understanding of truth?... do I pray for God's Spirit of truth in my life?... is my life a true reflection of my beliefs?... do I respect those who sincerely hold different beliefs to mine?... do I try to understand the beliefs of others?... do I try to share my vision of truth with others?... do I allow others freedom to accept truth, or do I put unjust pressures on them?... do I look and listen for God in my life?

... *'it is always ready to excuse, to trust, to hope'*...

Do I ever reflect on Christ's advice: 'Judge not and you shall not be judged'?... do I pay attention to Christ's comment: 'Let he that is without sin cast the first stone'?... am I quick to judge others?... am I rigid in my judgements of others?... do I try to understand the actions of others?... do I regard justice and mercy as being in conflict?... am I ready to accept others whatever their faults?... am I willing to trust others, even if they let me down?... am I prepared to help others to grow and to hope by placing trust in them?... am I able to forgive myself?... do I place my trust in God?... do I have a firm hope that God will give me his grace?... do I accept that God will give me his grace?... do I accept that I shall not be tried beyond my strength?... do I see Christ's triumph over death as a guarantee that I can overcome sin and death?...

... *'it is always ready to endure whatever comes'*...

Am I prepared to take up my cross daily and follow Christ?... do I accept that true love will always bring suffering? . . . do I grumble about the problems and difficulties of my life?... do I blame God for my sufferings and hardships?... how do I try to face doubt?... do I try to overcome my own bad habits?... is my love for those who are close to me such that I can cope with their unkindnesses, their weaknesses, their letting me down, their failures?... is my love for those who ignore and hurt me such that I can forgive them?... is my love for God such that I can accept persecution for speaking out in his name?... do I accept that there are three things that last: faith hope and love, and that the greatest of these is love?...

When we have reflected on the pattern of our lives in the light of the gospel we can then express our sorrow in prayer. Our own prayer is often the best, but some suitable prayers can be found on pages 295 to 300. A simple expression of sorrow coupled with a plea for help and forgiveness made to the whole communion of saints and to God, whom we have sinned against, is the *I Confess.*

I confess to almighty God,
and to you, my brothers and sisters,
that I have sinned through my own fault
in my thoughts and in my words,
in what I have done,
and in what I have failed to do;
and I ask blessed Mary, ever virgin,
all the angels and saints,
and you, my brothers and sisters,
to pray for me to the Lord our God.

Confession

The Greeting

When the penitent comes for confession the priest greets him in a friendly way and the penitent makes the sign of the cross.

In the name of the Father, and of the Son, and of the Holy Spirit. Amen.

The priest invites him to put his trust in God. There follow below a number of forms of greeting.

1. May God, who has enlightened every heart,
   help you to know your sins
   and trust in his mercy. **Amen.**

2. The Lord does not wish the sinner to die
   but to turn back to him and live.
   Come before him with trust in his mercy.
   (Ezekiel 33.11) **Amen.**

3. May the Lord Jesus welcome you:
   He came to call sinners, not the just.
   Have confidence in him. *(Luke 5.32)* **Amen.**

4. May the grace of the Holy Spirit
   fill your hearts with light,
   that you may confess your sins with loving trust
   and come to know that God is merciful. **Amen.**

5. May the Lord be in your heart
and help you to confess your sins with true sorrow. **Amen.**

6. If you have sinned, do not lose heart.
We have Jesus Christ to plead for us with the Father:
he is the holy One,
the atonement for our sins
and for the sins of the whole world.
(1 John 2.1–2) **Amen.**

7. Come with confidence to the Lord who invites all who labour and are overburdened to come to him for rest *(Matthew 11.29)*. **Amen.**

8. Be at peace, and know that nothing can separate you from the love of God made visible in Christ Jesus our Lord *(Romans 8.39)*. **Amen.**

9. Being dead to sin, may you be alive to God in Christ Jesus our Lord *(Romans 6.11)*. **Amen.**

10. May your mind and heart be renewed, 'so that you can put on the new self that has been created in God's way, in the goodness and holiness of the truth' *(Ephesians 4.23–23)*. **Amen.**

11. May the Lord Jesus, who 'learnt to obey through suffering' *(Hebrews 5.8)*, strengthen you, so that you may humbly confess your sins. **Amen.**

12. 'Let us be confident in approaching the throne of grace, that we shall have mercy from him and find grace when we are in need of help' *(Hebrews 4.16)*. **Amen.**

13. Know that however great the number of sins committed, the grace of God is even greater *(Romans 5.20)*. **Amen.**

14. 'If we acknowledge our sins, then God who is faithful and just will forgive our sins and purify us from everything that is wrong' *(1 John 1.9)*. **Amen.**

15. The Lord will never forget you *(Isiah 49.15)*, and will always care for you tenderly; come to him with faith and love. **Amen.**

16. May the Lord come to your aid, and make haste to help you *(Psalm 39(40).14)*. **Amen.**

17. Call to God for mercy and compassion, that you may be cleansed from your sins *(Psalm 50(51).1)*. **Amen.**

18. May God search you and know your heart, and lead you in the path of eternal life *(Psalm 138(139).23–24)*. **Amen.**

19. Come to God with faith and confidence, for his love for us is strong, and he is faithful for ever *(Psalm 116(117).2)*. **Amen.**

Readings from Scripture

The priest or penitent may now choose a passage from scripture to read aloud. Scripture is the Word of God, and can speak to us about ourselves and about the lives we lead, if only we are sufficiently at peace to listen. Before coming to celebrate this sacrament we can read and reflect on one of the passages below (or any other suitable text). If this same passage is read after the greeting, our confession may then be our response to the Word of God. We see ourselves in the light of this Word – a light that shines in the darkness of our lives.

Old Testament Readings

Love and Obedience

'See, today I set before you life and prosperity, death and disaster. If you obey the commandments of Yahweh your God that I enjoin on you today, if you love Yahweh your God and follow his ways, if you keep his commandments, his laws, his customs, you will live and increase, and Yahweh your God will bless you in the land which you are entering to make your own. But if your heart strays, if you refuse to listen, if you let yourself be drawn into worshipping others gods and serving them, I tell you today, you will most certainly perish; I call heaven and earth to witness against you today: I set before you life or death, blessing or curse. Choose life, then, so that you and your descendants may live, in the love of Yahweh your God, obeying his voice, clinging to him; for in this your life consists, and on this depends your long stay in the land which Yahweh swore to your fathers Abraham, Isaac and Jacob he would give them.'

Deuteronomy 29.15–20

Forgiveness

Yahweh sent Nathan the prophet to David. He came to him and said:

'In the same town were two men,
one rich, the other poor.
The rich man had flocks and herds
in great abundance;
the poor man had nothing but a ewe lamb,
one only, a small one he had bought.
This he fed, and it grew up with him and his children,
eating his bread, drinking from his cup,
sleeping on his breast; it was like a daughter to him.
When there came a traveller to stay, the rich man
refused to take one of his own flock or herd
to provide for the wayfarer who had come to him.
Instead he took the poor man's lamb
and prepared it for his guest.'

David's anger flared up against the man. 'As Yahweh lives,' he said to Nathan 'the man who did this deserves to die! He must make fourfold restitution for the lamb, for doing such a thing and showing no compassion'. Then Nathan said to David 'You are the man'. David said to Nathan, 'I have sinned against Yahweh'. Then Nathan said to David, 'Yahweh, for his part, forgives your sin; you are not to die.'

2 Samuel 12.1–7,13–14

Trust in God

The Lord is my shepherd;
there is nothing I shall want.
Fresh and green are the pastures
where he gives me repose.
Near restful waters he leads me,
to revive my drooping spirit.

He guides me along the right path;
he is true to his name.
If I should walk in the valley of darkness
no evil should I fear.
You are there with your crook and your staff;
with these you give me comfort.

You have prepared a banquet for me
in the sight of my foes.
My head you have anointed with oil;
my cup is overflowing.

Surely goodness and kindness shall follow me
all the days of my life.
In the Lord's own house shall I dwell
for ever and ever.

Psalm 22(23)

Confident Cry for Help

I lift up my eyes to the mountains:
from where shall come my help?
My help shall come from the Lord
who made heaven and earth.

May he never allow you to stumble!
Let him sleep not, your guard.
No, he sleeps not nor slumbers,
Israel's guard.

The Lord is your guard and your shade;
at your right side he stands.
By day the sun shall not smite you
nor the moon in the night.

The Lord will guard you from evil,
he will guard your soul.
The Lord will guard your going and coming
both now and for ever.

Psalm 120(121)

Out of the Depths

Out of the depths I cry to you, O Lord,
Lord, hear my voice!
O let your ears be attentive
to the voice of my pleading.

If you, O Lord, should mark our guilt,
Lord, who would survive?
But with you is found forgiveness:
for this we revere you.

My soul is waiting for the Lord,
I count on his word.
My soul is longing for the Lord
more than watchman for daybreak.

Because with the Lord there is mercy
and fulness of redemption,
Israel indeed he will redeem
from all its iniquity.

Psalm 129(130)

The Value of Wisdom

Love virtue, you who are judges on earth,
let honesty prompt your thinking about the Lord,
seek him in simplicity of heart;
since he is to be found by those who do not put him
to the test,
he shows himself to those who do not distrust him.
But selfish intentions divorce from God;
and Omnipotence, put to the test, confounds the
foolish.
No, Wisdom will never make its way into a crafty
soul
nor stay in a body that is in debt to sin;
the holy spirit of instruction shuns deceit,
it stands aloof from reckless purposes,
is taken aback when iniquity appears.

Wisdom is a spirit, a friend to man,
though she will not pardon the words of a
blasphemer,
since God sees into the innermost parts of him,
truly observes his heart,
and listens to his tongue.

Do not court death by the error of your ways,
nor invite destruction through your own actions.
Death was not God's doing,
he takes no pleasure in the extinction of the living.
To be – for this he created all;
the world's created things have health in them,
in them no fatal poison can be found,
and Hades holds no power on earth;
for virtue is undying.

Wisdom 1.1–6,12–15

Qualities of Wisdom

Within Wisdom is a spirit intelligent, holy,
unique, manifold, subtle,
active, incisive, unsullied,
lucid, invulnerable, benevolent, sharp,
irresistible, beneficent, loving to man,
steadfast, dependable, unperturbed,
almighty, all-surveying,
penetrating all intelligent, pure
and most subtle spirits;
for Wisdom is quicker to move than any motion;
she is so pure, she prevades and permeates all
things.

She is a breath of the power of God,
pure emanation of the glory of the Almighty;
hence nothing impure can find a way into her.
She is a reflection of the eternal light,
untarnished mirror of God's active power,
image of his goodness.

Wisdom 7.22–26

Forgive Each Other

Sarcasm and abuse are the mark of an arrogant
man,
but vengeance lies in wait like a lion for him.
The trap will close on all who rejoice in the downfall
of the devout,
and pain will eat them up before they die.

Resentment and anger, these are foul things too,
and both are found with the sinner.
He who exacts vengeance will experience the
vengeance of the Lord,
who keeps strict account of sin.
Forgive your neighbour the hurt he does you,
and when you pray, your sins will be forgiven.

If a man nurses anger against another,
can he then demand compassion from the Lord?
Showing no pity for a man like himself,
can he then plead for his own sins?
Remember the commandments, and do not bear
your neighbour ill-will;
remember the covenant of the Most High, and
overlook the offence.

Ecclesiaticus 27.28 – 28.7

Do Good; Avoid Evil

Take your wrong-doing out of my sight.
Cease to do evil.
Learn to do good,
search for justice,
help the oppressed,
be just to the orphan,
plead for the widow.

'Come now, let us talk this over,'
says Yahweh.
'Though your sins are like scarlet,
they shall be as white as snow;
though they are red as crimson,
they shall be like wool.'

Isaiah 1.16–18

Suffering and Peace

And yet ours were the sufferings he bore,
ours the sorrows he carried.
But we, we thought of him as someone punished,
struck by God, and brought low.
Yet he was pierced through for our faults,
crushed for our sins.
On him lies a punishment that brings us peace,
and through his wounds we are healed.

We had all gone astray like sheep,
each taking his own way,
and God burdened him
with the sins of all of us.

Isaiah 53.4–6

God is Rich in Forgiving

Oh, come to the water all you who are thirsty;
though you have no money, come!
Buy corn without money, and eat,
and, at no cost, wine and milk.
Why spend money on what is not bread,
your wages on what fails to satisfy?
Listen, listen to me, and you will have good things to eat
and rich food to enjoy.
Pay attention, come to me;
listen, and your soul will live.

Seek God while he is still to be found,
call to him while he is still near.
Let the wicked man abandon his way,
the evil man his thoughts.
Let him turn back to God who will take pity on him,
to our God who is rich in forgiving.

Isaiah 55.1–3,6–7

I Will Hope in God

I am the man familiar with misery
under the rod of his anger;
I am the one he has driven and forced to walk
in darkness, and without any light.
Against me alone he turns his hand,
again and again, all day long.

He has walled me in; I cannot escape;
he has made my chains heavy;
and when I call and shout,
he shuts out my prayer.
He has blocked my ways with cut stones,
he has obstructed my paths.

Brooding on my anguish and affliction
is gall and wormwood.
My spirit ponders it continually
and sinks within me.
This is what I shall tell my heart,
and so recover hope:

The favours of the Lord are not all past,
his kindnesses are not exhausted;
every morning they are renewed;
great is his faithfulness.
'My portion is the Lord' says my soul
'and so I will hope in him.'

The Lord is good to those who trust him,
to the soul that searches for him.
It is good to wait in silence
for the Lord to save.

Lamentations 3.1–3,7–9,19–26

'I Will be Your God'

The Lord says:
'I shall pour clean water over you and you will be cleansed; I shall cleanse you of all your defilement and all your idols. I shall give you a new heart, and put a new spirit in you; I shall remove the heart of stone from your bodies and give you a heart of flesh instead. I shall put my spirit in you, and make you keep my laws and sincerely respect my observances. You will live in the land which I gave your ancestors. You shall be my people and I will be your God.'

Ezekiel 36.25–27

God's Care For His Children

When you were a child I loved you.
I myself taught you to walk,
I took you in my arms;
yet you have not understood that I was the one
looking after you.
I led you with reins of kindness,
with leading-strings of love.
I was like someone who lifts an infant close against
his cheek;
stooping down to you I gave you your food.

from *Hosea 11.1,3–4*

The Gentleness of God

'But now, now – it is the Lord who speaks –
come back to me with all your heart,
fasting, weeping, mourning.'
Let your hearts be broken, not your garments torn,
turn to the Lord your God again,
for he is all tenderness and compassion,
slow to anger, rich in graciousness,
and ready to relent.

Joel 2.12–13

Gospel Readings

'Follow me'

As Jesus was walking by the Sea of Galilee he saw two brothers, Simon, who was called Peter, and his brother Andrew; they were making a cast in the lake with their net, for they were fishermen. And he said to them 'Follow me and I will make you fishers of men'. And they left their nets at once and followed him. Going on from there he saw another pair of brothers,

James son of Zebedee and his brother John; they were in their boat with their father Zebedee, mending their nets, and he called them. At once, leaving the boat and their father, they followed him.

Matthew 4.18–22

The Beatitudes

Seeing the crowds, Jesus went up the hill. There he sat down and was joined by his disciples. Then he began to speak. This is what he taught them:

'How happy are the poor in spirit;
theirs is the kingdom of heaven.
Happy the gentle;
they shall have the earth for their heritage.
Happy those who mourn:
they shall be comforted.
Happy these who hunger and thirst for what is
right:
they shall be satisfied.
Happy the merciful:
they shall have mercy shown them.
Happy the pure in heart:
they shall see God.
Happy the peacemakers:
they shall be called sons of God.
Happy those who are persecuted in the cause of
right:
theirs is the kingdom of heaven.

Happy are you when people abuse you and persecute you and speak all kinds of calumny against you on my account. Rejoice and be glad, for your reward will be great in heaven; this is how they persecuted the prophets before you.'

Matthew 5.1–12

The True Disciple

Jesus said:
'It is not those who say to me, "Lord, Lord", who will enter the kingdom of heaven, but the person who does the will of my Father in heaven. When the day comes many will say to me, "Lord, Lord, did we not prophesy in your name, cast out demons in your name, work many miracles in your name?" Then I shall tell them to their faces: "I have never known you; away from me, you evil men!" Therefore, everyone who listens to these words of mine and acts on them will be like a sensible man who built his house on rock. Rain came down, floods rose, gales blew and hurled themselves against that house, and it did not fall: it was founded on rock. But everyone who listens to these words of mine and does not act on them will be like a stupid man who built his house on sand. Rain came down, floods rose, gales blew and struck that house, and it fell; and what a fall it had!'

Matthew 7.21–27

He Takes Away Our Sickness

That evening they brought Jesus many who were possessed by devils. He cast out the spirits with a word and cured all who were sick. This was to fulfil the prophecy of Isaiah: He took our sicknesses away and carried our diseases for us.

Matthew 8.16–17

'Your Sins Are Forgiven'

Jesus came to his own town (Capernaum). Then some people appeared, bringing him a paralytic stretched out on a bed. Seeing their faith, Jesus said to the paralytic, 'Courage, my child, your sins are forgiven'.

And at this some scribes and pharisees said to themselves, 'This man is blaspheming'. Knowing what was in their minds Jesus said, 'Why do you have such wicked thoughts in your hearts? Now, which of these is easier; to say, "Your sins are forgiven", or to say "Get up and walk"? But to prove to you that the Son of Man has authority on earth to forgive sins,' – he said to the paralytic – 'get up, and pick up your bed and go off home'. And the man got up and went home. A feeling of awe came over the crowd when they saw this, and they praised God for giving such power to men.

Matthew 9.1–8

The Christian Way

Then Jesus said to his disciples, 'If anyone wants to be a follower of mine, let him renounce himself and take up his cross and follow me. For anyone who wants to save his life will lose it; but anyone who loses his life for my sake will find it. What, then, will a man gain if he wins the whole world and ruins his life? Or what has a man to offer in exchange for his life?'

Matthew 16.24–26

Forgive Without Limit

Then Peter came up to Jesus and said 'Lord, how often must I forgive my brother if he wrongs me? As often as seven times?' Jesus answered, 'Not seven, I tell you, but seventy-seven times.'

Matthew 18.21–22

'I Came to Call Sinners'

When Jesus was at dinner in his house, a number of tax collectors and sinners were also sitting at the table with Jesus and his disciples; for there were many of them among his followers. When the scribes of the Pharisee party saw him eating with sinners and tax collectors, they said to his disciples, 'Why does he eat with tax collectors and sinners?' When Jesus heard this he said to them, 'It is not the healthy who need the doctor, but the sick. I did not come to call the virtuous, but sinners.'

Mark 2.15–17

Jesus' Family

His mother and brothers now arrived and, standing outside, sent in a message asking for him. A crowd was sitting round him at the time the message was passed to him, 'Your mother and brothers and sisters are outside asking for you'. He replied, 'Who are my mother and my brothers?' And looking round at those sitting in a circle about him, he said, 'Here are my mother and my brothers. Anyone who does the will of God, that person is my brother and sister and mother.'

Mark 3.31–35

The Greatest

Jesus said to his disciples, 'You know that among the pagans their so-called rulers lord it over them, and their great men make their authority felt. This is not to happen among you. No; anyone who wants to become great among you must be your servant, and anyone who wants to be first among you must be slave to all. For the Son of Man himself did not come to be served but to serve, and to give his life as a ransom for many.'

Mark 10.41–45

The Greatest Commandment

One of the scribes put a question to Jesus, 'Which is the first of all the commandments?' Jesus replied, 'This is the first: Listen, Israel, the Lord our God is the one Lord, and you must love the Lord your God with all your heart, with all your soul, with all your mind and with all your strength. The second is this: You must love your neighbour as yourself. There is no commandment greater that these.' The scribe said to him, 'Well spoken, Master; what you have said is true; that he is one and there is no other. To love him with all your heart, with all your understanding and strength, and to love your neighbour as yourself, this is far more important than any holocaust or sacrifice.' Jesus, seeing how wisely he had spoken, said, 'You are not far from the kingdom of God'.

Mark 12.28–34

'Stay Awake!'

Jesus said to his disciples, 'Be on your guard, stay awake, because you never know when the time will come. It is like a man travelling abroad: he has gone from home, and left his servants in charge, each with his own task; and he told the door-keeper to stay awake. So stay awake, because you do not know when the master of the house is coming, evening, midnight, cockcrow, dawn; if he comes unexpectedly, he must not find you asleep. And what I say to you I say to all: Stay awake!'

Mark 13.33–37

'Be Cured!'

Now Jesus was in one of the towns when a man appeared, covered with leprosy. Seeing Jesus he fell on his face and implored him. 'Sir,' he said 'if you want to, you can cure me.' Jesus stretched out his hand, touched him and said, 'Of course I want to! Be cured!' And the leprosy left him at once. His reputation continued to grow, and large crowds would gather to hear him and to have their sickness cured, but he would always go off to some place where he could be alone and pray.

Luke 5.12–13,15–16

Be Generous in Forgiving

Jesus said, 'Be compassionate as your Father is compassionate. Do not judge, and you will not be judged yourselves; do not condemn, and you will not be condemned yourselves; grant pardon, and you will be pardoned. Give, and there will be gifts for you: a full measure, pressed down, shaken together, and running over, will be poured into your lap; because the amount you measure out is the amount you will be given back.'

Luke 6.36–38

Ask and You Shall Receive

Jesus said to his disciples, 'Suppose one of you has a friend and goes to him in the middle of the night to say, "My friend, lend me three loaves, because a friend of mine on his travels has just arrived at my house, and I have nothing to offer him"; and the man answers from inside the house, "Do not bother me... The door is bolted now, and my children and I are in bed; I cannot get up and give it you". I tell you, if the man does not get up and give it him for friendship's sake, persistence will be enough to make him get up and give his friend all he wants. So I say to you: Ask, and it will be given to you; search, and you will find;

knock, and the door will be opened to you. For the one who asks always receives; the one who searches always finds; the one who knocks will always have the door opened to him. What father among you would hand his son a stone when he asked for bread? Or hand him a snake instead of fish? Or hand him a scorpion if he asked for an egg? If you then, who are evil, know how to give your children what is good, how much more will the heavenly Father give the Holy Spirit to those who ask him!'

Luke 11.5–13

The Father's Love For His Son

Jesus told this parable: 'A man had two sons. The younger said to his father, "Father, let me have the share of the estate that would come to me". So the father divided the property between them. A few days later, the younger son got together everything he had and left for a distant country where he squandered his money on a life of debauchery. When he had spent it all, that country experienced a severe famine, and now he began to feel the pinch, so he hired himself out to one of the local inhabitants who put him on his farm to feed the pigs. And he would willingly have filled his belly with the husks the pigs were eating but no one offered him anything. Then he came to his senses and said, "How many of my father's paid servants have more food than they want, and here am I dying of hunger! I will leave this place and go to my father and say: Father, I have sinned against heaven and against you; I no longer deserve to be called your son; treat me as one of your paid servants." So he left the place and went back to his father. While he was still a long way off, his father saw him and was moved with pity. He ran to the boy, clasped him in his arms and kissed him tenderly. Then his son said, "Father, I have sinned against heaven and against you. I no longer deserve to be called your son." But the father said to his servants, "Quick! Bring out the best robe and put it on him; put a ring on his finger and sandals on his feet. Bring the calf we have been fattening, and kill it; we are going to have a feast, a celebration, because this son of mine was dead and has has come back to life; he was lost and is found." And they began to celebrate.'

Luke 15.11–24

Always Forgive Each Other

Jesus said 'If your brother does something wrong, reprove him and, if he is sorry, forgive him. And if he wrongs you seven times a day and seven times come back to you and says "I am sorry", you must forgive him.'

Luke 17.3–4

'Lord, Have Mercy'

Jesus spoke the following parable to some people who prided themselves on being virtuous and despised everyone else. 'Two men went up to the Temple to pray, one was a Pharisee, the other a tax collector. The Pharisee stood there and said this prayer to himself, "I thank you, God, that I am not grasping, unjust, adulterous like the rest of mankind, and particularly that I am not like this tax collector here. I fast twice a week; I pay tithes on all I get." The tax collector stood some distance away, not daring even to raise his eyes to heaven; but he beat his breast and said, "God, be merciful to me, a sinner". This man, I tell you, went home again at rights with God; the other did not. For everyone who exalts himself will be humbled, but the man who humbles himself will be exalted.'

Luke 18.9–14

‘Today You Will be With Me’

When they reached the place called The Skull, they crucified him there and the two criminals also, one on the right, the other on the left. Jesus said, ‘Father, forgive them; they do not know what they are doing’. One of the criminals hanging there abused him. ‘Are you not the Christ?’ he said. ‘Save yourself and us as well.’ But the other spoke up and rebuked him. ‘Have you no fear of God at all?’ he said. ‘You got the same sentence as he did, but in our case we deserved it: we were paying for what we did. But this man has done nothing wrong. Jesus,’ he said, ‘remember me when you come into your kingdom.’ ‘Indeed, I promise you,’ he replied, ‘today you will be with me in paradise.’

Luke 23.33–34,39–43

‘Neither Do I Condemn You’

The scribes and Pharisees brought a woman along who had been caught committing adultery; and making her stand there in full view of everybody, they said to Jesus, ‘Master, this woman was caught in the very act of committing adultery, and Moses has ordered us in the Law to condemn women like this to death by stoning. What have you to say?’ They asked him this as a test, looking for something to use against him. But Jesus bent down and started writing on the ground with his finger. As they persisted with their question, he looked up and said, ‘If there is one of you who has not sinned, let him be the first to throw a stone at her’. Then he bent down and wrote on the ground again. When they heard this they went away one by one, beginning with the eldest, until Jesus was left alone with the woman, who remained standing there. He looked up and said, ‘Woman, where are they? Has no one condemned you?' 'No one, sir' she replied. 'Neither do I condemn you.' said Jesus, 'go away, and don't sin any more.'

John 8.3–11

The Good Shepherd

Jesus spoke to them again:
'I tell you most solemnly,
I am the gate of the sheepfold.
All others who have come
are thieves and brigands;
but the sheep took no notice of them.
I am the gate.
Anyone who enters through me will be safe:
he will go freely in and out
and be sure of finding pasture.
The thief comes
only to steal and destroy.
I have come
so that they may have life
and have it to the full.
I am the good shepherd:
the good shepherd is one who lays down his life for his sheep.'

John 10.7–11

Death and Resurrection

Jesus said:
'I am the resurrection.
If anyone believes in me, even though he dies he will live,
and whoever lives and believes in me
will never die.'

John 11.25–26

Eternal Life

Jesus said to them:
'Now the hour has come
for the Son of Man to be glorified.
I tell you, most solemnly,
unless a wheat grain falls on the ground and dies,
it remains only a single grain;
but if it dies,
it yields a rich harvest.
Anyone who loves his life loses it;
anyone who hates his life in this world
will keep it for the eternal life.
If a man serves me, he must follow me,
wherever I am, my servant will be there too.
If anyone serves me, my Father will honour him.'

John 12.23–26

A New Commandment

Jesus said to his disciples:
'As the Father has loved me,
so I have loved you.
Remain in my love,
If you keep my commandments
you will remain in my love,
just as I have kept my Father's commandments
and remain in his love.
I have told you this
so that my own joy may be in you
and your joy be complete.
This is my commandment:
love one another,
as I have loved you.
A man can have no greater love
than to lay down his life for his friends.
You are my friends,
if you do what I command you.'

John 15.9–14

'Received the Holy Spirit'

In the evening of that same day, the first day of the week, the doors were closed in the room where the disciples were, for fear of the Jews. Jesus came and stood among them. He said to them, 'Peace be with you', and showed them his hands and his side. The disciples were filled with joy when they saw the Lord, and he said to them again, 'Peace be with you.

As the Father sent me,
so am I sending you.'

After saying this he breathed on them and said:

'Receive the Holy Spirit.
for those whose sins you forgive,
they are forgiven;
for those whose sins you retain,
they are retained.'

John 20.19–23

New Testament Readings

Christ Died For Us Sinners

We were still helpless when at his appointed time Christ died for sinful men. It is not easy to die even for a good man – though of course for someone really worthy, a man might be prepared to die – but what proves that God loves us is that Christ died for us while we were still sinners. Having died to make us righteous, is it likely that he would now fail to save us from God's anger? When we were reconciled to God by the death of his Son, we were still enemies; now that we have been reconciled, surely we may count on being saved by the life of his Son? Not merely because we have been reconciled but because we are filled with joyful trust in God, through our Lord Jesus Christ, through whom we have already gained our reconciliation.

Romans 5.6–11

Alive For God

We are dead to sin, so how can we continue to live in it? You have been taught that when we were baptised in Christ Jesus we were baptised in his death; in other words, when we were baptised we went into the tomb with him and joined him in death, so that as Christ was raised from the dead by the Father's glory, we too might live a new life. If in union with Christ we have imitated his death, we shall also imitate him in his resurrection. We must realise that our former selves have been crucified with him to destroy this sinful body and to free us from the slavery of sin. When a man dies, of course, he has finished with sin. But we believe that having died with Christ we shall return to life with him: Christ, as we know, having been raised from the dead will never die again. Death has no power over him any more. When he died, he died, once for all, to sin, so his life now is life with God; and in that way, you too must consider yourselves to be dead to sin but alive for God in Christ Jesus.

Romans 6.2–11

The Daily Struggle

I cannot understand my own behaviour. I fail to carry out the things I want to do, and I find myself doing the very things I hate. When I act against my will, it is not my true self doing it, but sin which lives in me. In fact, this seems to be the rule, that every single time I want to do good it is something evil that comes to hand. In my inmost self I dearly love God's Law, but I can see that my body follows a different law that battles against the law which my reason dictates. This is what makes me a prisoner of that law of sin which lives inside my body. What a wretched man I am! Who will rescue me from this body doomed to death? Thanks be to God through Jesus Christ our Lord!

Romans 7.15,20–24

Children of God

Everyone moved by the Spirit is a son of God. The spirit you received is not the spirit of slaves bringing fear into your lives again; it is the spirit of sons, and makes us cry out 'Abba, Father!' The Spirit himself and our spirit bear united witness that we are children of God. And if we are children we are heirs as well: heirs of God and co-heirs with Christ, sharing his sufferings so as to share his glory.

Romans 8.14–17

The Answer to All Law

Avoid getting into debt, except the debt of mutual love. If you love your fellow men you have carried out your obligations. All the commandments: You shall not commit adultery, you shall not kill, you shall not steal, you shall not covet, and so on, you summed up in this single command: You must love your neighbour as yourself. Love is the one thing that cannot hurt your neighbour; that is why it is the answer to every one of the commandments.

Romans 13.8–10

The Work of the Spirit

There is a variety of gifts but always the same Spirit; there are all sorts of service to be done, but always to the same Lord; working in all sorts of different ways in different people, it is the same God who is working in all of them. The particular way in which the Spirit is given to each person is for a good purpose. One may have the gift of preaching with wisdom given him by the Spirit; another may have the gift of preaching instruction given him by the same Spirit; and another the gift of faith given by the same Spirit; another again the gift of healing, through this one Spirit; one, the power of miracles; another, prophecy; another the gift of recognising spirits, another the gift of tongues and another the ability to interpret them. All these are the work of one and the same Spirit, who distributes different gifts to different people just as he chooses

1 Corinthians 12.4–11

A Portrait of Love

Love is always patient and kind; it is never jealous; love is never boastful or conceited; it is never rude or selfish; it does not take offence, and is not resentful. Love takes no pleasure in other people's sins but delights in the truth; it is always ready to excuse, to trust, to hope, and to endure whatever comes. Love does not come to an end. There are three things that last: faith, hope and love; and the greatest of these is love.

1 Corinthians 13.4–8,13

A New Creation

For anyone who is in Christ, there is a new creation; the old creation has gone, and now the new one is here. It is all God's work. It was God who reconciled us to himself through Christ and gave us the work of handing on this reconciliation. In other words, God in Christ was reconciling the world to himself, not holding men's faults against them, and he has entrusted to us the news that they are reconciled. So we are ambassadors for Christ; it is as though God were appealing through us, and the appeal that we make in Christ's name is: be reconciled to God. For our sake God made the sinless one into sin, so that in him we might become the goodness of God.

2 Corinthians 5.17–21

The Spirit is Our Life

Let me put it like this: if you are guided by the Spirit you will be in no danger of yielding to self-indulgence, since self-indulgence is the opposite of the Spirit, the Spirit is totally against such a thing, and it is precisely because the two are so opposed that you do not always carry out your good intentions. If you are led by the Spirit, no law can touch you. When self-indulgence is at work the results are obvious; fornication, gross indecency and sexual irresponsibility; idolatry and sorcery; feuds and wrangling, jealousy, bad temper and quarrels; disagreements, factions, envy; drunkenness, orgies and similar things. I warn you now, as I warned you before: those who behave like this will not inherit the kingdom of God. What the Spirit brings is very different: love, joy, peace, patience, kindness, goodness, trustfulness, gentleness and self-control. There can be no law against things like that, of course. You cannot belong to Christ Jesus unless you crucify all self-indulgent passions and desires. Since the Spirit is our life, let us be directed by the Spirit.

Galatians 5.16–25

Salvation A Free Gift

God loved us with so much love that he was generous with his mercy: when we were dead through our sins, he brought us to life with Christ – it is through grace that you have been saved – and raised us up with him and gave us a place with him in heaven, in Christ Jesus. This was to show for all ages to come, through his goodness towards us in Christ Jesus, how infinitely rich he is in grace. Because it is by grace that you have been saved, through faith; not by anything of your own, but by a gift from God; not by anything that you have done, so that nobody can claim the credit. We are God's work of art, created in Christ Jesus to live the good life as from the beginning he had meant us to live it.

Ephesians 2.4–10

The Fulness of God

This, then, is what I pray, kneeling before the Father, from who every family, whether spiritual or natural, takes its name: Out of his infinite glory, may he give you the power through his Spirit for your hidden self to grow strong, so that Christ may live in your hearts through faith, and then, planted in love and built on love, you will with all the saints have strength to grasp the breadth and the length, the height and the depth; until, knowing the love of Christ, which is beyond all knowledge, you are filled with the utter fulness of God. Glory be to him whose power, working in us, can do infinitely more than we can ask or imagine; glory be to him from generation to generation in the Church and in Christ Jesus for ever and ever. Amen.

Ephesians 3.14–19

The New Life in Christ

I implore you to lead a life worthy of your vocation. Bear with one another charitably, in complete selflessness, gentleness and patience. Do all you can to preserve the unity of the Spirit by the peace that binds you together. From now on there must be no more lies: You must speak the truth to one another, since we are all parts of one another. Even if you are angry, you must not sin; never let the sun set on your anger or else you will give the devil a foothold. Anyone who was a thief must stop stealing; he should try to find some useful manual work instead, and be able to do some good by helping others that are in need. Guard against foul talk; let your words be for the improvement of others, as occasion offers, and do good to your listeners, otherwise you will only be grieving the Holy Spirit of God who has marked you with his seal for you to be set free when the day comes. Never have grudges against others, or lose your temper, or raise your voice to anybody, or call each other names, or allow any sort of spitefulness. Be friends with one another, and kind, forgiving each other as readily as God forgave you in Christ.

Ephesians 4.1–3,25–32

Be Built on Christ

You must live your whole life according to the Christ you have received – Jesus the Lord; you must be rooted in him and built on him and held firm by the faith you have been taught, and full of thanksgiving. You have been buried with him, when you were baptised; and by baptism, too, you have been raised up with him through your belief in the power of God who raised him from the dead. You were dead because you were sinners: he has brought you to life with him, he has forgiven us all our sins.

Colossians 2.6–7,12–13

Life With Christ

Since you have been brought back to true life with Christ, you must look for the things that are in heaven, where Christ is, sitting at God's right hand. Let your thoughts be on heavenly things, not on the things that are on the earth, because you have died, and now the life you have is hidden with Christ in God. But when Christ is revealed – and he is your life – you too will be revealed in all your glory with him.

Colossians 3.1–4

The Witness of Jesus Christ

With so many witnesses in a great cloud on every side of us, we too, then, should throw off everything that hinders us, especially the sin that clings so easily, and keep running steadily in the race we have started. Let us not lose sight of Jesus, who leads us in our faith and brings it to perfection; for the sake of the joy which was still in the future, he endured the cross, disregarding the shamefulness of it, and from now on has taken his place at the right of God's throne. Think of the way he stood such opposition from sinners and then you will not give up for want of courage. In the fight against sin, you have not yet had to keep fighting to the point of death.

Hebrews 12.1–4

True Religion

You must do what the word tells you, and not just listen to it and deceive yourselves. To listen to the word and not obey is like looking at your own features in a mirror and then, after a quick look, going off and immediately forgetting what you looked like. But the man who looks steadily at the perfect law of freedom and makes that his habit – not listening and then forgetting, but actively putting it into practice – will be happy in all that he does. Nobody must imagine that he is religious while he still goes on deceiving himself and not keeping control over his tongue; anyone who does this has the wrong idea of religion. Pure, unspoilt religion, in the eyes of God our Father is this: coming to the help of orphans and widows when they need it, and keeping oneself uncontaminated by the world.

James 1.22–25

Faith and Good Works

Take the case, my brothers, of someone who has never done a single good act but claims that he has faith. Will that faith save him? If one of the brothers or one of the sisters is in need of clothes and has not enough food to live on, and one of you says to them, 'I wish you well; keep yourself warm and eat plenty,' without giving them these bare necessities of life, then what good is that? Faith is like that: if good works do not go with it, it is quite dead. This is the way to talk to people of that kind: 'You say that you have faith and I have good deeds; I will prove to you that I have faith by showing you my good deeds – now you prove to me that you have faith without any good deeds to show, you believe in the one God – that is creditable enough, but the demons have the same belief, and they tremble with fear. Do realise, you senseless man, that faith without good deeds is useless.'

James 2.14–20

'Be Holy, For I am Holy'

Free your minds of encumbrances; control them, and put your trust in nothing but the grace that will be given you when Jesus Christ is revealed. Do not behave in the way that you liked to before you learnt the truth; make a habit of obedience: be holy in all you do, since it is the Holy One who called you, and scripture says: Be holy, for I am holy.

1Peter 1.13–16

Walk in the Light

St John writes:

This is what we have heard from him,
and the message that we are announcing to you:

God is light; there is no darkness in him at all.
If we say that we are in union with God
while we are living in darkness,
we are lying because we are not living the truth.
But if we live our lives in the light,
as he is in the light,
we are in union with one another,
and the blood of Jesus, his Son,
purifies us from all sin.
If we say we have no sin in us,
we are deceiving ourselves
and refusing to admit the truth;
but if we acknowledge our sins,
then God who is faithful and just
will forgive our sins and purify us
from everything that is wrong.

1 John 1.5–9

Love Your Brother

Anyone who claims to be in the light
but hates his brother
is still in the dark.
But anyone who loves his brother is living in the light
and need not be afraid of stumbling;
unlike the man who hates his brother and is in the darkness,
not knowing where he is going,
because it is too dark to see.

1 John 2.9–11

Love is Active

My children,
our love is not to be just words or mere talk
but something real and active;

only by this can we be certain
that we are children of the truth
and be able to quieten our conscience in his
presence,
whatever accusations it may raise against us,
because God is greater than our conscience and he
knows everything.
My dear people,
if we cannot be condemned by our own conscience,
we need not be afraid in God's presence,
and whatever we ask him,
we shall receive,
because we keep his commandments
and live the kind of life that he wants.
His commandments are these:
that we believe in the name of his Son Jesus Christ
and that we love one another
as he told us to.
whoever keeps his commandments
lives in God and God lives in him.
We know that he lives in us
by the Spirit that he has given us.

1 John 3.18–24

God is Love

God is love
and anyone who lives in love lives in God,
and God lives in him.
In love there can be no fear,
but fear is driven out by perfect love:
because to fear is to expect punishment,
and anyone who is afraid is still imperfect in love.
We are to love, then,
because he loved us first.

1 John 4.16,18–19

Prayers of Sorrow

After reading of the Word of God, the penitent makes his confession. If he wishes he may say the *I Confess* (p. 259). The priest offers him advice and counsel, and gives him a penance to say or to do. The penitent expresses his sorrow in a prayer, either choosing one of the prayers below, or praying in his own words.

1. My God,
   I am sorry for my sins with all my heart.
   In choosing to do wrong
   and failing to do good,
   I have sinned against you
   whom I should love above all things.
   I firmly intend, with your help,
   to do penance,
   to sin no more,
   and to avoid whatever leads me to sin.
   Our Saviour Jesus Christ
   suffered and died for us.
   In his name, my God, have mercy.

2. Remember, Lord, your compassion and mercy
   which you shared long ago.
   Do not recall the sins and failings of my youth.
   In your mercy remember me, Lord, because of
   your goodness.

   (Psalm 24.6–7)

3. Wash me from my guilt
and cleanse me of my sin.
I acknowledge my offence;
my sin is before me always.

(Psalm 50.4–5)

4. Father, I have sinned against you
and am not worthy to be called your son.
Be merciful to me, a sinner.

(Luke 15.18; 18.13)

5. Father of mercy,
like the prodigal son
I return to you and say:
'I have sinned against you
and am no longer worthy to be called your son.'
Christ Jesus, Saviour of the world,
I pray with the repentant thief
to whom you promised Paradise:
'Lord, remember me in your kingdom.'
Holy Spirit, fountain of love,
I call on you with trust:
'Purify my heart,
and help me to walk as a child of light.'

6. Lord Jesus,
you opened the eyes of the blind,
healed the sick,
forgave the sinful woman,
and after Peter's denial confirmed him in your love.
Listen to my prayer:
forgive all my sins,
renew your love in my heart,
help me to live in perfect unity with my fellow Christians
that I may proclaim your saving power to all the world.

7. Lord Jesus,
you choose to be called the friend of sinners.
By your saving death and resurrection
free me from my sins.
May your peace take root in my heart
and bring forth a harvest
of love, holiness, and truth.

8. Lord Jesus Christ,
you are the Lamb of God;
you take away the sins of the world.
Through the grace of the Holy Spirit
restore me to friendship with your Father,
cleanse me from every stain of sin
in the blood you shed for me,
and raise me to new life
for the glory of your name.

9. Lord God,
in your goodness have mercy on me:
do not look on my sins,
but take away all my guilt.
Create in me a clean heart
and renew within me an upright spirit.

10. Lord Jesus, Son of God,
have mercy on me, a sinner.

11. My God, I am sorry and ask forgiveness for my sins.
By the help of your grace I will try not to sin again.

12. Lord Jesus,
you died that all men might be saved.
Accept my prayer of sorrow,
and give me strength
to amend my way of life.

13. Lord God,
our loving Father, you know all my weaknesses and failures.
I come to you with deep sorrow in my heart.
Forgive me,
accept me,
strengthen me.

14. Lord God,
I have failed my fellow men,
and have sinned against you.
Be merciful to me
and restore me to your friendship and to full fellowship of your Church.

15. Jesus Lord, I ask for mercy.

16. (This is a prayer for personal reflection)

I have fallen, Lord,
once more.
I can't go on, I'll never succeed.
I am ashamed, I don't dare look at you.
And yet I struggled, Lord, for I knew you were right near me, bending over me, watching.
But temptation blew like a hurricane
And instead of looking at you I turned my head away,
I stepped aside
While you stood, silent and sorrowful,
Like the spurned fiancé who sees his loved one carried off by his rival.
When the wind died down as suddenly as it had arisen,
When the lightning ceased after proudly streaking the darkness,
All of a sudden I found myself alone, ashamed, disgusted, with my sin in my hands.

I can't get rid of it.
I run from it, like the master of an unwanted and mangy dog, but it catches up with me, and rubs joyfully against my legs.
Everyone must notice it.
I'm so ashamed that I feel like crawling to avoid being seen.
I'm ashamed of being seen by my friend,
I'm ashamed of being seen by you, Lord,
For you loved me, and I forgot you.

I forgot you because I was thinking of myself,
And one can't think of several persons at once.
One must choose, and I chose.
And your voice,
And your look,
And your love hurt me.
They weigh me down,
They weigh me down more than my sin.

Lord, don't look at me like that,
For I am naked,
I am dirty,
I am down,
Shattered,
With no strength left.
I dare make no more promises,
I can only stand bowed before you.

Come, son, look up.
Isn't it mainly your vanity that is wounded?
If you loved me, you would grieve, but you would trust.
Do you think that there's a limit to God's love?
Do you think that for a moment I stopped loving you?
But you still rely on yourself, son.
You must rely on me.

Ask my pardon
And get up quickly.
You see, it's not falling that is the worst.
But staying on the ground.

(from *Prayers of Life*, Quoist)

The Absolution

Then the priest extends his hands over the penitent's head and says:

God, the Father of mercies,
through the death and resurrection of his Son
has reconciled the world to himself
and sent the Holy Spirit among us
for the forgiveness of sins;
through the ministry of the Church
may God give you pardon and peace,
and I absolve you from your sins
in the name of the Father, and of the Son, +
and of the Holy Spirit.

The penitent answers:

Amen.

The Dismissal

After the absolution the priest says to the penitent:

Give thanks to the Lord for he is good.
Penitent: **His mercy endures for ever.**

The Lord has freed you from your sins.
Go in peace.

Alternatively the priest may say one of the following prayers:

1. May the Passion of our Lord Jesus Christ,
the intercession of the Blessed Virgin Mary, and of all the saints,
whatever good you do and suffering you endure,
heal your sins,
help you to grow in holiness,
and reward you with eternal life.
Go in peace.

2. The Lord has freed you from sin.
May he bring you safely to his kingdom in heaven.
Glory to him for ever.

3. Blessed are those,
whose sins have been forgiven,

whose evil deeds have been forgotten.
Rejoice in the Lord,
and go in peace.

4. Go in peace,
and proclaim to the world
the wonderful works of God
who has brought you salvation.

Other scriptural prayers may be helpful for the penitent:

5. Go in peace, for the power of God has answered your prayer of faith. As scripture says: 'The upright man finds life through faith.' *(Romans 1.16)*

6. Give 'glory to him who is able to give you the strength to live according to the Good News.' *(Romans 16.25)* Go in peace to love and serve the Lord.

7. God be with you in peace. 'Be awake to all the dangers; stay firm in the faith; be brave and strong. Let everything you do be done in love.' *(1 Corinthians 16.13)*

8. Go in peace and show you are God's servant by your purity, knowledge, patience and kindness; and by your holiness and love. *(2 Corinthians 6.6)*

9. Go with joy in your heart; grow more perfect; live in peace, and the God of love and peace will be with you now and always. *(2 Corinthians 13.11)*

10. May the peace of the Lord Jesus Christ who sacrificed himself for our sins, to the glory of God the Father, be with you. *(Galatians 1.3)*

11. May the peace and mercy of God be with you and may you become a new person as one of God's people. *(Galatians 6.16)*

12. 'Blessed be God the Father of our Lord Jesus Christ, who has blessed you with all the spiritual blessings of heaven in Christ.' *(Ephesians 1.3)*

13. 'And may the peace of Christ reign in your hearts, because it is for this that you were called together as parts of one body. Always be thankful.' *(Colossians 3.15)*

14. 'May the God of peace make you perfect and holy; and may you be kept safe and blameless, spirit, soul and body, for the coming of our Lord Jesus Christ. God has called you and he will not fail you.' *(1 Thessalonians 5.23–24)*

15. 'Be at peace. Be happy at all times; pray constantly; and for all things give thanks to God, because this is what God expects you to do in Christ Jesus.' *(1 Thessalonians 5.14–18)*

16. 'May the Lord of peace himself give you peace all the time and in every way.' The Lord be with you now and always. *(2 Thessalonians 3.16)*

17. Be content, for you have received 'grace, mercy and peace from God the Father and from Jesus our Lord.' *(1 Timothy 1.2)*

18. 'Your faith has saved you; go in peace.' *(Luke 7.50)*

19. Let us rejoice, because this child was dead, and has come back to life; was lost and is found. Go in peace to love and serve the Lord. *(Luke 15.24)*

Thanksgiving

Psalms of Thanksgiving

After confession and absolution the penitent may thank God for his mercy and love. Such a prayer is a purely personal 'thank you', made in the words and in the way that seem most appropriate to the penitent. Some of the extracts from the psalms given below may help to express the right mood of thanksgiving. It is enough to choose a sentence or two that strike a sympathetic chord, and to reflect on them quietly and with joy.

I lie down to rest and I sleep.
I wake, for the Lord upholds me.

Psalm 3.6

Lord, who shall be admitted to your tent
and dwell on your holy mountain?

He who walks without fault;
he who acts with justice
and speaks the truth from his heart;
he who does not slander with his tongue;
he who does no wrong to his brother,
who casts no slur on his neighbour,
he who keeps his pledge, come what may.
Such a man will stand firm for ever.

Psalm 14(15).1–3,5

You will show me the path of life,
the fulness of joy in your presence,
at your right hand happiness for ever.

Psalm 15(16).11

The Lord is my light and my help;
whom shall I fear?
The Lord is the stronghold of my life;
before whom shall I shrink?

Psalm 26(27).1

I am sure I shall see the Lord's goodness
in the land of the living.
Hope in him, hold firm and take heart.
Hope in the Lord!

Psalm 26(27).13–14

Blessed be the Lord for he has heard
my cry, my appeal.
The Lord is my strength and my shield;
in him my heart trusts.
I was helped, my heart rejoices
and I praise him with my song.

Psalm 27(28).6–7

Happy the man whose offence is forgiven,
whose sin is remitted.

Now I have acknowledged my sins;
my guilt I did not hide.
I said: 'I will confess
my offence to the Lord.'
And you, Lord, have forgiven
the guilt of my sin.

So let every good man pray to you
in the time of need.
The floods of water may reach high
but him they shall not reach.
You are my hiding place, O Lord;
you save me from distress.

Psalm 31(32).1,5–7

The salvation of the just comes from the Lord,
their stronghold in time of distress.
The Lord helps them and delivers them
and saves them: for their refuge is in him.

Psalm 36(37).39–40

When my heart grew embittered
and when I was cut to the quick,
I was stupid and did not understand,
no better than a beast in your sight.

Yet I was always in your presence;
you were holding me by my right hand.
You will guide me by your counsel
and so you will lead me to glory.

What else have I in heaven but you?
Apart from you I want nothing on earth.
My body and my heart faint for joy;
God is my possession for ever.

Psalm 72(73).21–26

Cry out with joy to the Lord, all the earth.
Serve the Lord with gladness.
Come before him, singing for joy

Know that he, the Lord, is God.
He made us, we belong to him,
we are his people, the sheep of his flock.

Go within his gates, giving thanks.
Enter his courts with songs of praise.
Give thanks to him and bless his name.

Indeed, how good is the Lord,
eternal his merciful love.
He is faithful from age to age.

Psalm 99(100)

My soul, give thanks to the Lord,
all my being, bless his holy name.

My soul, give thanks to the Lord
and never forget all his blessings.

It is he who forgives all your guilt,
who heals every one of your ills.
The Lord is compassion and love,
slow to anger and rich in mercy.

Psalm 102(103).1–3,8

O give thanks to the Lord for he is good;
for his love endures for ever.

Psalm 106(107).1

I will thank the Lord with all my heart
in the meeting of the just and their assembly.

He has sent deliverance to his people
and established his covenant for ever.
Holy his name, to be feared.

Psalm 110(111).1,9

I love the Lord for he has heard
the cry of my appeal;
for he turned his ear to me
in the day when I called him.

I will walk in the presence of the Lord
in the land of the living.

Psalm 114(115).1–2,9

How can I repay the Lord
for his goodness to me?

Your servant, Lord, your servant am I;
you have loosened my bonds.
A thanksgiving sacrifice I make:
I will call on the Lord's name.

My vows to the Lord I will fulfil
before all his people.

Psalm 115(116).12,16–18

Lord, you have been good to your servant
according to your word.
Teach me discernment and knowledge
for I trust in your commands.
Before, I was afflicted and I strayed
but now I keep to your word.

Psalm, 118(119).65–67

Truly I have set my soul
in silence and peace.
A weaned child on its mother's breast,
even so is my soul.

Psalm 130(131).2

O give thanks to the Lord for he is good,
for his love endures for ever.
Give thanks to the God of gods,
for his love endures for ever.
Give thanks to the Lord of lords,
for his love endures for ever.

He remembered us in our distress,
for his love endures for ever.
He gives food to all living things,
for his love endures for ever.
To the God of heaven give thanks,
for his love endures for ever.

Psalm 135(136).1–3,23,25–26

I thank you, Lord, with all my heart,
you have heard the words of my mouth.
In the presence of the angels I will bless you.
I will adore before your holy temple.

I thank you for your faithfulness and love
which excel all we ever knew of you.
On the day I called, you answered;
you increased the strength of my soul.

You stretch out your hand and save me,
your hand will do all things for me.
Your love, O Lord, is eternal,
discard not the work of your hands.

Psalm 137(138).1–3,7–8

Praise God in his holy place,
praise him in his mighty heavens.
Praise him for his powerful deeds,
praise his surpassing greatness.

Let everything that lives and that breathes
give praise to the Lord!

Psalm 150.1–2,6